PADEREWSKI ESSAYS & POEMS

PADEREWSKI ESSAYS & POEMS

J. J. Paderewski (signature)

Edited by Maja Trochimczyk

MOONRISE PRESS

COPYRIGHT INFORMATION

The Library of Congress Publication Data:

I. Author. Maja Trochimczyk (b. 1957) editor and translator.
II. Title. Paderewski Essays & Poems

274 pages (xviii pp. prefatory matter, and 256 pp.); 6in x 9in. Written in English. With portraits, illustrations, calendar of life, list of works, and bibliography.

ISBN 978-1-945938-87-0 (hardcover)
ISBN 978-1-945938-88-7 (paperback)
ISBN 978-1-945938-89-4 (eBook, ePub format)

10 9 8 7 6 5 4 3 2 1

Ignacy Jan Paderewski's portrait by Davis and
Sanford, 1903. Maja Trochimczyk Collection

Table of Contents

Part III. About Paderewski—209
Edited by Maja Trochimczyk

Introduction

During his lifetime, Ignacy Jan Paderewski (6 November 1860 – 29 June 1941), traveled far from his roots in the Polish gentry estate in the districts of Podolia and Volhynia, formerly a part of the Polish-Lithuanian Commonwealth. Since the partitions and the fall of Poland in 1795 this area was under Russian rule, and now it is in the Ukraine.[1] The young musician went to study in Warsaw, Berlin, and Vienna. He crisscrossed the world with his pianos—first the Erard, then, in America, the Steinway—to conquer concert stages and his audiences' hearts, earning praise from music critics, honors from governments, and a fortune from ticket sales. Paderewski was the first "long-haired" idol of young women who crowded to his concerts, welcomed him in harbors, and even sought to cut locks of his hair for their scrapbooks of press clippings and concert programs.

Paderewski's triumphs on concert stages as a passionate romantic virtuoso of impeccable technique and profound musicality brought him on 20 concert tours of the U.S. and Canada and flourished over countless recitals in capitals and small towns across Europe, as well as series of performances in South America (1911), Australia and New Zealand (1904, 1927). Everywhere, his fans gave him gifts and wrote poems, some of which are collected in this volume.

Yet, the outbreak of the first Word War changed the direction of his life. A passionate patriot, he dedicated about 350 lecture-recitals in 1914-1918 to pleading for the Polish cause—aid for victims of war on lands occupied by Germany and Russia, advocacy for Poland's independence, and support for a Polish Army to be created in the U.S. to fight along with American troops in Europe.[2] After being trained in Canada, the Army of 22,000 was

---

[1] There are no current, comprehensive, scholarly Paderewski biographies available in English. The most readable and accurate is still Adam Zamoyski, *Paderewski. A Biography of the Great Polish Pianist and Statesman.* (New York: Atheneum, 1982).

[2] See Kazimierz Braun, "The Life and Works of Ignacy Paderewski," *Kuryer Polski* (17 August 2023). Reprinted with revisions in Braun's

shipped to France, joined by more volunteers (reaching about 80,000 soldiers), and went to defend newly independent Poland against the Soviet invasion in 1920. It was known as the "Blue Army" after the color of their uniforms, or the "Haller" army after the name of their general, Józef Haller (1873-1960). Who is aware today that it was, in fact, a Paderewski Army?

It was not an accident that a virtuoso pianist and composer became an unofficial leader of the American Polonia, beloved and respected by the community. It was not an accident that he was nominated as Poland's President of the Council of Ministers and Minister of Foreign Affairs as well as Delegate to the Versailles Peace Conference in 1919. After all, President Woodrow Wilson's Peace Plan's 13th Point mandating Poland's independence was written on the basis of a Paderewski Memorial. It took a lot of diplomatic relationships and political maneuvering to gain the attention of the President.

Alas, in Poland, Paderewski faced a formidable opponent in the person of Marshall Józef Piłsudski (1867-1935) a former socialist leader, turned dictator after his 1926 *coup d'etat*. So, Paderewski was no longer welcome in his beloved homeland; the credit for restoring the country's independence went elsewhere. He left and never returned; after settling on his Swiss estate in Riond Bosson, he often visited the California resort town of Paso Robles where he could prepare the repertoire for his return to the concert stage, heal his hands in the hot springs, and oversee almond orchards and vineyards. Despite misgivings, his return to the concert stage in 1922 was triumphant; Paderewski embarked on another set of grueling concert tours. He also made more excellent recordings, some of the best of his entire career. He was now a celebrated virtuoso and stateman, a modern immortal.

But he never returned to composing. Among over 70 of his compositions, the only opera *Manru* (the first "Wagnerian-style" music drama in Polish music history), was premiered in Dresden, then played in Nice, Monte Carlo, Cologne, Prague, Zürich, Bonn, Lwów, and Kraków (1901), before a triumphant tour of American stages in 1902: the premiere at the Metropolitan Opera in New

Three Paderewski Plays, edited by Maja Trochimczyk (Moonrise Press, 2025). I credit Prof. Braun for the idea of the "Paderewski Army."

York, followed by performances in Philadelphia, Boston, Chicago, Pittsburgh, and Baltimore.[3] Meanwhile, in Europe, *Manru* was staged in Cologne, Zurich, Geneva, Warsaw, Moscow, and Kiev. But who, today, remembers *Manru*, the tragic romance of a Gypsy and a Polish peasant girl from the Tatra Mountains? This music was so innovative that Richard Strauss sought to study its score, while working on the acclaimed music drama, *Salome*.

The dramatic *Manru,* the mammot, patriotic Symphony *Polonia,* the Piano Concerto—his major compositions were all forgotten; only some piano miniatures retained the favor of pianists. Was his music really so mediocre, or was there something else at play? Paderewski's reputation got even worse after WWII and the establishment of the "socialist" Polish People's Republic by the Soviet Union. How could an émigré, nobleman, and an enemy of Soviets be promoted by anyone within the ideologically-controlled country? However, discerning why and how was Paderewski's name erased from music history and the history of Poland is a topic for another occasion.

In this volume, I would like to reveal some aspects of his well-deserved rise to fame as a charismatic musician and his widespread recognition by poets, journalists, and writers who dedicated their poems to the acclaimed virtuoso. For many of them he was not just a Maestro or a Polish Patriot: he was a Genius, an Archangel, the Great Master, a Modern Immortal. This veneration transcended borders and generations, spanning fifty years, from 1890 to 1940. During that time, Paderewski was a celebrity of global fame.

In 2011, I searched online archives of the *New York Times* for any mentions of the name of Ignacy Jan Paderewski. I found that he was a topic of 7,820 articles in 120 years from 1891 to 2011. For comparison, I also looked at online records of other classical musicians active in the same period: only composers Sergei

---

[3] The names of cities based on Małgorzata Perkowska, *Diariusz koncertowy Ignacego Jana Paderewskiego.* (Krakow: PWM, 1990). Information about Strauss first cited in my chapter "Searching for Poland's Soul: Paderewski and Szymanowski in the Tatras," in *A Romantic Century in Polish Music*, Maja Trochimczyk, ed. (Moonrise Press, 2009, 179-219).

Rachmaninoff and Igor Stravinsky enjoyed greater fame. Among famous performers—pianists, singers, violinists, conductors, such as Maria Callas, Enrique Caruso, Leopold Stokowski, Pablo Sarasate, or Ferrucio Busoni—Paderewski occupied a uniquely elevated position.

TABLE 1: Paderewski's fame according to the New York Times. Comparison of the number of mentions from 1891 to the present.

FAMOUS MUSICIANS	NY TIMES	FAMOUS ARTISTS	NY TIMES
Igor Stravinsky	> 10000	Shirley Temple	> 10000
Sergei Rachmaninoff	>10000	Judy Garland	> 10000
PADEREWSKI	7820	Charlie Chaplin	> 10000
Walter Damrosch	7530	Humphrey Bogart	> 10000
Pablo Casals	6710	Douglas Fairbanks	> 10000
Marcella Sembrich	4900	Salvador Dali	> 10000
Leopold Stokowski	4690	Mae West	> 10000
Ferrucio Busoni	4680	Clark Gable	9660
Maria Callas	4610	Paul Klee	8230
Enrico Caruso	3910	Greta Garbo	8150
Liberace	3700	Wassily Kandinsky	8000
Vladimir Horowitz	3000	PADEREWSKI	7820
Pablo de Sarasate	2690	Buster Keaton	6560
Claudio Arrau	2470	Ingrid Bergman	6200
Josef Hoffman	2160	Mary Pickford	6120
Maurizio Pollini	1840	Pablo Picasso	4590
Karol Szymanowski	1690	Lillian Gish	4380
Vladimir de Pachmann	588	Pola Negri	1250
		Helena Modjeska	409

It may be worth noting that during the interwar period, The New York Times was edited by John Houston Finley, one of Paderewski's friends who wrote poems about him (see Essay 1). Thus, it could be said that the newspaper was partial to Paderewski due to the relationship between the pianist and the editor. It would be interesting to trace these mentions by year, to observe the peaks and valleys of popularity. Alas, it is not possible to count the number of mentions on The New York Times' archival pages, since this function was removed by 2025. Back in 2011, I reviewed some of these articles and noticed three distinct subjects: a) his performances (i.e., announcements and reviews), b) his political contributions and advocacy for Poland, and c) details of his life, such as his incredible generosity of donating to many distinct causes, as well as his marriage, travels, and trivia (his dog, or parrot).

My interest in Paderewski was not infused during musicology studies at the University of Warsaw (M.A. 1986), where I pursued a fascination with the work of the most experimental Polish composers, many of whom were my friends. I did not care about Paderewski during my doctoral studies at McGill University in Montreal, Quebec (Ph.D. 1994), where I focused on the concept of space in music and on the avantgarde development of "spatial music" by such Western composers as American Henry Brant, Canadian R. Murray Schafer, Greek Iannis Xenakis, and French Pierre Boulez. I started researching Polish music after becoming the Director of the Polish Music Center at the University of Southern California in Los Angeles in 1996. As I wrote in "My Way to Polonia – A Memoir," at that time, in music history research, I went back home, to my native language, and an immersion in Polish musical culture:[4]

> Ignacy Jan Paderewski was the topic of two full issues of the *Polish Music Journal* in 2001-2 and six articles of mine, examining his image as "an Archangel at the Piano," and idol of female audiences, his opera *Manru*, his career choices and concert tours, as well as his reception by poets (2001-2025).
>
> Searching for an "angle" that would endear the Polish Music Center to Californian Polonia and result in more donations, I discovered that Paderewski received an honorary doctorate from USC in 1923; the university archivist even located press clippings from that event. I decided to establish the Annual Paderewski Lecture-Recitals, inviting one famous Polish composer per year for a lecture, seminars, and concerts. In 2002, my first choice, pianist-composer Zygmunt Krauze, had the entire Helena Modjeska Art & Culture Club in the audience, amazing my USC colleagues, and resulting in

---

[4] "My Way to Polonia — A Memoir," in an anthology of memoirs *"I Remember When . . ." Memories from the Polish American Historical Association* James S. Pula, ed. (PAHA Books, 2025).

increased financial support for the Center. I'm glad that the Paderewski Lecture-Recitals continue until today.

Two studies of Paderewski that I wrote at USC are reproduced in this volume, accompanied by an article about a unique album of concert programs, photos and press clippings collected by one of his British female fans that I found in 2016 (Essay 3), and another article based on a study commissioned by Dr. Stephen Downes for an edited volume dedicated to the changing image of Poland outside its borders.[5] Dr. Downes invited me to revisit the topic of Paderewski in poetry since he knew my work from 2001. His invitation resulted in my visit to the Archiwum Akt Nowych in search of more poems, and the results can be seen here—I found these poems so interesting that I decided to publish them.

These English-language poems about Ignacy Jan Paderewski primarily come from two sources. A small subset was written for the 10th anniversary of Poland's independence and published in 1928.[6] These poems are discussed in my article "Paderewski in Poetry: Master of Harmonies or Poland's Savior?" a special, Paderewski-themed issue of the online *Polish Music Journal* 4:1 (Summer 2001). The poems themselves were reproduced in 'Paderewski and the Tenth Anniversary of Poland's Independence (1928), in the same issue of the *Polish Music Journal*.

The book contains selections from a set of sixty-six English-language poems, written between 1890 and 1940 and preserved in the holdings of Archiwum Akt Nowych (AAN, Archive of Modern Records) in Warsaw, Poland. These poems are a part of the Archiwum Ignacego Jana Paderewskiego 1880-1940 (Ignace Jan Paderewski Archive 1880-1940, henceforth "Paderewski Archive") that "contains the entire archival legacy" of the pianist-statesman and was donated to the AAN after Paderewski's death. On the AAN website the archive is described as "one of the most

---

[5] "Romantic, Sublime, Heroic, Immortal: Paderewski and Poland in Poetry" a chapter in Stephen Downes and Daniel Elphick, eds., *Constructing Polish Musical Identities Outside Poland Since 1880 – Sounding 'Polish'* (Suffolk, U.K.: Boydell Press, May 2026).

[6] *To Ignace Jan Paderewski, Artist, Patriot, Humanitarian.* (New York: The Kosciuszko Foundation, 1928).

valuable collections" of AAN that "contains tens of thousands of docu-ments, diplomas, letters, scores, and photographs, many of which are particularly valuable for understanding the culture and political life of Poland and the Polish diaspora. In addition, non-archival items related to I.J. Paderewski's life, including his orders, decorations, and so on, are also stored."[7]

Poems selected for inclusion come from the folder signature 2/100/0/8/3763, *Wiersze dedykowane I. J. Paderewskiemu* (Poems dedicated to I. J. Paderewski), where hundreds of poems in Polish, English, French, German and Italian (dated from 1882 to 1940) are organized alphabetically by the poet's last name. Looseleaf pages feature penciled-in, handwritten pagination and, occasionally, the poet's last name. This collection appears to be the work of Paderewski's persona secretary Sylvin Strakacz (1892-1973); creating such an alphabetic arrangement would have made sense during the composer's lifetime. The earlier poem from 1882 to 1890, not included here, are in Polish and were written at the outset of his virtuoso career. Some came in letters and greetings mailed to Paderewski's home in Riond-Bosson, Switzerland from Poland, the U.S., Canada, England, Scotland, France, and Australia. Some were clipped from newspapers or concert programs, some were handwritten, and some typed, with handwritten dedications. Of the English-language poems, thirty-one were by female poets, twenty-six by male poets, and nine remained anonymous.

This set of poems is complemented by those I found in other archives, including the Performing Arts Division of the New York Public Library, and the Los Angeles Public Library. One poem about Paderewski in Brighton is from *Paderewski Brighton Album* assembled in England by his faithful fan and admirer, Miss Michell, in 1890-1914. I bought it on eBay and discuss this document and its ramification in Essay 3 included after the poems. Last but not least, poems printed here feature the most recent tributes to Paderewski, written in 2010 and 2018 respectively by Kath Abela Wison and myself.

---

[7] Information from the website of the Archiwum Akt Nowych in Warsaw accessed 9/24/2025. https://www.aan.gov.pl/a,6,archiwum-ignacego-jana-paderewskiego-1880-1940.

Clearly, my interest in Paderewski poems is not entirely academic. Without formal training in poetry or English literature, I started writing poems in English in the early 1990s, but decided to present my poems in public for the first time only in 2007, thanks to the encouragement of Kath Abela Wison and my daughter, Anna Claire Harley-Trochimczyk, Ph.D. From there, I went on to publishing 11 books of poetry and becoming the President of California State Poetry Society. My hobby became my avocation and a favorite research topic, merging music history training with poetic interests.

Whie acknowledging individuals that helped me on this journey to admiring Paderewski, I would like to offer special thanks to Dr. Stefan Wilk and his wife Wanda Harasimowicz Wilk, the founders of the Polish Music Reference Center at the University of Southern California for following upon the recommendation made unanimously by Polish musicologists and historians (my academic advisor, Prof. Zofia Heman, and Dr. Teresa Chylinska, Prof. Wodzimierz Kotonski, and Zygmunt Krauze) to hire me as the Center's Director in 1995. While my tenure lasted for eight years, 1996-2003, the passion of Ms. Wilk for Polish music and her admiration for Paderewski were contagious and I diverted my career as a historian to these topics. Moving to California from Canada in 1996 was one of the most beneficial and transformative events of my life and I am profoundly grateful to the Wilks for that opportunity.

While working on my poetry anthology, *Chopin with Cherries: A Tribute in Verse* (2010), I discovered that organizing poetry readings accompanied with live music is the ideal way of presenting both, so I am deeply grateful to Dr. Wojciech Kocyan, for enchanting poets with Chopin's Mazurkas and Waltzes, and accompanying their dance with a Chopin Polonaise at the Ruskin Art Club. This was an unforgettable experience and an inspiration to continue marrying poetry with music. Prof. Kocyan is the Artistic Director of the Paderewski Music Society, established in 2008, and our Paderewski collaboration is certain to continue.

Next, I would like to thank the Archive of Modern Records in Warsaw, Poland for permission to reprint poems from the Paderewski Archive. I'm also immensely grateful to Emma Boyd, of Reader Services at the National Scottish Library, who transcribed several handwritten and hard-to-decipher poems and provided an annotated translation from Scots into English with explanatory notes needed by the readers. A talented graphic designer Urszula Beaudoin prepared two Paderewski signatures from the *Paderewski Brighton Album* for use as illustrations in the book. These lovely and elegant signatures also grace the pages of a companion volume, with three pays about Paderewski written by Prof. Kazimierz Braun (Moonrise Press, 2025).

I dedicate this collection of Paderewski poems and essays to the talented pianists that faithfully follow in his footsteps, with hours of hard work, persistency, and unyielding dedication. Their passion, talents and musicality are greatly appreciated by their listeners. Classical music lovers of their audiences may also want to learn how virtuoso pianists were perceived way-back-when and enjoy finding out "How Paderewski Plays."

Maja Trochimczyk
12 December 2025

PART I

PADEREWSKI POEMS

NOTES

The following poems, written in English, are organized in an alphabetical order by the last name of the author, starting with "anonymous" poems. The bulk of the verse (40 poems) comes from Archiwum Ignacego Jana Paderewskiego 1860-1940 (Paderewski Archive) in Archiwum Akt Nowych (AAN, Archive of Modern Records) in Warsaw, Poland, These documents contain his corresponddence, papers, and assorted memorabilia. The poetry collection bears signature number 2/100/0/8/3763 and features hand-written page numbers in pencil on each looseleaf page. Each poem selected for publication here bears a note about its origins and the page number in the archives. I discuss their contents and significance in Essay 4, partly based on my chapter "Romantic, Sublime, Heroic, Immortal: Paderewski and Poland in Poetry" in a volume edited by Stephen Downes and Daniel Elphick, *Constructing Polish Musical Identities Outside Poland Since 1880 – Sounding 'Polish'* (Suffolk, U.K.: Boydell Press, May 2026).

Several of the remaining 12 poems were written for the 10th anniversary of Poland's independence and published by the Kościuszko Foundation, in *To Ignace Jan Paderewski, Artist, Patriot, Humanitarian* (New York, 1928). These poems are discussed in my article. "Paderewski in Poetry: Master of Harmonies or Poland's Savior?" in a special issue, "Paderewski and Polish Émigrés in America;" of the online *Polish Music Journal* 4:1 (Summer 2001).

Finally, scattered poems were located among ephemera, press clippings and documents held by the New York Public Library and Los Angeles Public Library. One previously unknown poem was in the *Paderewski Brighton Album* (1890-1914, see Essay 3); for others I should thank the engineers of the modern search engines.

— Maja Trochimczyk

Impressions of a Paderewski Recital

The hall was bright 'neath the shimmering light
    With gold and crimson and blue.
Each place was filled and the people thrilled,
With one intent, as they forward bent,
    For a glimpse of a face that they knew.

There's a form at the door, there's a step on the floor,
    And the sound of applause that endures.
In heart-felt ovation and the pride of a nation,
Rise up with one thought and a token is wrought,
    Of the honor devotion assures.

* * * * * * * * *

Three hours had passed, though all too fast,
    The colorful throng had departed.
In the shadowy bend at the concert's end,
We gathered around as the soulful sound
    From ivory key board started.

We listened, enchanted, to chords that implanted
    By the cadence and mood of their art
Sweet fancies long sought in the realm of our thought.
But the vision that lingers, as it floats from his fingers
    Is reflecting the Master's own heart.

1925

— **Anonymous**
1925

NOTE: *Typescript of a poem, without the author's name. AAN Paderewski Archive, page 304.*

≡ 3 ≡

A Scotch Tribute

"For Paderewski!" So they said –
(Ma heid was in a creel)
"A guinea Teecket!" and for me?
I could hae danced a reel! –

I coonted weel the 'oors, ye ken
Till syne the nicht cam roon –
And I was in the muckle Ha'
Wi' eager folk aroon' –

But when the Player sat him doon
Then a' was still as deith –
Sae feared were we tae lose a note
We scarce could draw a breith! –

And first of a' – as soft and sweet
As weslin' wins that blaw –
A strain o' witchin' melody
Comes stealin' through the Ha' –

But see! The Maister swaps the
    keys
Till grander tones they take –
And aye his fingers faster speed
Till a' the strings awake –

And noo they shriek wi erdlich glee,
And noo they stoond in pain,
And noo they croon a lullaby
Tae soothe a fractious wean -

And noo they're dancing up and
    doon
Like wavelets on the shore –
And noo again: we close oor een
And hear the breakers roar! –

But best of a', I mind a lilt
Sae waefu' like and sweet,
It's dirling in ma hert the noo

"For Paderewski!" So they said –
(My head was in a creel)
"A guinea Ticket!" and for me?
I could have danced a reel! –

I counted well the hours, you
    know
Until then the night came round-
And I was in the large Hall –
With eager people around –

But when the Player sat him down
Then all was still as death –
So feared were we to lose a note
We scarce could draw a breath! –

And first of all – as soft and sweet
As western winds that blow –
A strain of bewitching melody
Comes stealing through the Hall

But see! The Master swaps the
    keys
Until grander tones they take –
And yes his fingers faster speed
Until all the strings awake –

And now they shriek with
    unearthly glee,
And now they stand in pain,
And now they sing a lullaby
To soothe a fractious child –

And now they're dancing up and
    down
Like waves on the shore –
And now again: we close our eyes
And hear the breakers roar! –

But best of all, I mind a lilt
So woeful like and sweet,
It's dirling in my heart the now

And maks me like tae greet!

And what of him wha had the skill
Tae open up oor een
Tae wonders o' the music World
That else we hadna seen?

Beethoven, Bach, and Rubenstein,
Liszt, Chopin and them a'
They passed afore us, ilka ane
In answer to his ca'

Tae "Paderewski", the divine –
We'll offer on our pairt
A gift auld Time can never dim
A grateful people's hert!

And makes me like to cry!

And what of him who had the skill
To open up our eyes
To wonders of the music World
That else we hadn't seen?

Beethoven, Bach and Rubenstein,
Liszt, Chopin and them all
They passed before us, each one
In answer to his call

To "Paderewski", the divine –
We'll offer on our part
A gift old Time can never dim
A grateful people's heart!

— **Anonymous**

NOTES: Handwritten poem in Scots, on pages 291-292 in AAN Paderewski Archive. Transcribed and translated from Scottish into English by Emma Boyd, Reader Services, National Library of Scotland. Her notes are below.

creel = 'confusion, perplexed' – in a creel, in confusion, in a state of perplexity, gen. applied to the head or senses
guinea = a type of coin (no longer used in the British currency system)
reel = a type of ceilidh dance
stealing = in this context, means working/making its way through
erdlich = there is no direct translation that we have come across but believe It to be a version of 'eldrltch' to mean 'unearthly'. The word erdlich appears in James Hogg's 1816 poem Mador of the Moor *with the glossary to this translating 'erdlich' as 'unearthly' too. Burns also uses 'eldritch' in some of his poems.*
stoond = we think this may just be 'stand' but it could also be a variant of 'stound' which translates as 'astound' but also has a connotation to terrify, which would fit in with the context here too.
mind = in this context means 'remember'
dirling = 'thrilling sensation', 'vibrating motion'
the now = this is often used in Scotland instead of saying 'just now'
like (last line) = in this context meaning 'feel like / want to'
Ilka = 'each, every, of two or more. Ilka bodie, everyone'

To Paderewski

What that my hands have played with the raiment of God!
What though universes have spun about my finger's tips!
What though moonlight flowed my veins
And came forth in a white song,
Ethereal as morning mist!
What though my soul conceived the sun!
And burst in a golden fury, triumphant!
What though, listening, I may impart
The lisping of young waves —
Or the froth of foam on the wave's crest
Cool as a phantom's kiss —
What of all this! —
Rather would I be
As a plough share
Sunk in the bosom of my land,
Making it fertile — for fruition.

_____

Behold, in the dark abode of day
Have I left some holy taper burning —
A scarlet, glowing flame
Before the altar of the day.
Then, am I satisfied
To become the holy veil
Therefrom arising to intermingle with the altar —
The common office of day
Whereon man pays tribute.
But I shall elude all this
Lifting me upward,
Leaving behind the golden glowing light.

— Anonymous
1924

NOTE: A typescript dated Feb. 20, 1924. AAN Paderewski Archive, p. 289.

To Paderewski

Shine thou, forth, thou star of genius,
    With thy Heaven-given light,
With success that crowns endeavor
    Peerless Poland's might.
Thou, whom nations will remember
    Establisher of Poland free,
Go——the pinnacle of music
    Played and written, lies in thee.
Paderewski, all we wish thee,
    The millions here who love thy art,
Is that the bliss that Thou bestowest
    Returns ten-fold into thy heart.

December 18, 1925

— Anonymous
1925

NOTE: Anonymous typescript. AAN Paderewski Archive, p. 305.

Lines to an Artist (I.J.P.)
On His Playing...

A spark from the sun
A bolt from the blue —
A brief glimpse of heaven —
Your playing —and you —

Like waves in the moonlight,
Flowers gemmed with dew,
An ideal world dawning —
Your playing — and you.

Like flames in the darkness,
Stars fiery blue —
Life's joys, griefs and ecstasies,
Elle est votre jouit —

— **A. B.**
1928

NOTE: *Handwritten poem signed with initials A.B., dated 11 June 1928. The last name "Bryer" is penciled-in in the top left corner. AAN Paderewski Archive, p. 7. The French phrase means "she is your joy."*

To Paderewski—Sovereign—Pianist (1)
(Sonnet)

I bow to thee, incomparable Pole
Thou art a flawless glass wherein we scan
The melancholy which we call Chopin,
Beethoven passionate, tumultuous soul
They cannot die, no bells for them shall knoll.
Whoever cheats mortality, they can
Supreme themselves against the doom of man
More thro' thy special genius, round and whole
Tonight, a million indeed eyes have seen
Thy hands, consummate past a living man's
Subtly portray in mastery serene
Beethoven, only patient genius scans
Master, with tremulous Schubert I have been,
Mine eyes have seen thy glory and Chopin's.

— A. F. Bates

NOTE: *Two typescript poems on the same page, signed A.F. Bates with the address "The Avenue BALBY, Nr. Leicester." AAN Paderewski Archive, p. 1. The initials A.F. were sometimes used by Katharine Lee Bates (1859-1929), the celebrated author of "America, the Beautiful" (1893), one of the most beautiful patriotic songs of the U.S. Born and raised in Massachusetts, she was a poet, journalist and educator, who studied at Oxford University and Wellesley College where she later became a professor. Among over 20 books the majority are poetry collections, with some literary criticism travelogues, and essays. The identification of the poet is not certain, but the town of Leicester is indeed in Massachusetts where Bates lived, so that's one clue.*

To Paderewski—Sovereign—Pianist (2)
(Sonnet)

Master, thy genius hurts, 'tis so intense
So faultless, crystal-pure, like dew that drips
On a far-mountain side from one flower's lips
The bees have found not. Oh! the sheer suspense
Betwixt the notes. Say, Master whither, whence
This magic? Past a sirens' luring ships
Where great Odysseus went, each bell that dips
And sways and swells to full magnificence.
Let me not call on angels for thy peer,
Cry out to some far heaven, vainly scan
The firmament to match thy clear
Soul-sounding deep-sea music; let Chopin
Be thy great harp and Israfel shall fear
Thy mastery, he, a seraph, thou a man.

— *A. F. Bates*

NOTE: Second of two typescript poems signed A.F. Bates with the address the Avenue BALBY, Nr Leicester." AAN Paderewski Archive, p. 1. "Israfel" is the name of the angel of music in Islam, one of the four archangels announcing the Day of Last Judgement.

Genius

Genius is no child of chance,
Product of whim, or circumstance,
Down through seething chaos hurled,
A haphazard destiny to unfurl,

With measured tread, and dauntless heart,
Unconquerable it moves, a thing apart,
Not from earthly flesh pots sprung
In the soul's travail its song is sung.

Crucible wherein a dross is consumed
To the throb of the universe attuned,
Interpreter of every living thing
Way-shower, prophet, winged king.

**— Dorothy Hull Beatty
1938**

NOTE: Typescript of a poem, with typed-in dedication: "Dedicated to Ignace Jan Paderewski, Los Angeles, April 1938, Dorothy Hull Beatty" and a handwritten signature below. AAN Paderewski Archive, p. 2.

I Am Music

(Dedicated to Columbia University)

I am the song of the Universe.

I am the gurgle of the sparkling silvery brooklet, the monotone of the falling waters of the mountain stream, the dance of the rain on the lonely cabin roof.

I am the patter of children's feet on a city street that offsets the dull clamor of busy commerce.

I am the harmonies of the earth and celestial bodies.

I am the voice of the reasoning power of the eternal love of God.

I am the unspoken, unarticulated voice of love.

I am the siren of the Universe,

I am the spirit that breathed the happiness of the Universe into existence.

I am the wooing voice that brings peace and order out of wreckage and chaos.

I inspired the Song of Salomon and Psalms of David.

I am the wordless, winning voice of the Almighty, the Eternal God.

I am the paradise of love in human feelings and emotions.

I both inflame and soothe.

I furnish comfort in the aged who has lost his life mate — and bring sweet dreams of yesteryear and childhood.

I lull peaceful babies to sleep and incite warriors to battle.

I soothe the vanquished in defeat and cheer the victor in success.

I congratulate the proud parent of the birth of a child and soothe him when one has passed to the Great Beyond.

I was the inspiring notes of the harp of old, blind Homer and aided him in composing his immortal verse.

I deeply touch the world with shame for the way they have treated past great masters, such as Mozart in the garret, and others.

I furnished cheer and comfort to my patron Saint Dante in his miserable exile.

I utilize the crude harp of the child, the coarse bagpipe of the
Scotch highlander, and the magic flute of the hillside
shepherds.

I melt audiences to tears through lovely lips and with drum and
fife I scale the Alps.

I am purity—truth—wholesomeness and you, when your heart is
true and your soul is merry.

I am the promoter of art and enlightenment.

I am the kind words of admonition from a father to his son.

I am the thoughts of an artist who works only for the betterment
of humanity and forgets himself.

I am the devoted lover speaking wooing words of magic fire to his
soul mate.

I am the sweetest and most enchanting chord that touches the
human ear.

I am the beautiful voice of love that a mother sings to her babe.

I am that hypnotic—something—that man can feel but cannot
see, and I am free by the Grace of God to both king and peasant.

I am the tamer of wild beasts and soother of the savage breast.

I am the inspiration of the human soul that radiates from the
stringed instrument of Pan, by lovers of beauty and mankind.

I AM THE HUMAN SOUL IN ACTION AND IN TUNE WITH THE
OMNIPOTENT INFINITE.

I am the chimes of the combined merry laughter of children.

I am the bitterness and salt in maiden's tear, or the illuminating
sunbeam from her soul in her laughter that rings in love.

I deeply touch the heart and soul and am deeply felt by both
friend or foe.

I am the song of the poet interpreted into the songs of ages.

I am poetry in harmony with God and the inspiration of the
infinite Universe.

I am the heavenly chord that enchants and entrances the human
soul.

I am the euphonious chords whispering through the summer
zephyrs, in the unpruned natural wildwoods.

I am the charming fascinator of the happiness and inner deep
feelings of nature's expression.

I furnish music in the awakening hour, in the song of the robin,

From the Heavens and echo the voice of paradise at eventide in
the sweet strains of the nightingale.

I supply your good-night anthem in the nightly carol of the
grasshopper.

I am the sweet lullaby at the cradle and the hymn of God's eternal
peace at the grave.

"I AM MUSIC."

— Berton Bellis
1925

NOTE: A printed flyer marked below the poem as "Reprinted from The
Billboard*," with a handwritten dedication scribbled diagonally across:
"To the Prince of Poland, Paderewski, Given very sincerely, Barton Bellis,
1925." AAN Paderewski Archive, p. 4.*

*The format of this poem with repeated "I AM" invocations resembles
the meditations by the founders of St. Germain Foundation, a spiritual
group with roots in Theosophy, established by Guy Ballard in America, and
known as the "I AM" movement, see Essay 4. Berton Bellis, an American
poet born in St. Louis, Missouri penned a well-known poem "Abraham
Lincoln" in 1919 and published* Select Poems from the Pen of Berton
Bellis *in 1924.*

Paderewski Plays the Moonlight Sonata

Oh, do not even whisper while he makes
A potent influence of dead master's chords,
Responsive in my soul, they come to life
And listening as the great musician plays,
Awaking images of wavelets, bright,
Of moonlit paths across vast faerie seas,
Gentle and playful, dancing silently,
And then a-sudden, wild and wilder soars
The tumult of the dashing billows, bent
With angry roar at upstart beings who dare
Despise, defy the Lord of land and sea.

The Patriot plays, we hearken to the spell:
The music that he makes a message brings —
We are immortal, in this faith we live.

— **Arthur Bryant**

NOTE: Handwritten, undated poem about Beethoven's Sonata in C-sharp minor, Op. 27, No. 2, with a note in bottom left corner: "with respectful homage." AAN Paderewski Archive, p. 6. Sir Arthur Wynne Morgan Bryan (1899-1985) was a well-known British historian and writer, author of biographies of Samuel Pepys and King George V, among other books. He served as a pilot in British Air Force in WWI, and later was a lecturer in history at Oxford University. Bryant published over 40 books that had a combined readership of over two million.

When Paderewski Plays

I journey far with Memory
When Paderewski plays
And in a spell of fancy walk
Of path of "Then-a-days."

A rhapsody of Liszt inspires
And Campanella rings,
Beethoven seems to breathe again
When Poland's minstrel sings.

The concert grand beneath his spell
Responds to every thrill
Vibrating in the master's hand,
Commanded by his will.

His tones of beauty sensuous,
Flow rich in melodies,
Ecstatic halleluiahs and
In harping symphonies.

Across our heartstrings tenderly
Emotions freely play,
Forgotten songs of other days,
That charm our cares away.

The long ago steals back again
Revealed in lights and shades,
And youth's sweet harp once more attunes
The lovers' serenades.

The deepest music of the soul
Comes when the journey's done,
'Tis richer when the heart grows old,
But sweeter when it's young.

Sing on, piano's patriot bard,
And charm the years away,
And make the heart of youth to sing
Forever and a day!

— **Will George Butler**
(before 1923)

PADEREWSKI DAY

This is international known as "Paderewski Day" and is under the auspices of a committee of one hundred musicians and patrons of music. To-day, Wednesday, November, at 3:00 o'clock, in Carnegie Hall, New York City, Paderewski will play his famous "Minuet" and all over the world it will be known as Paderewski Day. For this event in the metropolis, the seats have been sold out for three weeks and tickets are now at a premium of 25.00 and cannot be secured even at this price.

NOTE: A typescript of this poem with a name typed in and a handwritten signature bears and additional quotation in the bottom left corner: "When he seeks the pianoforte to sing, it is a chorus of ecstatic hallelujahs and harping symphonies.—Mr. Krehbiel in The Tribune." *Henry Edward Krehbiel (1854-1923) was the music critics of the Chicago Tribune to 1923. AAN Paderewski Archive, p. 8. One more handwritten copy of this poem with the Krehbiel quote is on p. 9 and a typeset copy in elegant font is on p. 10 of AAN Paderewski Archive. Another variant of this poem is printed anonymously, and included as p. 290 in AAN Paderewski Archive, where the poem is preceded by the note about Paderewski Day copied above. Will George Butler (1876-1955) was a prolific composer of over 200 songs, director of music programs at Mansfield State Normal School, later transformed into Mansfield State College in Pennsylvania.*

Polonia Resurgata

Just life and nothing more, poor Poland sought
Of those who ravished and reviled her. She,
Sublime in native generosity,
Endured the pain dismemberment had wrought;
For, though a love divine the Christ had taught,
Predacious rulers, deaf to mercy's plea,
Intent upon their vile rapacity,
laid low the land their ruthless greed had caught.

So bowed with grief was Poland's gentle head,
Upheld alone by hope that God in grace
Decreed that She, by dauntless heroes led,
Should rise again, and bright her happy face
Keep on the path to glory, might and place,
Inspired by peace of perfect union bred.

To the dauntless fighter
For Poland's right,
In and out of Poland.

— Adolphe de Castro

NOTE: Typescript of a poem, undated, with a handwritten signature. AAN Paderewski Archive, p. 11. Adolphe Danzinger de Castro (1859–1959), a Polish-Jewish-American poet, writer, and rabbi published five novels, four volumes of poetry, a collection of short stories and several texts on Jewish politics and culture. With a Ph.D. in oriental philology from the University of Bonn (1882), he emigrated to the U.S. a year later and lived in different cities, St. Louis, San Francisco, New York, before settling in Los Angeles. He served as U.S. Ambassador in Spain and resided for short periods in Scottland and Mexico.

Paderewski

Sunlight dancing on the leaves,
Spring rain dripping from the eaves,
Snow-capped mountains towering heights,
A mother's tender lullaby —
When Paderewski plays.

A jewel flashing in the sun,
The fading light when day is done,
A brooklet tinkling on its way,
The mighty ocean's surge and sway —
When Paderewski plays.

Minneapolis, May 8.

— Myrtle E. Cone
1924

NOTE: *Press clipping with a poem written in Minneapolis on 8 May (no year), affixed to a page with a handwritten signature and the following note: "Afterthoughts upon the most wonderful music to be conceived." Below, in the bottom left corner, the address and date: "626 E. 6th Street, Sioux Falls, South Dakota, April 15, 1924." AAN Paderewski Archive, p. 13.*

Paderewski

The stars that sang in Time's awakening
sent each to each upon their golden rounds,
    a messenger, to hold the chords profound,
    unbroken still, so David's magic string
loosened the evil fetters of his king!
So here — from what great star, divinely crowned? —
    Rapt in whose ecstasy of perfect sound
    Each ivory key becomes a living thing,
Aeolian murmurs of a mystic dream,
The gathering tempest mighty thunder-roll,
    A sob, a shivering sight, just breathed, and mute
    Strife, triumph, rapture, peace of Heaven supreme —
All, all are his, the Master's — twin of soul
With Israfel "whose heartstrings are a lute."

— **Ina Coolbrith**

NOTE: *Typeset in a beautiful font, this poem is found in AAN Paderewski Archive, p. 14. "Israfel" is the angel of music in Islamic tradition.*
    Ina Donna Coolbrith (1841-1928) was an American poet, writer, and librarian, active in the San Francisco Bay Area literary circles. The niece of Joseph Smith, the founder of the Mormon Church, she left the church and in 1915 was crowned as the first California Poet Laureate and the first poet laureate of any U.S. state. She published four volumes of poetry, including A Perfect Day *(1881) and* Wings of Sunset *(1929). See Aleta George,* Ina Coolbrith: The Bittersweet Song of California's First Poet Laureate *(Shifting Plates Press, 2015).*

Paderewski Plays at Lausanne Cathedral

I.
On pillars mounting to dark mystery
Some scribe, jealous of a silent God,
Forbids us, slaves of music, to applaud.
We wait like forest spirits robbed of glee
Till lo! Each pillar turns into a tree,
Swayed by a wind that laughs at rule and rod.
Because of magic rising from the sod,
And old Silenus talking gloriously.

He talks through Schumann's beauty, Chopin's tears,
Beethoven's quiet and the storm of Liszt,
Through Schubert's ongoing talks us up to spheres
Where our apt brows by Presences are kissed
And gloomy silence whirls away in fright,
On the loud torrent of the heart's delight.

II.
Master, and freeman of the world's free lands,
You, with no gesture of the hand that deigns
Suffering, like Chopin for a land in chains,
Laid by your art at Freedom's rough demands.
Now, though your hair, no aureole expands,
Of russet fame, the inner fire remains
With man's long sorrow sweetening your strains,
And his sure triumph thundering from your hands.

Who says, the snow has fallen on your head?
Nay, you have mounted to the soul's pure snow,
With eyes unflinching and unwavering tread,
By paths which only Alpine spirit knows,
Whose end is in the white accomplished peak
Where the immortals with immortals speak.

— James H. Cousins, 1928

NOTE: Typescript of a poem dated November 27, 1928. AAN Paderewski Archive, p. 17. James Henry Cousins (1873-1956) was an Irish-Indian writer, poet, critic, editor, and educator, the author of 20 books of poems and essays. He was inspired by the Theosophy movement, Hindu & Buddhist religions and their focus on spiritual enlightenment— the subject of many of his books, e.g., The Quest, The Wisdom of the West, The Bases of Theosophy, A Tibetan Banner, *and* A Bardic Pilgrimage.

When Paderewski Plays

I.
The brooklet's voice clear whispers
Gurgles on its pebbly ways.
The Mockingbird sings in unison
Its joyous roundelays.
The children's merry voices
Now seem to fill the air.
The sparrows twitter in the trees
Sweet harmony everywhere.

II.
Sudden, adown the rocky road
A horseman thunders past.
Clear and long from out the wood
shrills a single bugle blast.
Against the trampling horse's feet,
the booming of a gun,
The hunters' whoop and yelp of dogs
commingled into one.

III.
A whirlwind of tempestuous sound,
then all again is still
Save the low trinkle of a bell
from some distant hill.
Music in majestic roar,
or sighing in soft lays,
Ah, thus to list the soul entranced
while Paderewski plays.

— **Flora Fain Crist**
1923

*NOTE: A handwritten poem, dated 29 November 1923, Atlanta, Georgia.
AAN Paderewski Archive, pages 18 and 19. According to cemetery records,
a certain Flora Fain Crist was born in 1869 and died in 1954, in Atlanta,
Georgia, where she was also buried. This may have been the poet, since the
location is the same and the name seems rare enough.
https://www.findagrave.com/memorial/75880599/mattie-flora-crist*

To Paderewski

What mystic charm thou hast with thee
Thou enchanter of a human soul.
What tales thy music dost impart to me
of every age recounts to me its role.
I see a knight in silvery plume bedecked
Dash by on steed as black as is the dark.
I hear the tongues of war, when nations
     vengeance wreaked,
When in the turmoil man to God must hark
And then thy spell departs to lighter theme.
The simple country in the joyous time of spring,
The happy glades with apple blossoms gleam,
A summers night when e'ven the heavens sing.
Oh, could I ever hear thy all inspiring lay,
Could I fore'er be near when thou dost play.

— **Mary Francis Crosby**

NOTE: A handwritten poem without a date, AAN Paderewski Archive, p. 23.
Mary Francis Crosby, also known as Fanny J. Crosby (1820-1915), was a
prolific and long-lived poet, specializing in hymnody. A mission worker,
lyricist, and composer, she wrote over 8,000 hymns and gospel songs, of
which the most famous and still in use are: "Pass Me Not, O Gentle
Saviour", "Blessed Assurance", "Jesus Is Tenderly Calling You Home",
"Praise Him, Praise Him", and "To God Be the Glory." Her hymns were
often published under one of nearly 200 pseudonyms and reached over
100 million copies in print. Most commonly used American hymn books
included her work, associated with the spiritual revival movement.

Paderewski

Chicago, February 6th, 1916

Let the sun weep and the moon shed tears —
A sun god is ravaged,
Poland dying, and cold.

"We saw babies sucking beet-roots
Wrapped in rags —
Starvation, ruin, mould."

Let great elegance weep, fierceness and pride:
There, in front of Poland's flag.
Paderewski, passionate, cold.

And the light flamed of Poland's years.
And Chopin from her crags —
A clear, proud story told.

— Dorothy Dudley
1916

NOTE: Published in Poetry *10: 4 (July 1917): 189. Dorothy Dudley (1884-1962), was an American poet from Chicago, a graduate of Bryn Mawr College (1905). She and her sister, Helen, worked closely with the editor of the* Poetry *magazine, Harriet Monroe. Dudley's poems appeared also in* The Dial *and* The Nation. *She is the author of a biography of Theodore Dreiser,* Forgotten Frontiers: Dreiser and the Land of the Free *(New York: H. Smith & R. Haas, 1932).*

The Golden Bear

Team song of U.C. Berkeley Bears Football Team

1.
Oh, have you seen the heavens blue, heavens blue,
When just sev'n stars are shining through, shining through,
Right overhead a jovial crew?
They're joining hands to make the Bear.
Right overhead a jovial crew?
They're joining hands to make the Bear!
2.
And oh, that Bear's a glorious sight, glorious sight,
A-circling 'round the pole all night, pole all night;
And once you've seen him, you're all right,
You've seen our California Bear.
And once you've seen him, you're all right,
You've seen our California Bear!
3.
He has a very patient air, patient air,
He wears a Paderewski hair, 'rewski hair,
He's the center rush of the heavens I swear,
Our silent, sturdy Golden Bear.
He's the center rush of the heavens I swear,
Our silent, sturdy Golden Bear!
4.
Oh, have you seen our banner blue, banner blue?
The Golden Bear is on it too, on it too,
A Californian through and through,
Our totem, He, the Golden Bear.
A Californian through and through,
Our totem, He, the Golden Bear!

— Charles Mills Gayley

NOTE: Reproduced with a corrected spelling of Paderewski's last name (originally "Paderooski"). Written in 1895, it is the oldest song in the Cal Band's repertoire. Charles Mills Gayley (1858-1932) was born in Shanghai, studied in Michigan, and served as professor of Latin and English at the University of Michigan. Since 1889, he was as a professor of English Language and Literature at U.C. Berkeley for whom he wrote this song. calband.berkeley.edu/media/cal-songs/#Golden%20Bear.

[Untitled]

Thy fingers, skilled, upon the heartstrings play
While smiles and tears their changeful mood obey,
The soul's impassioned language they translate
And its weird poesy articulate.

Emblem of thee, this match-safe with these fires suppressed
That flame at sudden touch like thou, thy warmth concealing
Until the cold piano keys unlock thy breast,
Its hidden fires and wealth of poesy revealing.

— **Sara Groenevelt**
1892

NOTE: *Handwritten poem in two parts, dated February 3, 1892, New York City. AAN Paderewski Archive, pages 48 and 49. Sara Groenevelt (d. 1899) was a classical musician and poet, born into an affluent family, owners of a cotton plantation in Louisiana. She studied music in Leipzig and even performed Moscheles' Piano Concerto with the Gewandhaus Orchestra in 1867. She wrote poems under various pen names, publishing her work in* Louisiana Times – Democrat *and* Chicago Current.

Paderewski at Troy

Beside Scamander's stream in ancient Ilium
(From whose dim, moon-lit ramparts Troilus
Sighed toward the Grecian tents where Cressid lay)
Brave Hector, so 'tis said, derided him
Whose love for Helen gave to Homer's harp
The timeless Iliad: "O brother mine
The sounding lyre shall not avail thee now!"
Meaning, (I translate from forgotten Greek
With aid of Lang), that spear and sword alone
Will serve ascending man...
... (Strange, is it not
That all that's left of arms and men and song
Of that old fray is song?)....
...Last night, in Troy,
(Not Hasselik, all tumultuous, but Troy
Which sits beside a new-world's Simois)
I heard brave Hector's taunt again, and then
I heard reply: "Great Paderewski played
Not such a puny lyre as Paris twanged,
But one Christofori designed to sound
The thundering of battle, and, alike,
The peaceful breathings of an oaten pipe;
And hearing, thought: "Had this Red Polack stood
Beside old Priam on the Trojan walls
The battle lost immortally were won!"

— John Huston Finley
1928

NOTE: *Fragments of a longer poem, copied from in Finley's speech at the 1928 10th Anniversary of Poland's Independence by the Kosciuszko Foundation in New York, later published in* To Ignace Jan Paderewski: Artist, Patriot, Humanitarian *(New York: Kosciuszko Foundation, 1928). The speech is reprinted in "Paderewski and the Tenth Anniversary of Poland's Independence," ed. Maja Trochimczyk,* Polish Music Journal *4:1 (2001). Scamander and Simois were ancient rivers; "Troilus and Cressida" —Trojan lovers from Shakespeare's tragedy; Hector and Paris—Trojan princes; and Christofori—the maker of pianos, that replaced the lyre.*

To Paderewski

I salute you, Artist, Statesman, Patriot.
You've brought from out the air such symphonies
As God with all His earth-orchestral range
From cataract through sloughing wind to lark,
Could not produce without the skill of man.
But there's a symphony that you've evoked
From out the hearts of men, more wonderful
Than you have played upon your instrument.
Composed of the praises of mankind
For what you've nobly done to lead again
To its proud place amid earth's greatest States
Your land that gave the world Copernicus,
And for our freedom Kosciuszko gave.

As ancient Orpheus trod the aisles of hell
To rescue from its thrall Eurydice,
So you for Poland. But though Orpheus failed
You won. *Polonia Restituta* lives.

— **John Huston Finley**
1928

NOTE: *Published in* To Ignace Jan Paderewski: Artist, Patriot,
Humanitarian *(New York: Kościuszko Foundation, 1928) two copies—in
calligraphy with an illustration on the first page of the volume and in a
typewritten transcript of Finley's speech, the latter is reprinted in Maja
Trochimczyk, ed.,* Polish Music Journal *4:1 (summer 2001), online.*

*John Houston Finley (1863-1940) was an American politician, writer,
President of City College of New York, President of the State University of
New York, and long-time editor of the* New York Times *(1921-1938). He
received honorary doctorates from over 30 colleges and universities and
was honored by governments of 12 countries with a variety of distinctions.*

How Paderewski Plays

I.
If words were perfume, color, wild desire;
If poet's song were fire
That burned to blood in purple-pulsing veins;
If with a bird-like trill the moments throbbed to hours;
If summer's rains
Turned drop by drop to shy, sweet, maiden flowers;
If God made flowers with light and music in them,
And saddened hearts could win them;
If loosened petals touched the ground
With a caressing sound;
If love's eyes uttered word
No listening lover e'er before had heard;
If silent thoughts spake with a bugle's voice;
If flame passed into song and cried, "Rejoice, rejoice!"
If words could picture life's hopes, heaven's eclipse
When the last kiss has fallen on dying eyes and lips;
If all of mortal woe
Struck on one heart with breathless blow by blow;
If melody were tears and tears were starry gleams
That shone in evening's amethystine dreams;
Ah, yes, if notes were stars, each star a different hue,
Trembling to earth in dew;
Or, of the boreal pulsings, rose and white,
Made majestic music in the night;
If all the orbs lost in the light of day
In the deep silent blue began their harps to play;
And when, in frightening skies the lightnings flashed
And storm-clouds crashed,
If every stroke of light and sound were excess of beauty;
If human syllables could e'er refashion
that fierce electric passion;
If ever art could image (as were the poet's duty)
The grieving, and the rapture, and the thunder
Of that keen hour of wonder, —
That light as if of heaven, that blackness as of hell, —
How Paderewski Plays, then might I dare to tell.

II.

How the great master played! And was it he
Or some disembodied spirit which had rushed
From silence into singing; and had crushed
Into one startled hour a life's felicity,
And highest bliss of knowledge—that all life, grief, wrong,
Turn at the last to beauty and to song!

— **Richard Watson Gilder**
1891

NOTE: *This poem was published in Gilder's collection* A Book of
Music *(New York, The Century Co., 1906): 32-36.*
*Richard Watson Gilder (1844-1909) was an American poet, writer,
journalist, editor, and publisher. He served as managing editor of*
Scribner's Monthly *renamed* The Century Magazine *in 1881; he edited it
until his death and promoted some of the best American poets and writers.
Gilder published nine volumes of his own poetry, including* The Celestial
Passion *(1887),* In the Heights *(1905) and* A Book of Music *(1906).
Paderewski came to know him through the recommendation by actress
Helena Modjeska (1840-1909) and became close friends with the Gilder
family during his American concert tours.*

The Portrait of Paderewski

Hair of flaming sun!
Eyes of the mystic sea!
Archangel of our muse!
IGNACE Paderewski.

King of glorious Poland!
God made him fit to be
A nation's wish (fate willing)
IGNACE JAN PADEREWSKI.

— "Halka"
1917

NOTE: *This poem was printed in* The Musical Courier *on 22 February 1917; the press clipping was found in the Research Collection, Performing Arts Division, New York Public Library. The original publication was in the* Von Ende Bulletin *issued by the Von Ende School of Music, where pianist-composer and Paderewski's friend and collaborator Zygmunt Stojowski (Sigismond, 1870-1946) was a faculty member. "Halka" is a name of the tragic heroine of a popular Polish opera by the same title, composed by Stanislaw Moniuszko (1819-1873).*

When "Padi" Comes to Town

(Nearly a score of years ago, the writer composed the following lines at Salina, Kansas. "Padi" is used for the sake of rhythm.)

The air is filled with rumors
Of how the people come
From Dan to far Beersheba
To hear the mighty one.
And to see him pound the ivories
In finished style, you know
For a Barnum isn't in it
When Padi gives a show.

He comes in regal fashion
This king in music grand,
To gather in the shekels
From o'er this goody land.
And to dazzle the natives
With his brilliancy, I throw
For the people sit and marvel
When Padi gives a show.

It is said of Paderewski
When his charming music flows
That it hypnotizes women,
For so the story goes.
And it seems from my observing
As I watched his hands come down
That you might as we surrender
When Padi comes to town.

Somehow he makes you wonder
While you sit a'drinking in
The melodies of heaven
That come pouring out of him.

Why the angels up in glory
Ever sent him down below
For they surely want to be here
When Padi gives a show.

And now perhaps I'm dreaming
As I panse to earn just why
This music wizard leads me
From the earth up to the sky.
But, friend, no mortal being
With the soul attuned to praise
Should miss the things a'doing
When Paderewski plays.

— George W. Hootman
1931 (written in 1923)

NOTE: Typewritten poem with the note above the title and the last name
after the poem, with the location "Hotel Vendome, Minneapolis, Minn."
Dated in the bottom left corner, "April 19, 1931." AAN Paderewski Archive,
p. 57. Since Paderewski performed in Minneapolis in January 1923 during
his Eleventh American Tour, we can surmise that the poem was written
after that concert.
    George Warren Hootman (1861-1941) was associated with the
Georgian Poetry movement of the early 20th century. He published
Writings of a Roadman: A Collection of Letters (1909), A Collection of
Letters and Poems (1909) in two volumes, and Short Nature Sketches for
Children and Young People (1935). His work was also included in many
anthologies.

To Paderewski, Patriot

Son of a martyred race that long
Has honed its sorrow into song
And taught the world that grief is less
When voiced by Music's loveliness.
How shall its newer anguish be
Interpreted, if not by thee?

In whose heart dearer doth abide
Thy land's lost century of pride
Since triple tyrants tore in three
That nation of antiquity—
But could not lock with prison keys
The freeman's sacred memories.

Now when thy soil lies wrecked and rent
By cruel waves of warfare spent,
Till Jeanine [?] counts so many slain
It looks on Slaughter with disdain
However others grieve, thou show'st
The noble spirit suffers most.

Master with whom the world doth sway
Like meadow with the wind at play
May Heaven send thee, at this hour,
Such access of supernal power
That every note beneath thy hand
May plead for thy distracted land.

— Robert Underwood Johnson
1916

NOTE: This poem was handwritten, with the date (13 April 1916) in the lower left corner; reproduced in Józef Orłowski, Ignacy Jan Paderewski i Odbudowa Polski (Chicago: The Stanek Press, 1940), 124.

   Robert Underwood Johnson (1853-1937) was an American writer, poet and diplomat, passionate about international copyright law and land preservation (he worked on the creation of Yosemite National Park). He directed Hall of Fame at New York University, served as a long-time secretary of American Academy of Arts and Letters and was Ambassador to Italy, A recipient of many honors from six governments, he published eight volumes of poetry and other writings.

[To Paderewski, Untitled]

Paderewski, fare thee well!
Magician thou, of thousand themes,
From grand to gay, you make your way
And weave the web of golden dreams.

Oh, poet soul, oh, wizard hands
That weave such music as you will.
We that have heard and understand
Would keep you ever with us still.

For you are one of whom t'was said
"God sent his minstrels on this earth
That they might woo the hearts of men
And lure them back to heaven again."

Fare well!

— **Josephine & M.**
1904

NOTE: *A handwritten poem in a form of a letter to the pianist, penned during his tour of Australia in July 1904, when he gave five concerts in Melbourne. Signed by Josephine and M., with no last name, it is written on a card with printed home address, "Arral Clendon Roorak." This was an affluent suburb of Melbourne, filled with Edwardian and Victorian mansions. AAN Paderewski Archive, p. 104.*

Paderewski

(At the Dedication of Beechwood Playhouse, Scarborough, N.Y. January 12, 1917)

Upon the twilight stage
Of warmly neutral tones
A grand piano richly black
Against dim draperies
That hung in heavy folds.
And one who entered here
With simple dignity
To play as only he can play.
A lonely tragic figure,
Lonely as true genius ever is,
Tragic with sorrows weightier than his own.
Grave — with intense devotion to ideals.
A man of men and a musician rare,
Filled with the sacred flame.

Of the hush of expectancy there,
He pictured with eloquent tones,
With marvelous form and color,
The dreams of a musical soul!
We were swept by his passionate fire
In the ringing assault of great chords.
His tenderness thrilled us to tears
Or unlulled with a lingering *legato.*
In noble and beautiful themes
As broad and as deep as the ocean
He told us ineffable things,
Stirred our souls to a lofty emotion
And stilled us to peace.

A finale of meteoric splendor
And soon — all too soon — it was over!
We heard him no more
But the musical magic he wrought
Held us breathes and spellbound the while
And illumines our memory still,
like a star in a twilight of dreams.

— **Jessica H. Lowell**
1917

NOTE: Typeset poem in a clipping of an event program: the dedication of the Beechwood Playhouse in Scarborough, N.Y., dated 12 January 1917. AAN Paderewski Archive, p. 103.

Sonata Appassionata

(On Hearing Paderewski Play Sonata, Op. 57 by Beethoven in Lexington, Kentucky, January 26, 1923)

He called from dreariness and dearth
For the black night and rain-beleaguered earth
With the first sweep of his magician hands
Born on the flying steed of music — far
Beyond the palisades of stars on stars,
Out where the pure notes drift
On all lakes of silence through the silvery rift.
Of ultimate echoes against heaven's bar,
He set me on the antiphonal towers of God.
All frantic tears, all petulant demands,
On dark, discordant ways that man had trod
Into benignant harmony were brought
And time and pain were nought.

And in that majesty
Of mellow chords that uplifted me,
The miracle was wrought of three in one —
The maker of the peerless instrument,
Those golden strings and ivory keys were bent
Through subtleties of tone
Into the perfect symmetry of sound —
And the Creator of the passionate, profound
Sonata whose incomparable chords
Echo the singing hordes
Of serafim who swept this toneless night
With notes like light. —
And third, the Master, the Interpreter,
The giant soul who felt the mystic stir

Of ancient memories and the secret sweep
Of dim foreknowledge break beyond the deep
Of all the melodies that leap
From God to man across the chasm of time.
And with his touch sublime
Brought this transcendent beauty into birth—
All sorrowing, all loveliness, all mirth
Were linked in music's thrall
With All-in-All —

— **Lucia Clark Markham**
1923

NOTE: A typewritten poem by Lucia Clark Markham, of Lexington, Kentucky, dated 26 January 1923. AAN Paderewski Archive, p. 115.
    Lucia Clark Markham (1901-1962) was an American poet, teacher and physician, who spent most of her life in Lexington, Kentucky. She published a book of Sonnets *in 1944 and* Sonnets to the Beloved *in 1960. Her archives are in the Special Collections of The Filson Historical Society, Louisville, Kentucky.*

Lines to Monsieur Paderewski on Hearing Him Play at the Brighton Pavilion

And this the human hand can do,
    When guided by a God-touched heart!
Could sate our souls with melody
    The outcome of divinest art.
Our eyes in wonder strained to see
    Thy marvelous movements on the keys.
Our mind felt storms and sudden calms
    And swish of wind among the trees.

But something more was there — a flash
    Divine which told of hidden fires
From Heaven's altars to foretell
    To men the sound of angels' lyres.

Musician! Sent by God in mercy here
    To raise us, free us from the sordid chains
Of earthly care and sorrow, many a tear
    Is quenched or called for by thy touching strains.
Thou carriest the message to all hearts
    A vital spark to kindle into life
The finer instincts of our human kind
    And strengthen, help us, in our earthly strife!

— "M. E.A."
(ca.1890-1892)

NOTE: Handwritten poem in the Paderewski Brighton Album signed
with initials M.E.A. on p. 2 of the Album, compiled by Madeleine Michell,
1890-1914. Paderewski played at Brighton's Royal Pavilion between
1890 and 1891, later moving to The Dome, hence the proposed dates.

Paderewski

His face — the home of Sorrow,
His heart is Heaven half,
And when his hands caress the keys,
I hear a dryad laugh.

Oh! He is Music's lover,
And they are found in flight,
Forever kissing into life
Things redolent with light.

But when he thunders darkness,
I fly to exile lands,
And hide, and in God's shadow,
From Paderewski's hands.

— **Kate Slaughter McKinney**
1923

.

NOTE: A handwritten poem, AAN Paderewski Archive p. 116. The poem is signed with the full name plus address and date at the top left corner: "519 Monroe Lane, Montgomery, Alabama, 29 January 1923." Transcribed by Emma Boyd, Reader Services, National Library of Scotland.

Kate Slaughter McKinney (1859-1939), was a well-known Alabama poet, publishing under the pseudonym Katydid. In 1931, she became the Poet Laureate of the State of Alabama. Her books include Katydid's Poems *(1887).* Palace of Silver (1927), *and* The Weed by the Wall *(1911).*

O Great Master,

Your last clear note of earthly harmony,
Will vanish on the trembling air someday;
God will turn the page, and you will play
The first firm strain of your life's symphony
Upon eternal keys, and when you go
Beyond the voiceless of those who love
You, we shall wait in silence, while above
The fluted bird-note in the first, faint glow
Of April dawns, or mingled with far bells,
Through softly falling snow on Holy Eves,
Or borne upon the golden autumn leaves,
Shall come your old, sweet songs.

          No earth-voice tells
Your worth, oh, Master of the Muse! My tears
Flow tonight to meet the silent years.

         Reverently,

         Ester Jacoby Merrill

                  — Ester Jacoby Merrill
                            1939

NOTE: Handwritten poem in a format of a letter with a signature and, in the lower left corner, date and location: "Fairfield, Idaho, March 9th, 1939." AAN Paderewski Archive, p. 120.

Sonnet to Paderewski

Oh Paderewski! wondrous charmer thou,
Thine is a mystic, strange, elusive power
Which holds us spellbound — Which interprets life
In all its phases, seems to understand
Our secret sorrow, shares our highest hope
Touchest our sorest wounds. Touching dost soothe
And well-nigh heal them. All the past thou knowest
And mournest with us for the "might-have beens"—
Thou speakest words of peace — The peace of heaven —
Above the deepest tones of earth's unrest,
Anew, the gates of joy thou openest wide
And bids't us enter in to claim our own.
Great Seer of Music! While my muse thus humbly
    sings thy fame —
Ten thousand hearts with one accord (delight)
    ignite to Praise thy name.

— **Alice May Moir**
1899

NOTE: *Handwritten poem, signed by Alice May Moir (or Muir, the writing is unclear) with information about her location and date 15 December 1899: "(late of Edinburgh, Scotland)/ 823 Lexington Avenue / New York / 15th Dec 1899." AAN Paderewski Archive, p. 123. Transcribed by Emma Boyd, Reader Services, National Library of Scotland..*

The Maestro

— To Paderewski

From the thunder of the tempest
To the sky lark in its bliss,
From the depths of human agony
To the touch of Cupid's kiss,
We will follow him enraptured
Where Elysian billows swell,
That burst in glorious anthems
Where the hosts of Eden dwell.

Ablaze in all his glory,
Imperial with his peers,
Evolving with the ages
And growing with the years,
Superb, this uncrowned sovereign
Attuned to God and man
Comes heralding to mortal ears
The strains from spirit-land.

**— Juliet C. Olin
1931**

NOTE: *Typewritten poem, with a handwritten signature, date of February 6, 1931, and street address in Montgomery, Alabama. AAN Paderewski Archive, p. 128.*

This poem may have been written by Juliet Starke Cook Olin (1858-1951), born in Lowndes County, who died in Montgomery, Alabama. https://www.findagrave.com/memorial/99440369/juliet-starke-olin

Immortal

This Great Genius — Soul of Poland
Did Ably Lead his Race
Its armed opponent to front
With indominable face.

A wonderful Composer,
A superb artist of renown,
He laid his fortune in the Scales
To pull the tyrants down.
Premiered a while — he founded
A Nation that will last
And though by foes surrounded
Poland hath visions vast.
A People none can overthrow
Since God hath brought them through the woe.

Immortal Paderewski,
You have given your Land a Place
Among the Leading Nations
That Time will not efface.
And the Centuries will acclaim you
As a Soul of supreme Grace.

— **William Kimberly Palmer**
1928

NOTE: *This typeset poem, with an elaborate border, has a note printed below the text: "Dedicated to Col. Edward Mandell House, The Friend of Poland, by William Kimberly Palmer, Chicopee, Massachusetts, U.S.A., March 1934 A.D." Below this note is a handwritten signature, and on top penciled-in last name and page number. AAN Paderewski Archive, p. 141.*

Ignace Paderewski (1940)

The Master teaches not "the harp"
Since his loved land was overrun.
The stabbing pain was all too sharp
And sorrow blotted out the sun.

The wrath that gleamed in his a'ged eyes
Was as when storms round Alp-peak play,
When earth, oppressed 'neath smothering skies,
Heav'n's fulmens will no more obey.

Then was he young through that brief hour,
Who strongly love are only young.
A youth, in his lapel a flower,
A youth — gay, noble, sad, high strung!

But laid a weary sadness soon
its heavy hand upon his brow
and — oft' at dusk — but ev'n at noon —
Mid agehood's grief his head will bow.

The Master will not teach "the harp"
When his loved land is made to bleed.
We coax with cooings, dare be sharp,
He looks away, he will not heed.

— **Einar Atair Paulenton**

NOTE: *Typescript signed with initials, with typescript note containing the name Einar Atair Paulenton or Paulenten (the copy is unclear), that was the pseudonym of E.A. Peterson. AAN Paderewski Archive, p. 145.*

Poland and Paderewski

There was a silence as of death—/
    the nations watched, the righteous mourned,
Where on her bier with hushed breath /
    dear Poland lay—the wept, the scorned.
In all the darkened air no sound /
    save muffled drum and funeral bell:
Deep-chorded Chopin's anthem found /
    refrain but in the tears that fell —
Until the music of your soul, /
    great Master of the Harmonies,
Broke on her listening ear to roll /
    with echoing note across the seas.
Across the seas, across the years, /
    with Oh, what hope renewed she heard
That summoning from night and tears —/
    the voice of your rekindling word!
Mother to son, she called; and son /
    to mother hastening fore came...
Now mark the mighty chords /
    that run to music of her golden name!
Now mark the hand that strikes the chord—/
    and strikes the shackles off! O, hand
Of filial love, of flashing sword, /
    that lifts and waves with one command!
What music ever man hath made/
    is like unto this music now
That rings with challenge unafraid. /
    against the breakers of the vow?
What music ever heard of men /
    is sweeter than these chords that wake
Within her prisoned heart again —/
    the sound of yokes that fall and break!

    ... She rises, beautiful, renewed! /
    She lifts her golden voice—she sings—

And in her song, sweet plenitude /
of love, O, son, your bright name rings!

[signed] — Charles Phillips,
Notre Dame University, Notre Dame,
Indiana, May 16, 1928.

— **Charles Phillips**
1928

NOTE: Two pages of the autograph of this poem are reproduced in: To
Paderewski: Artist, Patriot, Humanitarian *(New York: Kosciuszko
Foundation, 1928), no page number. All the pages have the same heading:
"Greetings to Ignace Jan Paderewski on the Tenth Anniversary of the
Independence of Poland." The transcription includes the original's
signature, date and location; the verses are too long so they are divided in
half with a / mark. A copy is in AAN Paderewski Archives, p. 107-8.*

*Charles Phillips (1880-1933) was Paderewski friend and biographer
author of* Paderewski: The Story of A Modern Immortal *(1933). With an
M.A. from St. Mary's College in California, he successively work as the
editor of the* Northwestern Chronicle *in St. Paul, MN, the* Monitor *in San
Francisco, and the* New Century *in Washington D.C.. He served with the
American Red Cross Committee to Poland, 1919-1922, and on the special
committee of the National Catholic Welfare Council to Mexico in 1925. As
Professor of English at the University of Notre Dame, 1924-1933, he helped
found the University Theatre.*

To Paderewski

— After Years

Poet dreaming o'er the keys,
Playing soulful melodies.
Give us Chopin's gold to-night—
Gold inwrought with jewels bright.
Preludes, etudes, nocturnes, all,
Let them spark, glimmer, fall.
Poet dreaming beauty's dream,
Give us vision, art's clear beam.

Years ago I heard you play;
Spring it was—I know 't was May—
And still that art and still
Are blooming, singing in your heart;
And at your name the past returns,
And beauty like a clear flame burns.
Poet, dreaming dreams impearled,
Pour out beauty on the world!

Ernest Powell

NOTE. Typescript with handwritten signature, "Ernest Powell," and the location, "Marshall, Texas," without a date. AAN Paderewski Archive, p. 150.

Jan Ignace Paderewski

Then I heard a strain of music
So mighty, so pure, so clear,
That my very soul was silent
And my heart stood still to hear.
It rose in harmonious rushing
Of mingled voices and strings,
And I tenderly laid my message
On music's outstretched wings.
And I heard it float farther and farther,
In sounds more perfect than speech.
Farther than sight can follow,
Farther than soul can reach.
And I know that at last my message
Has passed the golden gate,
So my heart is no longer restless
And I am content to wait.

— **Procter**

NOTE: *Typescript in a brochure with a Paderewski portrait, AAN Paderewski Archive, p. 173.*

To Paderewski's Dog

The little dog is dead and some will
    smile
That noted people should have
    paused a while
Putting their fame and money quite
    aside
To weep because a little dog has
    died.
But of the thousands who will read
    the tale —
Though there must be the few who
    laugh and rail,
There will be many a famous pros-
    perous man
And common hungry beggar stop
    to scan
The news, to learn how this small
    dog comes on
And know true grief on finding he
    is gone.
For, oh, how many a one of us
    has cried,
Because some little dog that loved
    us died.

— Jean Hennepin Render
1930

NOTE: Typescript, with name and address in a handwritten annotation:
"Jean Hennepin Render, 726 South Whittier St. Los Angeles, CA."
AAN Paderewski Archive, p. 174.

When Paderewski Came to Town

The sparrow on the housetop sat
    And Heaved a heavy sigh —
And with his little claw he dashed
    A tear-drop from his eye.

"Oh, foolish bird, what ails you so?"
    A passing sparrow said;
"Why is it that you weepeth thus
    And sadly hang your head?"

"I weep" — the little sparrow sighed,
    And dashed more tears away —
"Because I've seen a one Best Bet,
    That I can never play."

"Oh, what a happy bird I'd be,"
    He wailed in bleak despair,
"If I could only build my nest
    In Paderewski's hair."

**— Grantland Rice
(1908)**

NOTE: Press clipping with a poem from The Tennessean *paper, in Grantland Rice column "Tennessee Uns" mentioning the date of April 10, no year. AAN Paderewski Archives, p. 175.*

Henry Grantland Rice (1880-1954) was an American poet and a well-known sports writer, originally from Tennessee, whose reports appeared in The Tennessean *between 1907-1911 (Paderewski played in Nashville on 25 March 1908, hence the assigned date). Rice also wrote for* New York Evening Mail, New York Tribune, *the* Collier's *and appeared on Paramount broadcast newsreels. The poem is followed by "PUGILISTIC NOTES" of which the first is an actual report about boxing and the second reads as follows:*

"Paddy Rueski, the Russian welterweight, will fight six rounds with piano tonight. The piano has a shade on Paddy around the legs, but Russian is there with the reach and the punch, and should enter ring a 1-3 favorite."

When Paderewski Plays

His eyes pierce as a shaft of light
And see far, into the night
And on through space, among the spheres —
Is there the music that he hears?

His hand he raises from the key
To guide the wafted melody,
And from the taut, vibrating string
Ethereal voices call and sing.

With nodding head, he seems aware —
His lips move, as in silent prayer
Speaking to things we cannot see —
The master of sublimity!

A flash of hands, a crashing chord
As lightning-gash across the sward
And with a throb life seems to be
Enveloped by his ecstasy.

The ocean checks its mighty roll
Time stops — the earth becomes a soul,
The stars, responsive to his theme —
Clustered in brilliant silence — gleam!

Where he has sought and caught the key
Of a celestial symphony.

— Windsor V. Richberg
1934

*NOTE: Typescript poem, with a handwritten date in the bottom left
corner: "26 October 1934." Below is a dedication: "In grateful memory of
the decades of enjoyment. Windsor Richberg." The bottom left corner has
a pencil note with the address: "145 Hyde Park Road, Chicago, Ill." AAN
Paderewski Archive, p. 176.*

Paderewski

Sacrifice is nature's plan,
Strains both sad and gay
Not fully realized by man,
But God must have His Holy Way.

Giving forth his life's blood,
With hope of better things,
He must work and he must wait
To stand with Kings.

From the instrument beloved,
Guided by his master's hand,
Delicate, forceful tones,
Obeying his commands.

Music for the soul
Calls the world to listen,
Shows the brother-hood of man,
And makes sad eyes to glisten.

Then, his country called him,
This man, so great and true,
He did not stop to question
What will my music do?

After duty came the music —
Flashing, floating, fair,
Ringing out free tones of love,
Filling all the air.

**— Josephine Rita Sargeant
1923**

NOTE: Typescript of a poem, dated 1923. AAN Paderewski Archive, p. 181.

Mr. Ignace Paderewski,
Morges, Switzerland

I am going to wait and hear you on the air,
I know you are the grandest pianist anywhere,
I am very sorry to learn that you are ill,
Hope you are better soon, the engagement to fill.
There are none like you anywhere that I know.
Heard you many times, many years ago,
So it made me very sorry to know that you are sick,
Hope you get better now, really very quick,
And it would please me much to get your reply.
No one will be more delighted than I,
For I know that you're the master of the art.
If I only had your photograph,
It would be very dear to my heart.

With kindest regards,

Yours very truly,

B. Sterling

3909 Main St. Houston, Texas

— B. Sterling

NOTE: *Typescript poem typed all in caps, with handwritten signature above the typed-in name; no date. AAN Paderewski Archive, p. 193.*

Chanson d'été

(Song of the Summer)

'Mid pauses of dream and revelry,
 Steals a laughing wind upon the morn,
By green-blue glistening lengths of sea,
 Whose ripples are like the waving corn.

Yet the green-blue sea but wears a mask
 To woo the young wind to cease its quest,
And nothing further of day to ask
 Than cool, mute sleep on the sea's broad breast.

But the wind, in its boyish lust of strife,
 Leaps back, full wary of sea and cloud,
For it wills to keep its laughing life,
 To arrant pleasure and freedom vowed.

So it slips away from sea and strand,
 To seek new places of gay delight,
Where clover blossoms make sweet the land
 And bees sip honey from dawn till night.

Yet, laughing wind who flees from your foes
 For the love of mirth and liberty.
Why lie you hushed by a wild red rose
 Whose only power is coquetry?

**— William Struthers
1907**

*NOTE: Poem in a press clipping, dated on the margin in handwriting,
"Boston, Saturday, May 25, 1907." AAN Paderewski Archive, p. 198.*

The Last Pure Chords of a Chopin "Berceuse"

— To Paderewski

Over a thread of undulant vibration,
Whose monotone lies cunningly concealed,
You weave, young mother fancy, an emotion,
Of tonal patterns, fairy wafts congealed.
Blithe, tender, pensive strains from early days,
A fragrance kept from carefree julish ways —
Silver-clean and gossamer-delicate,
And soft, as nest-bird's coo to her fond mate!

But now the lullaby has sung its length,
The baby sleeps and while its eyelids close,
From 'neath the elfin moon, in throbbing strength,
Breaks forth a deep, true mother-voice — a rose
Of harmony, whose first pathetic chord
Bleeds with child-pangs and wounds of that sharp sword,
Which pierced sad Mary's bosom nigh the Cross.
Yet, that's the second chord — yes, not the last!
What sense of sweetest gain from little loss!
A transformation that, by magic stealth,
Reveals the mother-heart in fullest wealth —
Listen! The agony and doubt are past —
All, all resolved — a seraph's dream of peace —
Into ineffable trust in Love's release!

— William Struthers
1907

*NOTE: A handwritten poem with a location and date in bottom left corner
"Philadelphia, November 11, 1907." AAN Paderewski Archive, p. 197.*

Paderewski

Poland on the map is small
But her history is great,
Heroes rally at her call,
Genius brightens all her state.

There was Paderewski born,
Country sights and sounds he knew,
Early in is youth was torn
From his arms his mother true.

She bequeathed sweet Music's art
To the child she left behind.
How he held it to his heart
In his later life we find.

Austria's capital he sought
And woo'd his high idea long,
Fitted by this, his art was brought
To concert stage and public throng.

He played in Paris and New York,
Berlin and many cities more,
The great pianist was the talk
Of music lovers the world o'er.

Interpretation is his field —
Bach, Beethoven, Schumann, Liszt
Their divinest treasures yield
To his skill of hand and wrist

"How easy," was the comment made
Of one of Chopin's preludes given,
"Yes, easy" Paderewski said,
"After seven years I've striven."

His audience is soon forgot,
To his own soul he seems to play.
If his own soul commands him not,
He little cares what others say.

He has richly stored his mind,
Many languages he speaks,
More of truth he longs to find,
Deeper knowledge ever seeks.

Living master of the keys,
His supremacy is sure.
Toil and genius that could seize,
Also holds the prize secure.

By the grave of wife and son
He has stood. Can busy years
And the triumphs he has won
Make him quite forget the tears?

No! The baptism of pain.
In his music he reveals.
To his art it is great gain —
He transfigures all he feels.

His compositions brought his pain
Have you heard his "Minuet"?
"Polish Fantasy" lifts his name
To a higher level yet.

His "Fugue and Variations" sound
Through all the orchestra one strain.
His "Voyager" is outward bound,
To other lands beyond the main.

His opera "Manru" won success
Conducted by his very self,

It pleased the audience and the press
And won him praise and honest pelf.

By fair Lausanne in Switzerland
A portion of his time is spent,
There many interests he has planned
Let's hope they bring him sweet content!

**— Elisabeth Tousey
(after 1901, before 1909)**

NOTE: *Signed typescript, AAN Paderewski Archive, pp. 252-255. The title does not have a date. A second copy with the date in the title ("Paderewski – 1859") with a wrong birth year of the pianist, is in an anonymous typescript, also in AAN Paderewski Archive, p. 302-303. The ballad enumerating Paderewski's musical achievements ends the list of his compositions with the music drama* Manru *of 1901 and does not mention his Symphony* Polonia *of 1909, hence the proposed dating of the poem.*

Paderewski in Gold

Gold halo of curls on his portraits
Gold crowns of kings of old above the keys
Gold riches of his fortune, spent and growing —
Gold heart beneath it all

The gleam of gold ring on his finger
The gleam of brilliance in his eyes
The gleam of fame that still surrounds him —
Gold heart beneath it all

The dream of music in his youth
The dream of kindness at his prime
The dream of Poland, free and mighty —
Gold heart beneath it all

His heart is gold, so bright and pure
Immortal music he brought to teach
Us all to live his noble vision —
Truth, Goodness, Beauty —
Gold heart beneath it all

— Maja Trochimczyk
2018

NOTE: *Written in January 2018 for the Keynote Lecture on "Paderewski and Poland's Independence" given at the Polish Embassy in Washington, D.C. during the Annual Conference of the Polish American Historical Association. An earlier version published on the* Chopin with Cherries *blog. Revised in 2025.*

To Paderewski. A Sonnet

Hush, what frenzy those earned hands do phrase,
That fecundates the circumambient air,
With absinthian, voluptuous despair,
Then, — onward the delirious fancy strays,
In labyrinth of loveliness delays,
In misty lands obscure, a region where
Exquisiteness is orthodox, — not rare.
Wan face above the black piano raised.
Scarred seraph! Dragoman of realm so quaint,
Forlorn, you must be sweetly drunk with gloom,
That from this ebon wood, this sonant loom,
Your hands pluck out such precious, poised, complaint.
August, aloof, autumnal now he stands,
The Master, — with his tired, orchestral hands.

— **Elva W. Williams**

NOTE: Typescript, with a handwritten signature: "Elva W. Williams, 641 Post Street, San Francisco." No date. AAN Paderewski Archive, p. 272.

What Paderewski Taught Me about Being

good
he tells me
the heart moves

for what has been taken
for what is left
for what has been given

moves like the ocean
sometimes like a mountain
constantly in greeting

a nation for what is right
the dearly loved
what he always wanted

his words
my pulse the same
surprises

from the edge
of her seat
a woman leans forward

Trembles
holds back
rushes forward

holds
a breath
time waits

washed always
in silence
silence for what is not

the woman breathes out
whish of wind
essence of man

dark and light
rubato of being
becomes being again

— **Kath Abela Wilson**
2010

NOTE: *Written by a California-based poet in 2010 for the Paderewski and Chopin Conference held at Loyola University Chicago. Published in* Cosmopolitan Review, *3:2 (4 July 2011).*

Poland's Resurrection

Oh, Poland, fair nation, thy hour has come:
Thy thraldom is o'ver, thy freedom is won.
Thy foes lie stricken by God's holy will,
Arise from thy tomb upon Golgotha's hill.

Throw off the shackles that bound thee tight,
Come forth in thy majesty, splendor and might.
Take up thy place among nations once more,
Thou "Bulwark of Christendom" in the days of yore.

"Sentinel of Europe." "Chivalrous knight."
The Turk and the Tartar always ready to fight,
To protect Christianity and defend the Cross,
Against desecration, tyranny, and loss.

Thy vic'try at Vienna by Sobieski the Great
Saved the nations of Europe from the terrible fate.
Alas, Thou fallest to the prey of their greed
Thy body they massacred in return for your deed.

But we greet thee, Poland, we greet thee today,
As thy freedom is won in this awful fray,
In thy struggle for liberty, justice and right,
Against persecution and despotic might.

Arise, then, a fair nation, long thought to be dead
From thy tomb of martyrdom and proclaim that instead
Show to the World why again thou must live
Thy suffer-iage and enemies forget and forgive.

Kosciuszko and Sobieski they beckon to thee,
Thou must, oh, Poland, henceforth be free,
To resume the mission and arduous task,
That crowned with glory thy brow in the past.

Arise, then, Poland, thou art not dead,
Of all of Slavonia stand at the head,
In brotherly love, the shining light,
To lead the Slav nations in peace and the right.

Thy past is recorded in a dim tragic story,
Deathless thy fame, undying thy glory,
And judging the future by the light of the past,
A glorious thereafter awaits thee at last.

Godspeed thy mission, and hasten the day,
When history again must truthfully say
You've suffered so much and went through pain
To be of real service to mankind again.

— **Anthony Zaleski**
1918

This poem was written in the year of 1918, on the signing of the Armistice, when the author was twenty years old.

— A. Zaleski, A.B., L.L.B.

DEDICATION

To the honorable Ignace Jan Paderewski, distinguished Pole of international fame. Poland's own son, patriot, statesman, and ambassador of good will to the world at large, this poem is respectfully dedicated in appreciation on the invaluable services rendered in the restoration of Poland's independence, and in the further acknowledgement of the universal fame, achieved in the realm of music.

— Anthony Zaleski, A. B., L.L.B.

NOTE: A three-page typescript, with the dedication on the first page and the poem on the following two. AAN Paderewski Archive, pages 280-282.

Poland, Past and Present

By I. J. PADEREWSKI

JUST PUBLISHED

SOLD FOR THE BENEFIT OF THE

POLISH VICTIMS RELIEF FUND

AEOLIAN BUILDING, NEW YORK CITY

Autographed Edition de Luxe, Ten Dollars the Copy

" I AM performing a difficult, painful, even humiliating, but sacred duty. I am endeavoring to arouse some interest in the fate of my people, who in this war suffered most of all. Faithful to Poland's tradition, true to the spirit of our ancestors, I am not seeking assistance for those of my blood only, or of my religion, but for all, without any distinction of race, of creed, or of opinion—for all who are sharing in common my country's unspeakable misfortune."

Paderewski's text about the suffering Poland in a flyer of the Polish Victims' Relief Fund, ca. 1916.

PART II

PADEREWSKI ESSAYS

J. J. Paderewski (signature)

By Maja Trochimczyk

1.
Paderewski in Poetry:
Master of Harmonies or Poland's Savior?[1]

I. Poetry of Music and Patriotism

Poetry is just one of the ways in which the intense public fascination with "the immortal"[2] pianist-composer-statesman, Ignacy Jan Paderewski (1860-1941) was expressed during his lifetime. Since his triumphant entry onto the international music stage, Paderewski was the subject of poems, often florid or erudite, always enthusiastic. The "Paderewski-themed" poetry highlights its authors' responses to various aspects of their subject's multi-faceted career—the pianistic virtuosity, compositional talent, and the musician's patriotic zeal. This paper will examine the range of these responses and the image of Paderewski that was constructed in selected works by American and Polish poets, including verses by: Waldemar Bakalarski (a poem of 1941); John H. Finley (1863-1940; poems of 1914 and 1928); Richard Watson Gilder (1844-1909, poem of 1906); Robert Underwood Johnson (1853-1937, poem of 1916); Henryk Merzbach (poem of 1888); Charles Phillips (1880-1933, poem of 1928); Julian Adolf Święcicki (poem of 1899); and Marian Gawalewicz with Maryla Wolska (1873-1930; poem of 1899). Of the American writers, only the names of Gilder and Phillips appear in Paderewski biographies; the former—as a personal friend and supporter, the latter—as a biographer.

An overview of the Paderewski-themed poetry highlights two transformations of the subject matter, after 1918 and after 1941, as well as characteristic differences between the images of the great virtuoso presented in Poland and in the U.S. The first turning point marks the time of Poland's rebirth after World War I when the country regained independence following a period of over 120 years when it was divided between Russia, Prussia, and Austria. It

---

[1] A revised version of a paper first published in *Polish Music Journal* (online) 4:1 (Summer 2001).

[2] The term "modern immortals" was often used in reference to famous people, such as Ghandi or Einstein. Paderewski was added to such "immortals" in the title of his biography by Charles Phillips, *Paderewski. The Story of a Modern Immortal.* (New York: Macmillan, 1933).

was universally believed this event would not have been possible without the efforts of Paderewski.[3] Simultaneously, this historical moment marks the end of Paderewski's career as a composer: his last work, a patriotic anthem *Hej, orle biały! [Hey, white eagle]* was written as the hymn of the Polish Army in the U.S. in 1917. The second, more obvious, milestone in Paderewski's poetic reception marks the event of his death, which was commemorated in a series of elegies by his compatriots.

Before Paderewski's intense involvement in the patriotic campaign on Poland's behalf in the U.S. (1915-1918), ending with the historical event of the country's sovereignty in 1918, poems about him followed three thematic paths: (1) "synaesthetic responses," i.e., attempts to capture in elaborate verbal imagery the fleeting impressions of Paderewski's musical performances (represented by a poem by Richard Watson Gilder), (2) "erudite responses," i.e., venerations of Paderewski's musical genius cast in classical terms, with complex references to Greek antiquity (poems by John H. Finley), and (3) "patriotic responses" connecting Paderewski to Polish musical traditions, expressing his role in Polish culture as a "new Chopin," or an internationally recognized "Master" whose art could raise awareness of Polish history and culture, with the expected result of assisting Poland in its resurrection as an independent state. The third approach connected Paderewski to his musical roots in the achievements of Poland's greatest pianist-composer, Fryderyk Chopin, but simultaneously transformed the artistic goals of composing and performing music into a patriotic mission (poems by Swięcicki, Merzbach, and Wolska).

---

[3] This subject has been examined in several dissertations written at American universities: David J. Morck, *Ignace Paderewski and the Re-Birth of the Polish State, 1914-1919*, (M.A. thesis, California State University, Fullerton, 1994); Joseph T. Hapak, *Recruiting a Polish Army in the United States, 1917-1919*, (Ph.D. diss., University of Kansas, 1985); Mieczyslaw B. Bienkowski-Biskupski, *The United States and the Rebirth of Poland, 1914-1918*, (Ph.D. diss., Yale University, 1981). Authors of Paderewski's political biographies wrote about it in Poland: Marian Marek Drozdowski, *Ignacy Jan Paderewski. Zarys biografii politycznej* [Outline of a political biography] (Warsaw, 1979; Eng. trans., 1981, enlarged 1988); Henryk Przybylski, *Paderewski: Między muzyką a polityką* [Paderewski: Between music and politics] (Katowice: Unia, 1992).

After Poland became an independent country and during the period of Paderewski's increased political prominence in the 1910s and 1920s, numerous laudatory verses appeared, praising the musician as a voice of the nation in elaborate linguistic constructions linking sound, music, patriotism, etc. These poems form a category of politically-oriented (4) "commemorative" or "laudatory responses", praising Paderewski's musical talent in general terms, while emphasizing his dedication to the national cause (including poems by Finley, Johnson, and Phillips). In that period, I have not found additional testimonies to the electrifying power of Paderewski charisma at the piano expressed so eloquently as in Gilder's earlier verse. A 1934 poem, "Immortal Jan Ignace Paderewski", might be an exception, but its text was not available for the present study.[4]

This paucity of "synaesthetic" descriptions of the music's impact on its listeners in the inter-war period indicates a change in the tone of public response to Paderewski's persona and the nature of his appearances. This transformation was even more profound after his death—an event to which his Polish compatriots reacted with sorrow in (5) "elegiac responses," i.e. farewells to a great musician-statesman whose art was seen as primarily serving patriotic purposes. Two examples of such mourning poetry by Poles and Polish emigrants are listed below, neither one of particularly high artistic merit (by Bakalarski and Strakacz-Appleton).

---

[4] A copy of this poem, held in the library of Brown University, was issued as a broadside in Chicopee, Massachusetts. Paderewski did not give concerts in the U.S. in 1934, as his wife died that year and he did not travel far; in 1933 he performed in New Haven, Conn.; Boston, New York, Chicago, Pittsburgh, & Washington, D.C. Małgorzata Perkowska, *Diariusz koncertowy Paderewskiego* [Paderewski's concert diary] (Kraków: PWM, 1990), 189.

II. Paderewski's Triumphs and Patriotic Hopes

Paderewski's first international triumphs took place in Paris in the spring of 1888.[5] After the enthusiastic reception of his performances there, he traveled to Belgium, where—invited by Francois-Auguste Gevaert, the director of the Brussels Conservatory—he gave a concert on 14 April 1888. He returned to Brussels in December 1888 for three concerts; at that time, the Polish expatriates in Belgium honored his successes with a reception in a private home. The event included a performance by Paderewski and violinist Jozef Wieniawski. On the same occasion, the vice-president of the Polish Charitable Society in Brussels [Polskie Towarzystwo Dobroczynnosci], Henryk Merzbach, a writer and editor, recited the following poem that he wrote for Paderewski:[6]

> Płyn, młody mistrzu, po tym oceanie
> Burz, namiętnosci, rozkoszy i chwały...
> Graj nam a narod niech zmartwychwstanie
> Chocby na chwilę, wierząc w ideały...
> Twa gra nas brata z niebem i z krajem,
> Przyjm więc serdeczne nasze uwielbienie.
> Swiat da ci sławę, my ci serce dajem —
> Nowy Chopinie.

Translation:
> *Sail, o young master, on this ocean*
> *Of storms, passions, delights and glory...*
> *Play for us and let the nation resurrect*
> *if only for a moment, believing in ideals...*
> *Your music unites us with heaven and with our country,*
> *So please accept our heartfelt worship.*
> *The world will give you fame, we give our heart —*
> *to you, new Chopin.*

---

[5] Details about Paderewski's travels and performances are taken from two main sources: Andrzej Piber, *Droga do sławy: Ignacy Paderewski w latach 1860-1902* [The path to fame: Ignacy Paderewski in the years 1860-1902] (Warsaw: PIW, 1982) & Perkowska, *op. cit.*
[6] Piber, *op. cit.*, p. 166. Piber's note probably includes a wrong date of publication of this poem in *Dziennik Poznański* according to Dr. Barbara Zakrzewska—for whose assistance in this matter I am grateful.

This poem, published in Poland in *Dziennik Poznański* (No. 289 of 16 December 1889), set the tone for the Polish reception of Paderewski, mixing hopes for the nation's resurrection with praise for the "young master", who had inherited the prophetic gifts of Chopin. The nation's resurrection mentioned by Merzbach finds a visual expression in a postcard from the late 19th century, issued by Wydawnictwo Salonu Malarzy [The Publishers of the Salon of Painters] in Krako w (see Figure 1 below). In this image, a series of ghosts of the Polish kings arise from the mysterious mist surrounding Paderewski playing the piano while a supernatural light emanates from the instrument.

Figure 1: "I.J. Paderewski - Improwizacya" (Evocation of Chopin's Music). Postcard, Wydawnictwo Salonu Malarzy Polskich, Kraków, n.d. (late 19th c.) Maja Trochimczyk's Collection.

The virtuoso spent the following two years on concert tours in Europe, taking him from Paris, to Vienna, London, Budapest, and back to Brussels.[7] On 3 March 1891 he gave a recital for the "Cercle artistique et litte raire" with eleven pieces on the program: Beethoven's Sonata, Op. 111, Schubert's Impromptu in A-flat, Op. 142, No. 2 and a Minuet; Liszt's arrangement of Schubert's Lied *Erlkönig*; Chopin's Ballade in F major Op. 38, Mazurka, and Polonaise in B-flat major, Op. 71. No. 2; Anton Rubin-

---

[7] See Perkowska, *op. cit.*, p. 42; Piber, *op. cit.*, p. 166, 543

stein's *Barcarolle* Op. 93; his own *Humoresques de concert* Op. 14; and Liszt's unspecified *Hungarian Rhapsody*. In gratitude, a group of Poles from Brussels signed the following poem dedicated to Paderewski and presented it to him on 5 March 1891:[8]

Paderewskiemu

Znowu do nas powracasz, poeto muzyki,
Tak wracają na wiosnę słonce i słowiki.
Skromne nasze tułacze i biedne poddasze,
Lecz dajem Ci, co mamy—tęskne serca nasze.

Translation:
Again you return to us, you, the poet of music,
As the sun and the nightingales return in the spring.
Modest and poor is our place of exile [lit. "homeless garret"],
But we give you what we have—our longing hearts.

While not more than a florid greeting, this short poem expresses the hopes that Poles attached to Paderewski as a fellow compatriot, a living connection to their homeland, and a possible harbinger of Poland's freedom.

After triumphant tours in Europe and the U.S. and thirteen years of absence from his native country, Paderewski returned to Warsaw for a series of concerts held in the winter of 1899. The concerts were characterized by an intense fascination with an artist who rose to international prominence abroad. Musical events were interspersed with various honorary celebrations, award dinners, and tributes. A dinner held on 15 of January 1899 in Warsaw had a most distinguished list of participants.[9] The guests of honor included Poland's most famous novelist, Henryk Sienkiewicz and the founder of the Warsaw Philharmonic, industrialist Leopold Kronenberg.[10] Paderewski was seated between them, with a watercolor by Stanisław Lentz marking his place at the table. The

---

[8] The poem is cited from Piber, p. 543; the original is found in Paderewski Archive in Warsaw's Archiwum Akt Nowych, file no. 587, p. 1.
[9] See Piber, *op. cit.*, p. 337.
[10] Henryk Sienkiewicz (1846-1916) wrote a series of popular historical novels, including *The Flood* and *Quo Vadis?*; the latter received a Nobel Prize for literature. Leopold Julian Kronenberg (1849-1937), a banker, industrialist and composer, heir to the family fortune, invested in railroads and sponsored the building of the Warsaw Philharmonic.

image portrayed the virtuoso at the piano from which the spirit of Chopin was emerging—thus expressing, in a tangible form, the vision of Paderewski as a "new Chopin" articulated earlier by Merzbach.

The proceedings opened with a recitation of another "Paderewski" poem, written by Julian Adolf Święcicki (a poet of little distinction in Polish literary history). The text was later published in *Ignacemu Janowi Paderewskiemu. Album Podpisów* preserved in Paderewski Archive in the Archiwum Akt Nowych in Warsaw. Besides the poem, the album included signatures and greetings of the most eminent members of the Polish cultural milieu including: writer Aleksander Głowacki (Bolesław Prus); playwright Lucjan Rydel; conductor-composer Emil Młynarski; composer Zygmunt Noskowski; music historian Aleksander Polinski; music historian Ferdynand Hoesick; and music lover and philanthropist Aleksander Rajchman (co-founder of the Warsaw Philharmonic). Święcicki's poem, though hardly a memorable work of art, expressed sentiments felt by many Poles upon Paderewski's return to his homeland:

> Wyleciałes jako orle z gniazda
> młodych skrzydeł doswiadczyc potęgi [...]
> Nie dlatego w swiat biegłes wytrwale,
> By zyc orgią i kąpac się w szale [...]
> By z wędrowki mozolnej a długiej
> Przyniesc Polsce swoj wieniec zasługi [...]
> I juz jasnosc Twej gwiazdy nie skona,
> Bo ojczyzna Twą sławą... wsławiona.
> Translation:
> *You flew out as an eaglet from the nest*
> *To experience the power of young wings [...]*
> *You did not ceaselessly travel round the world*
> *[lit. "run persistently"]*
> *To live in orgies and bathe in ecstasies [...]*
> *Yet you went on a long and arduous journey,*
> *to bring back, for Poland, your wreath of honor [...]*
> *Now the brightness of your star will not die,*
> *Because your homeland is made famous through your fame.*

The mention of "orgies" and "ecstasies" is a reference to the eccentric interests of Young Poland luminaries, the symbolist writer Stanisław Przybyszewski (preoccupied with intense spirituality and emotionalism, the demonic world, eroticism and self-expression) and the painter Władysław Podkowinski (1866-1895), whose monumental and borderline-kitschy painting "Szał uniesien" [The Frenzy of Ecstasy] was displayed amidst great public controversy in 1894.[11] The painting depicted a raving, naked woman riding a huge, wild, black horse through tumultous darkness. In a fit of rage, Podkowinski tried to destroy this painting during its exhibition; a year later, in 1895, he committed suicide leaving on his canvas a bleak interpretation of Chopin's *Funeral March* from his Sonata in B-flat minor.

No doubt, Poles were relieved that Paderewski, in contrast to his wildly bohemian compatriots such as Podkowinski, traveled around the world without similar artistic excesses, focusing instead on musical excellence and increasing the international stature of his country. His personal, artistic and financial achievements were seen as successes of the whole nation, both in Poland and among Polish emigres in the countries that he visited. A Warsaw daily, *Kurier Warszawski,* was supposed to publish Swięcicki's poem, but it was censored by the Russian authorities to such an extent that the cuts deeply changed its meaning. As a result, the poem's publication was postponed for twenty years: it was finally issued in no. 15 of 15 January 1919, two months after Poland regained independence (11 November 1918) and a day before Paderewski started his official duties as Poland's first prime minister, or "President of the Council of Ministers" (hence his subsequent honorific title of "Mr. President").

Another poem, also dating from the period of Paderewski's triumphant return to Poland in January 1899, was published in no. 19 of *Kurier Warszawski,* on 19 January 1919, three days after Paderewski was inaugurated into office. In the poem, entitled simply *Paderewski,* odd strophes were penned by a little-known poet Marian Gawalewicz and even-numbered strophes were written by a well-respected lyrical poet of the Young Poland movement, Maryla Wolska (1873-1930).[12] Paderewski's biogra-

---

[11] Tadeusz Dobrowolski, *Malarstwo Polskie* (Wrocław: Ossolineum, 1989): 178-183.

[12] Maryla, or Maria Wolska, née Młodnicki (1873-1930) studied painting in Munich and Paris, but later dedicated all her efforts to poetry. She held

pher, Andrzej Piber, cites the following example of Wolska's contribution:[13]

Pozar nad czołem, a w oczach mgła
Mistyczne cienie kładła.
Przed nim elegia smutna szła
I tęsknych mar widziadła...
Za nim się snuł marzący tłum,
Melodią wniebowzięty,
I szedł za czarem jego dum
Przez dzwięcznych fal odmęty...
I szedł za czarem jego słow,
Zaklętych w tony rzewne
I wołał w głos: "O, graj! O, mow!"
I spiącą wskrzes krolewnę!"

Translation:

The fire above his forehead and the mist in his eyes
Spread out the mystic shadows.
Before him a sorrowful elegy walked
And phantoms of lonesome spirits...
Behind him wandered a dreamy crowd
Transfixed with heavenly melodies,
Thus they followed the charm of his song
Through the depths of sonorous waves...
Thus they followed the charm of his words,
Spellbound into longing tones
Thus they called out loud: "Oh, play!, Oh, speak!"
And resurrect the sleeping princess!"

Again we encounter an image of mystical mists and sorrowful spirits that could be (and were) read as references to the legendary past of Poland's greatness, a nation now awaiting its rebirth into a sovereign country. Thinly veiled allusions to national matters in Wolska's poem include the image of the "sleeping princess" — borrowed from such classic fairy-tales as "Sleeping Beauty" by Charles Perrault (1696) or "Snow White" by the Brothers Grimm

---

a literary salon in her mansion in Lwów; her poetry draws upon characteristic *fin-de-siècle* themes of pessimism and misgivings of death
[13] Piber cites only one strophe by Wolska from this joint poem; it is found in the notes on p. 583 of his 1982 study, *op. cit.*

(1812).[14] Both fairy-tale maidens were saved from their death-sleep by courageous princes; in Perrault's story this deadly slumber lasted over a hundred years—hence the parallel to Poland's enforced "sleep" while the country waited for the return of its freedom since its fall and partitions in 1795. Paderewski, cast in the role of his country's lover and savior, was to "resurrect" the Polish princess, thus performing a task usually assigned to God himself (but realized by the "Prince Charming" in the fairy tales). This elevation of a musician and composer to the realm of legends and tales is a common thread in subsequent Paderewski-themed poems.

Simultaneously, the idea of Poland being asleep while waiting for its resurrection was widespread at the end of the 19th century. A Polish folk tale from that period described a legend of the sleeping knights, who—hidden in the caves in the Tatra Mountains—for a hundred years waited for the call to arms that would wake them from their dreams.[15] The postcard included below (see Figure 2) presents another version of this patriotic slumber: the sleeping knight, ready for combat, in full armor and with national colors, is guarded by an angel who would, hopefully, awake him at the time of struggle. The image, probably created by Maksymilian Piotrowski (1813-1875), an artist whose patriotic paintings depicted Polish legends and events from the country's history, was published in Galicia at the end of the 19th century.[16] The image could have been created after the fall of the January Insurrection (1863), the last, violent attempt at regaining Poland's liberty.

---

[14] Perrault and Brothers Grimm, in *The Mammoth Book of Fairy Tales*, edited by Mike Ashley (London: Robinson, 1997). "Little Snowdrop; or, Snow White and the Seven Dwarfs," by The Brothers Grimm p. 271-280; and "Sleeping Beauty" by Charles Perreault, p. 417-426.

[15] The Polish tale about sleeping knights under the rocky peak of Giewont may be found in *Na Skalnem Podhalu* [On the Rocky Foothills] by Kazimierz Przerwa-Tetmajer (1865-1940), published at the end of the 19th century (Warsaw: Nakł. Gebethnera i Wolffa, 1902, 2nd ed.); numerous later reprints use a variant of the title caused by changed spelling: *Na Skalnym Podhalu*.

[16] The postcard is signed by A. Piotrowski, the middle name of Maksymilian Piotrowski was Antoni; see Dobrowolski, *op. cit.*, 168.

Figure 2: A. Piotrowski: Sleeping Knight. Postcard, c. 1900. Maja Trochimczyk Collection.

III. Gilder and Musical Symbolism

Outside his native country, Paderewski's poetic reception was not limited to occasional tributes filled with praise and expressions of national hope. His tours of America resulted in several poems of distinct artistic quality written by Richard Watson Gilder, John H. Finley, Robert Underwood Johnson, and Charles Phillips. These names are not well known to Polish music scholars; Finley and Johnson, for instance, do not appear in Paderewski biographies. Gilder is mentioned as the composer's associate and personal friend in Andrzej Piber's study of Paderewski's early years and in Adam Zamoyski's biography, both of 1982. Phillips is referred to solely as Paderewski's biographer.

According to Andrzej Piber, Paderewski's contacts with Richard Watson Gilder (1844-1909) resulted from the latter's long-lasting friendship with the Polish actress Helena Modrzejewska (known in the U.S. as Modjeska).[17] Adam Zamoyski writes that the Polish pianist soon became a good friend of the poet, considering Gilder's

---

[17] Richard Watson Gilder (1844-1909); see *The Cambridge History of English and American Literature: An Encyclopedia in Eighteen Volumes,* ed. by A.W. Ward, A.R. Waller, W.P. Trent, J. Erskine, S.P. Sherman, and C. Van Doren (New York: G.P. Putnam's Sons; Cambridge, England: University Press, 1907-21). Piber, *op. cit.,* 214-215.

house to be his "real home during those first years in America."[18] In Gilder's home Paderewski had the opportunity to meet Mark Twain and Andrew Carnegie, among other prominent members of American society, but the contacts between the two men were not limited to socializing.

In the 1890s, Gilder served as the secretary of the Washington Arch Committee gathering funds for this monument; he approached Paderewski to ask for donations. According to Andrzej Piber, the pianist decided to designate to this purpose all the income from the final concert of his first, triumphant tour of the U.S. (1891-1892). The fundraiser was held at the Metropolitan Opera on 28 March 1982 with the participation of the Boston Symphony Orchestra. The event included, besides the music (i.e. piano concerti in A minor by Schumann and Paderewski, as well as a solo Hungarian Rhapsody by Liszt), a special ceremony during which Gilder and Parker Goodwin, members of the Washington Arch Committee, offered Paderewski a wreath in national colors of both nations. On the same day, the Washington Arch Committee passed a resolution thanking Paderewski for the greatest individual contribution to the fund ($4,300). Gilder was a co-signer of this declaration that also bestowed upon Paderewski a gift of two national flags that were used to decorate the hall during the celebration.

This footnote to Polish-American friendship appears in an entirely different light upon realizing that its protagonist, Richard Watson Gilder, published numerous volumes of poetry and that many of his poems dealt with other arts, painting, acting, and music. He wrote about actresses Helena Modjeska and Eleonora Duse, composers Beethoven and Chopin, MacDowell and Paderewski.[19] A volume of poetry about music, *A Book of Music*, was published in 1906; drafts

---

[18] Zamoyski, op. cit., 101, 124. The biographer's statements are based on Gilder's *Letters*, Rosamond Gilder, ed. (New York: 1916), p. 216.

[19] See Herbert F. Smith, in *Dictionary of Literary Biography, Volume 64: American Literary Critics and Scholars, 1850-1880*, John W. Rathburn, Monica M. Grecu, eds. (The Gale Group, 1988. pp. 71-77). See also R. W. Gilder, *The Poems of Richard Watson Gilder* (Boston, New York: Houghton Mifflin, 1908); *Five Books of Song* (New York: The Century Co., 1894); *The Fire Divine* (New York: The Century Co., 1907).

of the poems are held in the Gilder Collection at Princeton Library.[20]

It is clear, just from the range of his artistic subjects, that Gilder's response to art was of a synaesthetic nature; he attempted to find connection between colors and sounds, shapes and emotions. Such interpenetration of multi-sensory experiences is present, for instance, in his definition of the sonnet:

The Sonnet (In Answer to a Question)

What is a sonnet? 'T is the pearly shell
That murmurs of the far-off murmuring sea;
A precious jewel carved most curiously;
It is a little picture—painted well.
What is a sonnet? 'Tis the tear that fell
From a great poet's hidden ecstasy;
A two-edged sword, a star, a song—ah me!
Sometimes a heavy-tolling funeral bell.
This was the flame that shook with Dante's breath;
The solemn organ whereon Milton played,
And the clear glass where Shakespeare's shadow falls:
A sea this is—beware who ventureth!
For like a fjord the narrow floor is laid
Deep as mid-ocean to the sheer mountain walls.

Gilder believed in poetry's capabilities to express hidden emotions and impressions of its author in a perfectly crafted form; as a poet he is associated with the "genteel" tradition, the representatives of which avoided erotic or stark subjects, attempting to edify rather than shock and bewilder their readers. Music, the "wordless art," is a poet's supreme challenge. Verses that Gilder penned about Paderewski, after having ample opportunities to hear him in public concert halls and at home, reveal the depth of synaesthetic links in his response to music:[21]

---

[20] Richard Watson Gilder, *A Book of Music* (New York, The Century Co., 1906).

[21] The poem, published in *A Book of Music* was cited by Arthur V. Sewall during the ceremonial dinner for Paderewski in 1928 and included in *To Paderewski, op. cit.;* the speech is reprinted in Part II of "Paderewski and the Tenth Anniversary of Poland's Independence," ed. Maja Trochimczyk, *Polish Music Journal* 4:1, 2001.

How Paderewski Plays

If words were perfume, color, wild desire
If poet's song were fire
That burned to blood in purple-pulsing veins;
If with a bird-like trill the moments throbbed to hours;
If summer's rains
Turned drop by drop to shy, sweet, maiden flowers;
[...]
If melody were tears and tears were starry gleams
That shone in evening's amethystine dreams;
Ah, yes, if notes were stars, each star a different hue,
Trembling to earth in dew;
Or, of the boreal pulsings, rose and white,
Made majestic music in the night;
If all the orbs lost in the light of day
In the deep silent blue began their harps to play;
[...]
If ever art could image (as were the poet's duty)
The grieving, and the rapture, and the thunder
Of that keen hour of wonder,
That light as if of heaven, that blackness as of hell, —
How Paderewski Plays then might I dare to tell.

Gilder's poem about Paderewski's talent as a performer belongs in a cycle of his works celebrating great musicians. In this extended simile the poet brings up a range of synaesthetic comparisons of music with natural phenomena and surreal, enchanting imagery. The poem is sophisticated and richly associative, filled with imagery of nature's power and beauty, from cosmic orbs to dew drops, from storm-clouds to eclipse and aurora borealis. The complete verse includes no less than eighteen "ifs" comparing Paderewski's art with natural wonders and emotional states: mortal woe, tears, rapture... The romantic intensity of this poem is well balanced with its elaborate form. Irregular phrase length piques the interest of listeners or readers awaiting the unexpected resolution; the poem seems written to be read aloud or recited. Paderewski's musical gifts, according to Gilder, reach beyond the realm of natural forces and human comprehension.

IV. Finley and Classical Erudition

A different approach to praising Paderewski's musical talents was taken by John Huston Finley (1863-1940).[22] He wrote two poems for the Polish pianist, separated by over a decade and expressing different concerns. Both poems reveal Finley's life-long preoccupation with classical antiquity and a modern revival of Greek culture. Finley was a professor, writer, and editor of enormous influence on early 20th-century America.[23] With a broad array of interests, ranging from the classics, through modern poetry, to American history and politics, Finley was highly successful as a college professor (at Princeton University) and president (at City College of New York, until 1913). The following decade saw him as an administrator, i.e. the Commissioner of Education of the State of New York (until 1921). After resigning from that post, Finley became an associate editor, and then in 1937, the editor-in-chief of the *New York Times*.

During his distinguished career, Finley engaged in a large array of charitable activities, working for the Boy Scouts of America, the Commission for the Blind, the Red Cross in Palestine, and the American Biography project (sponsored by the American Council of Learned Societies). He received thirty-two honorary doctorates from the U.S. and Canada. Finley believed that the study of Greek and Latin provided the best foundation for liberal education, and that good education improved society and increased the personal quality of life. His interests in Greek antiquity extended beyond books—he was one of the leaders in the project of reconstructing the Parthenon in Athens. His list of publications contains a range of titles that speak for themselves:[24]

---

[22] Biographical data about Finley are based on an entry in *Dictionary of American Biography, Supplements 1-2: To 1940.* (American Council of Learned Societies, 1944-1958. Reproduced in Biography Resource Center. Farmington Hills, Mich.: The Gale Group, 2001; http://www.galenet.com/servlet/BioRC).

[23] See Marvin Gettleman, *An Elusive Presence: The Discovery of John H. Finley and His America* (Chicago: Nelson-Hall, 1979).

[24] The publications are selected from items found in the OCLC online catalog, WorldCat.

- *The French in the Heart of America* (New York, C. Scribner's Sons, 1915);
- *Our Need of the Classics* (Princeton, 1919);
- *American Democracy from Washington to Wilson: Addresses and State Papers* with James Sullivan (New York: Macmillan Co., 1919);
- *Duties of Schools When the Nation is at War* (New York: National Security League, 1918);
- *The Guide to Literature* (Garden City, N. Y.: Doubleday, Page and Company, 1926);
- *The University Library* in 24 volumes, co-edited with Nella Braddy, and Christopher Morley (Garden City, N. Y.: Doubleday, Page and Co., 1927).

Finley's fascination with ancient Greece is clearly noticeable in his poem written after Paderewski's performance in the town of Troy, New York on 27 March 1914. This concert was part of an extended tour through the Eastern states that lasted from 14 March to 22 April 1914 and ended with Paderewski's return to Europe in May that year. The tour alternated between two programs, one with Paderewski's Piano Concerto in A-minor and another with a range of solo works.[25] Paderewski performed the concerto: in Boston, Philadelphia, Washington, Baltimore, New York, Brooklyn, Providence, R. I., and Chicago. The solo recital consisted of the following compositions:

- Liszt's arrangement of Bach's Prelude & Fugue in A minor;
- Beethoven's Sonata Op. 27 no. 2 in C-sharp minor;
- Schumann's *Fantasiestücke* Op. 12;
- Liszt's arrangements of Schubert's *Erlkönig* and *Soirées de Vienne* in A major;
- Chopin's Ballade in A-flat major Op. 47;
- Chopin's Nocturne in B major Op. 62 no. 1;
- Chopin's Polonaise in A-flat major Op. 53;
- Liszt's arrangement of Wagner's *Isoldes Liebestod*; and
- Liszt's Hungarian Rhapsody (not numbered).

This mammoth program was repeated in Newark, NJ.; Troy, NY; Harrisburg, PA; Hartford, CT; Rochester, NY.; Erie, PA; Kansas City,

---

[25] Details about the tour are based on information from Perkowska, *op. cit.*, 136, & *passim*.

MO.; and Wells-Bijou Theatre in an unknown location (on 22 April, the last concert of the tour). Paderewski had earlier presented the same set of pieces minus the opening Liszt-Bach arrangement at a concert in Madison, Wisconsin, on 13 December 1913, and also during a tour of the West in January 1914 (in Colorado Springs; Boise City, Idaho; and Vancouver, Canada).

While attempting to capture the musical qualities and emotional impact of this concert, Finley decided—instead of describing the music and its effects on the listener, as Gilder would have done—to elevate Paderewski to the realm of mythical heroes by comparing him with the Greeks and Trojans from Homer's *Illiad*. Undoubtedly, the town's name, "Troy," inspired this ode to the ancient greatness and its modern reincarnation in Paderewski. Finley wrote:

> Beside Scamander's stream in ancient Ilium
> (From whose dim, moon-lit ramparts Troilus
> Sighed toward the Grecian tents where Cressid lay)
> Brave Hector, so 'tis said, derided him
> Whose love for Helen gave to Homer's harp
> The timeless Iliad: "O brother mine
> The sounding lyre shall not avail thee now!"

Extended excerpts from this poem are included in Finley's speech of 1928 given at the Testimonial Dinner for Paderewski, organized by the Kosciuszko Foundation, on 16 May 1928, at the Hotel Commodore in New York City. The dinner celebrated both the 10th anniversary of Poland's regained independence and Paderewski's widely recognized and pivotal role in this historical event. The program included speeches and musical interludes such as songs by Paderewski.

Speakers featured Samuel M. Vauclain—an industrial potentate who was a founder of the Kosciuszko Foundation; the Foundation's current president, writer Henry Noble MacCracken who served as the Toastmaster; Jan Ciechanowski—Minister of Poland to the United States; two scholars—Arthur V. Sewall and Dr. John H. Finley; and Paderewski himself. The texts of their addresses were published in a testimonial book containing the program of the event and over two hundred congratulatory messages to the pianist-statesman, from representatives of American government and institutions, as well as by a multitude of Polish-American organizations. The book, entitled *To Ignace Jan Paderewski; Artist; Patriot; Humanitarian,* was issued in 1928 by the Kos ciuszko Foundation.[26]

Figure 3: Artur Szyk, Paderewski and President Woodrow Wilson, *designing the borders of future independent Poland, from Polish American Fraternity series of 1938. Note Tadeusz Kościuszko and Kazimierz Pułaski, the Polish heroes of American Revolution in the background, and Poland's map on the table. Maja Trochimczyk Collection.*

As a celebratory project, the volume of Paderewski greetings has a notable predecessor: for the 150th Anniversary of the American Revolution the citizens of Poland signed a mammoth collection of 111 volumes of greetings including over 5,500,000 signatures (more than one sixth of the country's population in 1926). The

---

[26] This speech including the whole poem is reprinted in Part II of "Paderewski and the Tenth Anniversary of Poland's Independence" in *Polish Music Journal* 4:1 (2001)..

congratulatory greetings were initiated by two Polish-American organizations, the American-Polish Chamber of Commerce and Industry in Poland (active since 1921), and the Polish-American Society, established in 1919 by Paderewski. The document included the signatures of representatives of Polish government, both central and regional, various religious and social organizations, educational institutions, including universities and schools. The project was an extension of a Polish custom of honoring eminent citizens with a commemorative album ("Księga Pamiątkowa").

Like the offering from the Polish nation to the Americans, though on a much smaller scale, the Paderewski volume includes congratulatory messages, poems, and speeches. The texts published in the 1928 volume present a range of voices praising Paderewski for the greatest political achievement of his life, i.e. the restoration of the sovereign state of Poland after over 120 years of the country being partitioned between Russia, Prussia and Austria. Though he served as Poland's Prime Minister for less than a year in 1919, his elevated political standing and immense public recognition in the U.S. even after resigning from the government, may be gleaned from the list of people who sponsored the testimonial dinner and who wrote congratulatory greetings.

Several presidents of the U.S. sent in their messages: Calvin Coolidge (in the office at that time), Herbert Hoover, Franklin D. Roosevelt, as well as Ellen Bolling Wilson (who may have been an "acting president" during her husband illness in 1919-1921). In congratulating Paderewski, 25 American governors joined high ranking government officials, including the Secretaries of State, War, Labor, Agriculture, the Chief of Staff, the Mayor of New York, and members of the Senate and the Congress. All the branches of the American government were represented—the executive, legislative, and judiciary. Their tributes frequently took the form of personal, handwritten letters. Numerous messages came from philanthropists and musicians, as well as Polish Americans (e.g., Ralph Modjeski, engineer and son of famous actress Heena Modjeska). Representatives of American culture included musicians (Walter Damrosch, Josef Hoffman); benefactors and patrons of the arts (Elizabeth Sprague Coolidge, Frederic Juilliard, John D. Rockefeller); presidents and chancellors of universities

(Columbia University, Cornell University, Catholic University of America, Wellesley College, University of Pittsburgh, and Yale University); presidents of American organizations (the American Legion) and the clergy (the auxiliary bishop of Detroit, Joseph C. Plagent and others).

Polish-American organizations, charities, and publications usually sent in letters from the whole committees, signed by the officers in the name of all their members. The list of such organizations represented in *To Paderewski* includes: Macierz Polska [Polish Alma Mater]; Polska Rada Opieki Społecznej w Ameryce [Polish Council of Social Welfare in America]; Unia Polska [Polish Union] of Wilkes-Barre; Unia Sw. Jozefa [St. Joseph's Union] of Pittsburgh; Zjednoczenie Kapłanow Polskich w Stanach Zjednoczonych [The Union of Polish Priests in the U.S.]; paramilitary youth organization Sokolstwo Polskie w Ameryce [Polish Hawks in America]; Zjednoczenie Polsko-Narodowe [Polish National Union]; Zjednoczenie Polskie Rzymsko-Katolickie [Polish Roman Catholic Union] with its 200,000 members; Związek Narodowy Polski [Polish National Alliance] and its chapters in Chicago, Cleveland, Detroit, South Bend; Związek Polakow w Ameryce [Union of Poles in America] of Cleveland, Ohio; Koło Polskie w Nowym Yorku [The Polish Circle in New York]; Polish Singers Alliance of America; Stowarzyszenie Inzynierow Polakow w Ameryce [Association of Polish Engineers in America]; Polish-American Society of Warsaw, Poland; Polish College in Athol Springs, New York; St. John Kanty College in Ezic, Pa.; and Higher School of Holy Trinity, Chicago.

Polish-American publications were well represented by: *Czas; Dziennik Chicagoski; Dziennik Związkowy— Zgoda; Głos Narodu; Goniec Polski; Górnik; Gwiazda; Gwiazda Polarna; Rolnik; Jaskółka; Kultura* from Stevens Point; WI; *Jedność; Jedność Polonia; Kronika; Kurjer; Kuryer Codzienny* of Boston; *Monitor Clevelandzki; Wiadomości Codzienne* (Cleveland; Ohio); *Pittsburczanin; Przewodnik Katolicki;* and *Rekord Codzienny of Detroit.*

The commemorative volume also published what amounted to a "high society" roster in the form of Paderewski dinner's committee sponsors, led by Herbert Hoover—Honorary Chairman and featuring a veritable who's who of American politics, industry, business, and culture.27

To return to Finey poem and its Homeric setting, the Scamander (now: Karamenderes) was the river near the ancient Troy (its ruins are in modern Turkey), a proud metropolis under siege by the Greeks. This was the site of the tragic romance of Troilus and Cressida, immortalized by William Shakespeare and mentioned to prove the writer's erudition. The poem refers to the protagonists of Homer's epic, two brothers, sons of Priam, the king of Troy: the patriotic warrior, mighty Hector and the selfish and charming musician, Paris, who seduced Greek queen Helene and, by doing so started the Trojan wars. If not Paris but Paderewski had been there, with his vastly superior instrument (the piano invented by Christofori), the Trojan wars would have ended quite differently— or so claims Finley:

> I heard brave Hector's taunt again, and then
> I heard reply: "Great Paderewski played
> Not such a puny lyre as Paris twanged,
> But one Christofori designed to sound
> The thundering of battle, and, alike,
> The peaceful breathings of an oaten pipe;
> And hearing, thought: Had this Red Polack stood
> Beside old Priam on the Trojan walls
> The battle lost immortally were won!"

The poem is a game of sophistication and erudition; Finley's allusions include the names of Christofori, the Italian inventor of the piano, and of Andrew Lang (1844-1912), the venerated English translator of the *Illiad*.28 Without a thorough knowledge of the ancient epic, its heroes, stories, and locations, Finley's narrative, effectively replacing Paris with Paderewski and reversing the course of the whole Trojan war, would be incomprehensible. The poet's choice of substituting one musical seducer with another one—adored for his physical beauty (including startlingly "red" or "golden" hair) and personal charisma as much as for his musical

---

27 The list is reproduced in my introduction to the Paderewski-themed issue of the online *Polish Music Journal* 4:1 (2001).

28 Andrew Lang's translation of Homer's *Illiad* was first published in 1905 and repeatedly reprinted with illustrations in the 1930s

talents—reveals his erudition and insight. It is not only the power of sound emitted by a better instrument that gave Paderewski an advantage over his ancient predecessor, though obviously the dynamic range of the grand piano far exceeds that of the ancient lyre or kythara.[29] It is also the strength of Paderewski's musical talents apparent in the choice and scope of his concert program, lasting well over three hours, that gave him an advantage over his mythological counterpart, i.e. Paris, and his adversary, i.e. the Greek attacker of Troy, Achilles. Thus, in Finley's poem Paderewski entered mythology and became an "immortal."

The American author wrote another poem about the Polish pianist in 1928, again drawing a metaphor from the rich treasury of Greek mythology. Finley read this poem as a part of his speech during the ceremonial dinner celebrating Paderewski's role in the regaining of Poland's sovereignty on the occasion of the tenth anniversary of this event. In the second poem, Finley again drew from ancient Greek mythology as he compared Paderewski to a demi-god, Orpheus, attempting to bring back from Hades his wife, Eurydice, who had died and whose spirit was imprisoned in the Underworld. Orpheus failed despite the magic of his music that enchanted the guardians of Hades and allowed Eurydice to pass; he failed because of a lack of self-restraint, or loving her too intently, or having too much curiosity... Explanations of the immensely popular Orpheus myth differ. Nonetheless, it is clear, to Finley at least, that Paderewski succeeded in the quest for his Eurydice:

> You've brought from out the air such symphonies
> As God with all His earth-orchestral range
> From cataract through soughing wind to lark
> Could not produce without the skill of man.
> [...] As ancient Orpheus trod the aisles of hell
> To rescue from its thrall Eurydice,
> So you for Poland. But though Orpheus failed
> You won. Polonia Restitute lives.

In Latin, "Polonia Restituta" means "rebuilt" or "restored" Poland; it is also the name of the new country's most important state honor,

---

[29] For an in-depth study of all aspects of Greek music, see Thomas J. Mathiesen, *Apollo's Lyre: Greek Music and Music Theory in Antiquity and the Middle Ages* (University of Nebraska Press, 1999).

awarded to individuals that assisted the country on its way to freedom. The name of this distinction was well-known to those present at the New York ceremony where the poem was presented in public: several holders of "Polonia Restituta" medals were in the audience, including writer Charles Phillips and composer Zygmunt Stojowski. Therefore, Finley's casual use of this Latin phrase did not require extraordinary sophistication of his listeners; neither was the use of the myth of Orpheus-Paderewski and Euridice-Poland as complex and unintelligible as the references to the epic of *Illiad* had been in the earlier poem.

While still recognizing the significance of Paderewski's musical achievements and praising them in extraordinary similes, Finley described Paderewski's political actions as constituting the most important achievement of his life. Apparently, not much could compare with restoring a country to the political map of Europe. Besides Orpheus and Euridice, the poem also mentions two illustrious Poles—the astronomer Nicolaus Copernicus, and the hero of the American Revolutionary War as well as a fighter for Poland's independence, general Tadeusz Kosciuszko. The inclusion of the names of these two men whose actions profoundly changed the world are not accidental. By shifting attention from the musical to the political, the poet articulated a hierarchy of human achievements described later by Hannah Arendt in *The Human Condition*.[30]

According to the philosopher, whose views were influenced by the bitter experiences of World War II, the Holocaust, and a personal confrontation with totalitarianism, "action" takes precedence over "contemplation," or "labor," or "production" as the most worthy form of human behavior. Arendt described her ideal of a politicized "Vita Activa," pursued by free, fully individualized subjects in the "agora" of a public space. This active life contrasted with the lives

---

[30] Hannah Arendt, *The Human Condition* (Chicago: University of Chicago Press, 1958). See also Daniel Mano, *Relating Vita Activa and Vita Contemplativa Hannah Arendt on the Human Condition* (Ph. D. diss., University of Waterloo, 1992); H. Arendt and Melvyn A. Hill, *Hannah Arendt, the Recovery of the Public World* (New York: St. Martin's Press, 1979).

of the physically productive "Homo Faber" and the merely hard-working "Animal Laborans." As Arendt wrote:[31]

> With word and deed we insert ourselves into the human world, and this insertion is like a second birth, in which we confirm and take upon ourselves the naked fact of our original physical appearance. [...] To act, in its most general sense, means to take an initiative, to begin (as the Greek word *archein*, "to begin," "to lead," and eventually, "to rule," indicates), to set something into motion (which is the original meaning of the Latin *agere*). In acting and speaking, men show who they are, reveal actively their unique personal identities and thus make their appearance in the human world. [...] The political realm rises directly out of acting together, the "sharing of words and deeds." Thus action not only has the most intimate relationship to the public part of the world common to us all, but is the one activity which constitutes it.

It is perhaps not a coincidence that Arendt's theory arose from her study of ancient philosophers and that Finley was so thoroughly immersed in their writings. While appreciating Paderewski as a man of political action rather than a creative artist and musician in the 1928 poem, Finley expressed his personal philosophy of liberalism and political involvement. Similarly to Paderewski, Finley took a path away from academic contemplation of the past towards an active involvement in the present, including both charity and politics. Another, celebrated instance of such a shift from the realm of "contemplation" towards "action"—though limited to charitable pursuits—was provided by Dr. Albert Schweitzer, who abandoned his research of J.S. Bach and a career as an organist and music historian for the sake of medical studies and working in a leper colony in Africa. Since the choices made by Finley and Paderewski both involved political motivation, it was harder to view both men as "modern saints." Therefore, their impact on their societies has been underappreciated.

At present, the figure of John Huston Finley is of great interest to the historians of American literature and education. The revival of his heritage may be seen in calls to return to the "great books" tradition of liberal education that he championed for American students. In contrast, Paderewski's generous vision of a large, powerful and multi-ethnic Poland was destroyed by the Nazis and

---

[31] The quotation is from Arendt, *op. cit.*, pp. 176, 179, and 198.

Soviets. His reputation as a creative artist has also suffered numerous setbacks and rarely, if ever, is he venerated as an incomparable musical genius and a "modern immortal."

Figure 4: Portrait of Paderewski by H. T. Beckert from Orłowski, 1940.[32]
Based on a popular image of Paderewski while giving a speech in 1915.

V. Johnson's Tribute to a Patriot

When Robert Underwood Johnson (1853-1937) wrote his tribute to Paderewski in 1916, the composer's transformation into a statesman, living a "vita activa," had already begun.[33] Since 1915

[32] Józef Orłowski, *Ignacy Jan Paderewski i Odbudowa Polski* [I.J. Paderewski and the Rebuilding of Poland] vol. 2 (Chicago: The Stanek Press, 1940).

[33] Robert Underwood Johnson, American poet and diplomat. Biographical information may be found in *World Authors, 1900-1950* Martin Seymour-Smith and Andrew C. Kimmens, eds. (Wilson, H.W., 1996); Alden

Paderewski was involved in an extensive publicity campaign on behalf of Poland: during the years of World War I he gave over 350 speeches about the country's need to become an independent state and preceded every concert with a half-hour talk on this subject. By continually and persistently shaping public opinion, while simultaneously engaging in seeking support in the highest political circles, Paderewski sought to achieve just one, main goal: the liberty for his country. His efforts were rewarded when President Woodrow Wilson added Poland's sovereignty to his conditions for peace after World War I.

The connection between Robert Underwood Johnson and Paderewski was probably established through Richard Watson Gilder: Johnson worked for the *Scribner's Monthly* (later transformed into the *Century Monthly Magazine*) where he served as associate editor and Gilder was the editor-in-chief. After Gilder's death, Johnson took over this post until retiring in 1913. A poet, editor, and diplomat, with family roots reaching far back into colonial times, Johnson was a literary celebrity, often called the unofficial poet laureate of the United States.[34] He published several volumes of poetry, frequently commemorating eminent individuals and events; he also co-edited the four-volume series of *Battles and Leaders of the Civil War.* Among his other pursuits were the international copyright movement, the creation of literary organizations, such as the Academy of Arts and Letters, and the preservation of American land and natural resources in national parks (with John Muir, the founder of the Sierra Club). Despite his appreciation of Paderewski's patriotism, Johnson's favorite European country was Italy; he worked for the Italian War Relief Fund of America, and after the war served as the American ambassador to Italy.

Whitman, *American Reformers: An H.W. Wilson Biographical Dictionary* (Wilson, 1985).

[34] The American office of "poet laureate" was established by the U.S. Congress only in 1985; the position is temporary and involves serving as a poetry advisor to the Library of Congress. In the British tradition, the "poet laureate" had the task of writing verses about the royal family; the first official poet laureate was John Dryden (1668).

Johnson's poem, *To Paderewski, Patriot* was hand-written on one page and its photographic reproduction is included in Orłowski's collection of documents published in 1940.[35] The four strophes of the poem consist of six verses each, with the parallel rhyme structure of *aabbcc,* recurring in each strophe. The poem's awkwardly angular symmetry results also from the identity of rhythmic patterns in each line and the placement of the accents on the last, single syllable. The poet described the composer as:

> Son of a martyred race that long
> Has honed its sorrow into song
> And taught the world that grief is less
> when voiced by Music's loveliness.

In Johnson's poem, Paderewski was the "bearer of memories" of his torn and suffering country that survived by cherishing remembrances of past glory through its "lost century of pride." The poem included references to national travails and defeats; it concluded with an expression of hope that Paderewski's "God-sent" musical gifts would serve and advance the Polish cause:

> Master with whom the world doth sway
> Like meadow with the wind at play
> May Heaven send thee, at this hour,
> Such access of supernal power
> that every note beneath thy hand
> May plead for thy distracted land.

The date of 13 April 1916 locates the poem's likely origin in Washington, D.C. On that day Paderewski gave a recital at the National Theatre in the American capital.[36] The simplistic formal features of Johnson's ode to Paderewski's patriotism do not make his product appear very attractive at the threshold of the modernist era (it was written in the same year as James Joyce's first major book, *A Portrait of the Artist as a Young Man*).[37]

---

[35] Józef Orłowski, *Ignacy Jan Paderewski i Odbudowa Polski, op. cit.* p. 124.
[36] Data about the concerts from Perkowska, *op. cit.,* 141.
[37] James Joyce (1882-1941), *A Portrait of the Artist as a Young Man* (New York: Huebsch, 1916; London: Egoist, 1917); *Ulysses* (London: Egoist, 1922; New York: Random House, 1934).

However, we should note that Johnson's poetry had at least one prominent musical admirer, i.e. the American father of musical modernism, Charles Ives (1874-1954). In the 1920s, Ives wrote songs to four poems by Johnson, including a longer excerpt of *The Housatonic at Stockbridge*, as well as *At Sea, Luck and Work*, and *Premonitions*. In Johnson, Ives found a fellow Transcendentalist; the composer also shared the poet's interests in nature and its healing power. Paderewski's interests had a different common trait with Johnson's—i.e. classical-romantic aesthetic, characterized by an emphasis on the profundity of emotion and the comprehensibility of musical (or poetic) form. Johnson's fascination with the romantic "giants" of English-language poetry active in the first half of the 19th century, such as Shelley, Tennyson, and Keats, was reflected in Paderewski's belief that the greatest composers belonged to the early romantic period and included Beethoven, Schumann, Schubert, and Chopin.[38]

VI. Phillips, Paderewski and Poland

The final English-language poem to be considered in this overview was written by Charles Phillips (1880-1933), known to Paderewski scholars as the author of his popular biography, *The Story of a Modern Immortal*, published in 1933.[39] Phillips was a writer and poet, working as a professor of English at the University of Notre Dame (1924-1933), where his archives are now located. The Paderewski poem was penned for the celebration of Poland's tenth anniversary of independence and as a tribute to Paderewski's role in this development during the celebratory dinner in New York in 1928. The same occasion was commemorated in verse by John H. Finley; as mentioned earlier these poems were included in an album of greetings.[40] In *Poland and Paderewski*, Charles Phillips described the long-suffering country's resurrection as resulting from Paderewski's actions:

[38] For references to Paderewski's efforts to promote these composers, see Piber, *op. cit.,* 293, 375; Zamoyski, *op. cit.,* 134.

[39] Charles Phillips, *Paderewski, the Story of a Modern Immortal* (New York: MacMillan, 1933; reprint New York: Da Capo Press, 1978; reprint lists the publication date as 1934). This biography is listed in every subsequent book on Paderewski.

[40] Selected items are in Part I of "Paderewski and the Tenth Anniversary of Poland's Independence" *Polish Music Journal* 4:1 (2001).

There was a silence as of death—
the nations watched, the righteous mourned,
Where on her bier with hushed breath
dear Poland lay—the wept, the scorned.
In all the darkened air no sound
save muffled drum and funeral bell:
Deep-chorded Chopin's anthem found refrain
but in the tears that fell—
Until the music of your soul,
great Master of the Harmonies,
Broke on her listening ear to roll
with echoing note across the seas.
[...]
... She rises, beautiful, renewed!
She lifts her golden voice—she sings—
And in her song, sweet plenitude of love,
O, son, your bright name rings!

Since Paderewski's first title to fame was his performing talent as a musician, Phillips abundantly draws from musical imagery in his text. It is Paderewski's "kindling voice" that stirs Poland, his "mother," back to life; it is the sound of music transcending any other human music that echoes in the breaking of the chains of the imprisoned country. As an international aid worker for one of the war victims' relief agencies in Poland, Phillips had an opportunity to see the destruction and rebirth of Poland after World War I. He spent two years (1919-1920) directing the Polish relief efforts and wrote a book about the country. As a result of his charitable activities, he was awarded the *Polonia Restituta* medal. During the period spent in Poland, Phillips witnessed first-hand the nation's reaction to Paderewski's arrival and the outpouring of gratitude addressed towards the musician-statesman. The first year of Phillips's work there coincided with the composer's brief sojourn as the President of the Polish Council of Ministers.

Paderewski's initial months in power were filled with public expressions of support and gratitude; crowds welcomed him during all his public appearances; he was portrayed in the press as Poland's savior. Two laudatory Polish poems discussed earlier, written in 1899 by Swięcicki and Wolska, were finally published at that time.

A detailed review of archival material is likely to increase the number of known occasional verse praising Paderewski's achievements. By the time Phillips wrote his poem (1928), Paderewski's active role in the Polish government had ended, and his erstwhile supporters abandoned him, disappointed with his lack of success in negotiations of Poland's borders at the Peace Conference and contentious issues arising with the country's neighbors, Czecho-Slovakia and Germany.

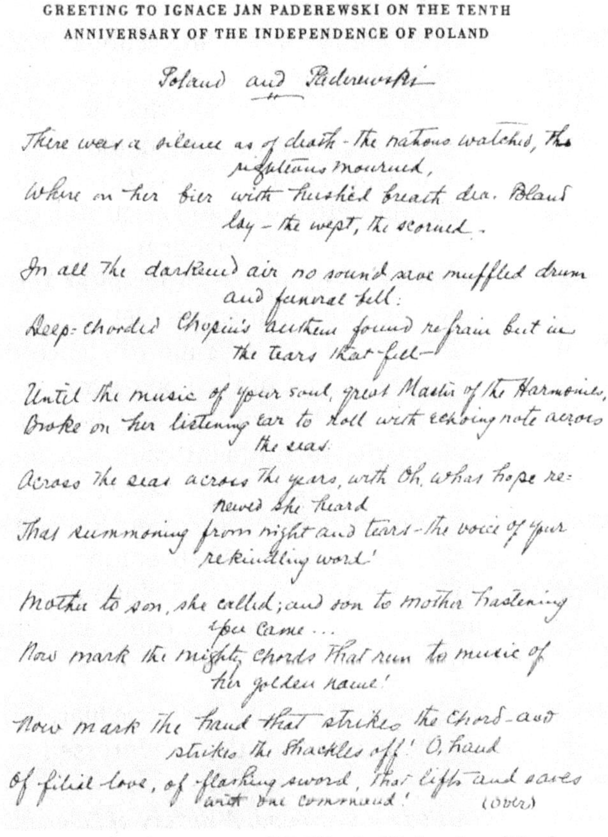

GREETING TO IGNACE JAN PADEREWSKI ON THE TENTH
ANNIVERSARY OF THE INDEPENDENCE OF POLAND

Poland and Paderewski

There was a silence as of death - The nations watched, the
righteous mourned,
Where on her bier with hushed breath dead. Poland
lay - she wept, she scorned.

In all the darkened air no sound save muffled drum
and funeral bell:
Deep-chorded Chopin's anthem found refrain but in
the tears that fell—

Until the music of your soul, great Master of the Harmonies,
Broke on her listening ear to roll with echoing note across
the seas.

Across the seas, across the years, with Oh, what hope renewed she heard
That summoning from night and tears - The voice of your
rekindling word'

Mother to son, she called; and son to mother hastening
you came ...
Now mark the mighty chords that run to music of
her golden name'

Now mark the hand that strikes the chord - and
strikes the shackles off' O, hand
Of filial love, of flashing sword, that lifts and saves
at one command! (over)

Figure 5: The first page of Phillips's "Poland and Paderewski."
New York: Kościuszko Foundation (1928).

Moreover, in 1926, Paderewski's main political rival, Jozef Piłsudski, orchestrated a *coup-d'etat* that overturned the legally-elected government for the sake of a Piłsudski-controlled regime that was supposed to "heal" the disarray in the country (hence its

Latinized nickname of "Sanacja").[41] These political circumstances further diminished the recognition of Paderewski's political achievements in his home country and abroad. In these circumstances, the excessive praise found in Phillips's poem and other tributes to the pianist-patriot seem partly designed to rectify the historical record and recover his reputation, while countering the relentless propaganda of Piłsudski supporters. Needless to say, the portrayal of Piłsudski in Phillips's biography of the composer was far from appealing.

In his laudatory poem, Phillips's statement about Paderewski's voice calling out across the ocean to Poland may seem pure poetic license. However, it is far more accurate than it would appear: Paderewski's last composition was an anthem for the Polish Army in the U.S. that he was organizing in 1917-1918 in order to increase Poland's presence in the battles of the Great War and to give credence to the country's claim to a seat at the Peace Conference that was to define the new European order after the war. The composer penned the text for his anthem on a letterhead page from the Gotham Hotel in New York, his venue of choice during his American tours.[42] The manuscript of the poem's text is not dated; the music was composed in 1917 and the song immediately sent out to be performed in the recruitment camps in the U.S. and Canada. According to the catalog of Paderewski's manuscripts by Perkowska and Pigła, there are two sources for this song, entitled in both *Orzeł Biały* [White Eagle]: a 1918 edition, New York: T. Wronski (arrangement for male choir and piano or brass band); and an undated arrangement for mixed choir and brass band, copied by Henryk Opienski.[43]

The four-strophe song, with the incipit "Hej, orle biały" [Hey, white eagle!] which is usually used as a title, is addressed to Poland's

---

[41] See Norman Davies, *God's Playground: A History of Poland* (New York: Columbia University Press, 1982), vol. 2. For discussions of Paderewski and Piłsudski see Marian Marek Drozdowski, *Ignacy Jan Paderewski. Zarys biografii politycznej* [Outline of a political biography] (Warsaw, 1979; Eng. trans., 1981, enlarged 1988).

[42] Paderewski's undated manuscript of the song's text and the first page of the 1918 edition by T. Wroński are on pp. 12-13 of Orłowski, *op. cit.*

[43] Małgorzata Perkowska and Włodzimerz Pigła, "Katalog rękopisów I. J. Paderewskiego," *Muzyka* 33: 3 (1988): 53-70.

emblem, a proud bird of prey, that is encouraged to soar and lead Poles to valiant action. The Polish text—transcribed from Paderewski's handwriting—is followed by an anonymous translation published in the volume by Orłowski (1940), with literal translations inserted in square brackets. The tone of the whole may be inferred from the following fragments:

> Hej, orle biały, ongi tak zraniony,
> Zbyt długo brzmiały pogrzebowe dzwony,
> Rozpaczy szały i załosne tony.
> Wiedz nas na smiały czyn, nieustraszony.

> Translation:
> *On, white eagle, once so severely wounded!*
> *Too long have rung the mourning chimes*
> *[lit. "resounded funereal bells"],*
> *Lasted the mad despair and crying tunes*
> *[lit. "despair's frenzy and mourning tunes"].*
> *Lead us to brave and fearless deeds.*

The final two strophes are addressed directly to Polish troops and present them with their goals. The soldiers are to fight for freedom, for Polish access to the sea, for the recovery of the past glory of Poland's two most powerful royal dynasties, the Piasts and the Jagiellons, and for universal liberty:

> Hej na boj, na boj, gdzie wolnosci zorza,
> Hej na boj, na boj, za polski brzeg morza.
> Za Polskę wolną od tyranskich tronow,
> Za Polskę dumną — Piastow, Jagiellonow.

> Hej, na boj, na boj! Taka wola Boza!
> Hej, na boj, na boj! Za Gdansk i brzeg morza!
> Za Ziemie całą, tę ojczyznę naszą,
> Za wolnosc wszystkich, za waszą i naszą.

> Translation:
> *On to fight! to fight! Where liberty is dawning!*
> *On to fight for the Polish shore of sea!*
> *For Poland free from tyrants' fetters [lit. "thrones"]!*

> *[additional line, missed in translation:*
> *"For Poland—proud—of Piasts and Jagiellons."]*

On to fight! Such is God's will!
On to fight! For Gdańsk and seashore!
For all our land, our native land,
For the liberty of all, for yours and ours!

The last line is a reference to the motto embroidered on national flags since the 1848 Spring of the Nations, when Polish troops led by General Jozef Bem fought in the Hungarian uprising against the Hapsburgs. Overall, Paderewski's poetic effort follows the conventions of a military song, expected to be simple, easily comprehensible, uplifting, and encouraging bravery.

Figure 6: Paderewski's autograph of the text for "Hej, orle biały." Polish Museum of America. Reproduced from Józef Orłowski, op. cit., (1940), 12.

Alas, the text leaves much to be desired in terms of its literary quality. The rhymes are too obvious, the elevated language borders on the grotesque (e.g. "rozpaczy szały," i.e. the frenzy of despair). However, Paderewski's vision of a powerful Poland modeled on the multi-ethnic kingdoms of Poland's Golden Age, hinted upon in several lines of his anthem, is notable for its far-reaching quality and political savvy. Paderewski, raised in the eastern part of Poland, where the towns were predominantly Jewish, villages—Ukrainian, and manors—Polish, was opposed to the notion that

Poland could ever become an ethnically-united "nation-state." He knew that large ethnic minorities were interspersed throughout Poland's territory and that the country could not have been defined in narrow ethnic terms without serious internal and external strife.[44] In addition, Paderewski's territorial emphasis on creating Poland with full access to the Baltic Sea and the inclusion of the port-city of Gdansk was prescient in the light of the awkward, and ultimately dangerous, construct that emerged as a result of the Versaille Peace Treaty: a free city of Danzig, and a corridor of Polish land separating two German enclaves. It was the Polish resolve not to give in to Hitler's demands for a corridor of land that would have connected both German-held parts of the seashore that provided him with an excuse to attack Poland and start World War II in 1939.

Despite the political wisdom apparent in his vision of a large, multi-ethnic and powerful Poland, Paderewski's patriotic song has not been widely recognized or very popular. It rarely appeared in printed collections of military songs in Poland or abroad. Of the sources I consulted, Paderewski's hymn of the Polish Army was not included in any currently used anthologies or CD collections. Yet, it marks a decision that changed the course of Paderewski's career and ultimately influenced his standing as a composer and statesman: as a Polish national hero he disappeared from the annals of music history, as a piano virtuoso and an "idol" of the crowds, he was not a typical politician either. Paderewski's *Hej, orle biały*, thus occupies a peculiar place among the "last works" by composers, that include monumental symphonies (Beethoven, Bruckner, Mahler), and the unfinished *Kunst der Fuge* (Bach).

VII. Paderewski Elegies

By 1941, Paderewski's own music was nearly forgotten, perhaps with the exception of the "immortal" Minuet. The war-themed symphonies performed during World War II included Shostakovich's *Leningrad Symphony* and Aleksander Tansman's

---

[44] While Paderewski's name was used for various political causes, especially by the nationalist faction of Roman Dmowski, he did not fully share Dmowski's nationalistic views and was supportive of the role of minorities in the independent country. See Zamoyski, *op. cit.*, 143-144.

Polish Rhapsody was receiving performances throughout the U.S. instead of Paderewski's Symphony in B minor, *Polonia*.[45]

The aging artist was still highly recognized as the living symbol of Poland's independence and invited to chair the National Council, the kernel of the Polish government-in-exile. No wonder then, that Paderewski's death in 1941 resulted in an outpouring of patriotic poetry. According to Marian Marek Drozdowski, who studied Paderewski's political career, a poem by Włodzimierz Bakalarski was often recited in military camps in Switzerland, Scotland, Wales, and the Near East, through 1942-43.[46]

> Niech wszystkie wierzby w kraju się rozpłaczą
> I te przydrozne i te nad strumieniem...
> Gdy Cię oczami w zaswiatach zobaczą,
> jak szopenowskim będziesz kroczył cieniem.
> Lekko trąc liscmi, a na wiatru strunach
> wypiesc akordy, co łkają Ci w duszy.
> Niech Wiosna Ludow przebudzi się w łunach
> i całą łunę w fundamentach ruszy.
> Niech się Mazowsze rozspiewa, rozdzwoni,
> w takt kujawiaka, mazurkiem ułanskim...
> [...] A wtedy zbrojnie ruszą wszystkie stany
> i duch Twoj będzie znow przewodził ludem...
> Gdy zagrasz swiatu—Mistrzu Ukochany -
> Rewolucyjną Szopena etiudę!!!

> Translation:
> *Let all the willows in the country weep*
> *those by the roads and those by the streams...*
> *when they see you—with their eyes—in the otherworld*
> *as you walk in Chopin's shadow.*
> *[...] When—*

---

[45] Aleksander Tansman's *Rapsodie polonaise* (1940) connected the melodies of the Polish and British national anthems, as an expression of hope that Britain would come to the rescue of its beleaguered ally. The work was performed in the U.S. through the war years.

[46] See Marian Marek Drozdowski, "Reakcje świata na śmierć Paderewskiego," in Wojciech Marchwica & Andrzej Sitarz, eds., *Warsztat kompozytorski, wykonawstwo i koncepcje polityczne Ignacego Jana Paderewskiego* [Composers workshop: Performance and political conceptions of Ignacy Jan Paderewski] (Kraków: Musica Iagiellonica, 1991), 20-34. The poem is cited on pp. 24-25.

with the sounds of the sonata, in the moonlight silence—-
Poland will be filled with the tender sorrow,
cast the threads of alarm into heaven!
And then all the states [i.e. classes of society] will rise to arms
and your spirit will again lead your people...
when you will play for the world—you, our Beloved Master—
[will play] Chopin's Revolutionary Etude.

Bakalarski describes Paderewski's most popular pieces as reflections of Poland's landscape and its regions: the dances resound in the central area of Mazovia, the Tatra Album resounds with echoes in the mountains from which the music originated, and the waves of the Baltic Sea sway in the gentle rhythm of the ever-popular Minuet (in G major). There is an allusion to the "moonlight silence" i.e. the *Moonlight Sonata*—the subtitle of Beethoven's Piano Sonata Op. 27 no. 2 and the title of the only movie in which Paderewski acted (1937).[47]

The grand finale, though, is reserved for Chopin's music: it is the tones of Chopin's Revolutionary Etude that would result in the patriotic resurgence, not Paderewski's own *Hymn of the Polish Army*, or his Symphony *Polonia*. For Paderewski, it seems, Chopin's shadow was too large to be cast off. Despite his repeated efforts at creating a national opera (*Manru*), symphony (*Polonia*), or piano repertoire (various collections of dances and program pieces), Paderewski's presence in the popular imagination, even among his compatriots was primarily as a performer. It is also worth noting that his political achievements in securing Poland's independence a quarter century earlier are not even mentioned in Bakalarski's final tribute to the charismatic patriot and inspired musician.

Personal sentiments about the nature of death and dying witnessed by a child are found in a personal elegy published by the daughter of Paderewski's secretary, Sylvan Strakacz, Anne Strakacz-Appleton. The Polish text of this poem is found in her "Wspomnienie o Paderewskim" in the anthology of Paderewski

---

[47] The black-and-white *Moonlight Sonata* was released in 1937 in England; it includes a twenty-minute Paderewski recital with Chopin's Polonaise Op. 53, Liszt's *Hungarian Rhapsody*, Beethoven's *Moonlight Sonata* and Paderewski's Minuet in G major.

studies edited by Wojciech Marchwica and Andrzej Sitarz (1991).[48] Strakacz-Appleton writes:

> Pozegnał nas usmiech zza progow człowieka.
> W nim wszystko spoczęło: i droga daleka,
> i koniec tak bliski, i krzyz bohatera
> o ktory się ludzkosc bezsilna opiera;
> i gwiazda za ktorą krol idzie wybrany
> by drogę wskazywał tym nędzniej odzianym.

Translation:
Our last farewell was the man's smile from beyond the threshold.
Everything rested in it: the long way,
the imminent ending, and the cross of the hero
that provides the support for powerless humankind;
the star that is followed by the king chosen
in order to show the way to those dressed more poorly.

While still belonging to the genre of "elegiac poems" and touching upon mystical themes of religious nationalism (with veiled references to Christianity and a quotation of a title of Juliusz Słowacki's play, *Król Duch* [The King Spirit]), Strakacz-Appleton's expression of personal grief exemplifies a new category of poetry dedicated to the pianist-composer. It could be called "personal-sentimental response," for lack of a better label. Simultaneously, its heart-felt sentiments indicate a return to the earnest devotion of Paderewski's early listeners, like Polish exiles in Belgium who, in awkwardly rhymed lines, "gave him their hearts." For his Polish compatriots, Paderewski was the country's favorite son and its "savior;" this role of the "new Chopin" was far more important than his engagement in purely musical pursuits—i.e. his image as "Master of Harmonies" praised by Gilder, Finley, and Phillips. In poetic reception of Paderewski in Polish culture, politics triumphed over art.

---

[48] Anne Strakaczówna-Appleton, "Wspomnienie o Paderewskim," [Remembering Paderewski], in Marchwica, Sitarz, eds., *op. cit.*, 5-19.

Essay 2.

An Archangel at the Piano:
Paderewski's Image and His Female Audience

Maja Trochimczyk

1. The Creation of the Angelic Myth

Hair of flaming sun!
Eyes of the mystic sea!
Archangel of our muse!
IGNACE Paderewski.

King of glorious Poland!
God made him fit to be
A nation's wish (fate willing)
IGNACE JAN PADEREWSKI.

This poetic fragment, published in the *Musical Courier* in 1917, was penned by a young student at the Von Ende School of Music in New York, who identified herself only with a pseudonym "Halka."[1] The name, borrowed from an infatuated heroine of Stanisław Moniuszko's national opera of the same title, indicated that the writer was a young woman of Polish descent.[2] Paderewski's young admirer chose to present herself as a tragic lover who committed suicide when her beloved married a different woman. The work remains in the repertoire of Polish opera theaters but is not well known in the West; the student who chose "Halka" as her pseudonym must have been acquainted with Polish culture.

---

[1] First published with the same title in *Polish American Stud*ies 67:1 (Spring 2010): 5-44. The press clipping is from the *Musical Courier* dated 22 February 1917, found in the Research Collection, Performing Arts Division, New York Public Library. Paderewski's friend and former student, pianist-composer Zygmunt Stojowski (1870-1946) directed the Von Ende School of Music at the time. I first copied this poem in "Rediscovering Paderewski," an editorial to the "Unknown Paderewski" issue of the online *Polish Music Journal*, 4:2 (2001).

[2] Stanisław Moniuszko (1819-1872), composed *Halka* in 1848 for its Wilno premiere and revised it for a subsequent performance in Warsaw (1858). He is regarded as the "father of national opera" in Poland.

"Halka's" awkward poetic description of Paderewski's charismatic beauty was almost prophetic in its juxtaposition of his image as a mysterious, dazzling "archangel" and his emergent public persona as a "king"—or rather, as in 1919, a Prime Minister—of Poland.[3] Among numerous European pianists touring the U.S. at the turn of the twentieth-century, Ignacy Jan Paderewski (1860-1941) occupied a unique position of a musical and political celebrity. Over the years, the young virtuoso was transformed into a noble statesman revered for his role in the "resurrection" of Poland, a country reborn after a hiatus of 123 years.[4] Paderewski's role as Poland's President of the Council of Ministers and the first Minister of Foreign Affairs (1919) resulted from his recognition by the Allied Powers as Poland's main spokesperson and representative on the international arena during World War I. His direct involvement in Polish government did not last long, but he preserved the honorary title of "Mr. President" until the end of his life.

---

[3] Political biographies of Paderewski include Anita Prazmowska, *Ignacy Paderewski: Poland* (London: Haus, 2009); Marian Marek Drozdowski, *Ignacy Jan Paderewski. Zarys biografii politycznej* [Outline of a political biography] (Warsaw, 1979; Eng. trans., 1981, rev. 1988) and Henryk Przybylski, *Paderewski: Między muzyką a polityką* [Paderewski: Between music and politics] (Katowice: Unia, 1992). See also Mieczysław B. Biskupski "Paderewski, Polish Politics, and the Battle of Warsaw, 1920," *Slavic Review* (1993): 503-513; and "Paderewski as Leader of American Polonia, 1914-1918," *Polish American Studies* 43, No. 1 (1986).

[4] Adam Zamojski, *Paderewski* (New York and London: Atheneum, 1982); Andrzej Piber, *Droga do Sławy: Ignacy Jan Paderewski w latach 1860-1902* [Way to fame: Ignacy Jan Paderewski in the years 1860-1902] (Warsaw: PIW, 1982); Małgorzata Perkowska, *Diariusz koncertowy Ignacego Jana Paderewskiego* [Paderewski's Concert Diary] (Kraków: PWM, 1990); Andrzej Sitarz and Wojciech Marchwica, eds., *Warsztat kompozytorski, wykonawstwo i koncepcje polityczne Ignacego Jana Paderewskiego* [Composers workshop: Performance and political conceptions of Ignacy Jan Paderewski], (Kraków: Musica Iagellonica, 1991); Małgorzata Perkowska and Maja Trochimczyk, "Selected Bibliography: Ignacy Jan Paderewski," *Polish Music Journal* 4, no. 2 (winter 2001), online; Maja Trochimczyk, "Searching for Poland's Soul: Paderewski and Szymanowski in the Tatras" in M. Trochimczyk, ed., *A Romantic Century in Polish Music* (Los Angeles: Moonrise Press, 2009), 179-219.

In this study, I will focus on the earlier, idealized image of the "immortal"[5] Paderewski: an astoundingly beautiful, golden-haired young archangel, depicted in images and words by the media and his admirers, including Polish, German, British and American painters and poets.[6] While examining the creation of this angelic image and its role in the reception of Paderewski's music, I will take into account the issues of his appearance and the resultant imagery, the format and repertoire of his recitals, and the reception of his artistic persona in music criticism and literature, especially in poetry.[7] I will show how the pianist consciously cultivated his appearance and structured his recitals and repertoire to maximize the emotional impact on his audiences. As scholar Annegret Fauser recently demonstrated, similar artistic "image-making" was practiced by other performers, for instance a harpsichord player,

---

[5] The term "immortal" is used in reference to Paderewski by Charles Phillips in *Paderewski: The Story of a Modern Immortal* (New York: Da Capo, 1978; original edition, New York: The Macmillan Co., 1933).

[6] The term "master of harmonies" comes from a poem by Charles Phillips, entitled *Poland and Paderewski* (1928) and included in a book of tributes celebrating Paderewski's role in the regaining of Poland's independence in 1918, *To Paderewski: Artist, Patriot, Humanitarian* (New York: Kosciuszko Foundation, 1928).

[7] See Jeffrey Kallberg, *Chopin at the Boundaries: Sex, History, and Musical Genre* (Cambridge, Mass.: Harvard University Press, 1996): "The Harmony of the Tea Table: Gender and Ideology in The Piano Nocturne" (pp. 30-61); "Small Fairy Voices: Sex, History, and Meaning in Chopin" (pp. 62-88). In these essays, Kallberg noted the emergence of the otherworldly, angelic image of Chopin and its links to the association of the piano with the sphere of domesticity inhabited by women; he also pointed to the peculiarly gendered characteristics of the nocturne. The gendered characteristics of piano performance and repertoire have been studied from different perspectives, beginning from Arthur Loesser, *Men, Women, and Pianos: A Social History* (New York, 1954); Judith Tick, "Passed away is the Piano Girl: Changes in American Musical Life, 1870-1900," in *Women Making Music: The Western Art Tradition, 1150-1950*, Jane Bowers and Judith Tick, eds. (Urbana: University of Illinois Press, 1986), 325-348; Richard Leppert, "Sexual Identity, Death, and the Family Piano," *19th-Century Music* 16 (1992): 105-128; and most recently in James Parakilas, ed. *Piano Roles: Three Hundred Years of Life with the Piano* (New Haven: Yale University Press, 1999, second ed. 2002), esp. chapters 3-5, pp. 77-186.

Wanda Landowska who "styled herself as a high priestess in the cult of Bach."[8]

Paderewski's archangelic image and mythology was created early and, I believe, purposefully, by the famous Polish actress Helena Modrzejewska (1840-1909).[9] Twenty years Paderewski's senior, Helena, known as Modjeska in the U.S. (this name will be used henceforth),[10] first met the young pianist in the home of Dr. Tytus Chałubinski (1820-1889) in the mountain resort of Zakopane in Poland. As she recollected in her memoirs, during the summer vacations of 1884, Chałubinski introduced the 24-year-old "frail-looking" pianist as "our second Chopin."[11] Modjeska remembered him with "an aureole of profuse golden hair and delicate, almost feminine features" and observed that he "looked like one of Botticelli's or Fra Angelico's angels, and he seemed so deeply wrapped up in his music that this intensity was almost hypnotic... He used to come often to our villa and it was impossible to keep him away from the piano ... We had many chats and I advised him to appear in public. I knew he would make a name and fortune. His poetic face, combined with his genius, was bound to produce brilliant results."[12]

Modjeska's emphasis on two keys to success—"poetic face" and "genius"—emphasizes the twin factors that still determine the way to fame in the music world, charisma and talent. The actress's encounter with the pianist took place in Poland in 1884, before

---

[8] Annegret Fauser, "Creating Madame Landowska," in *Women and Music A Journal of Gender and Culture* - 10 (2006), pp. 1-23.

[9] Helena Modrzejewska, was born Jadwiga Helena Misel and changed her name for the stage while starting her theatrical career in Poland. She married Karol Bozenta Count Chłapowski in 1868 and immigrated to California in 1876. *Memories and Impressions of Helena Modjeska: An Autobiography* (New York: Macmillan, 1910). See Beth Holmgren, *Starring Madame Modjeska: On Tour in Poland and America* (Indiana University Press. 2011).

[10] Modjeska debuted in English in 1877 and appeared in 260 roles including 17 in Shakespeare's dramas. Modjeska's Californian years and Paderewski encounters are discussed in her memoirs, *op. cit.* (1910).

[11] Modjeska, *Memories*, 466.

[12] Modjeska, *Memories*, 466, 468.

Paderewski's first travels to study with Theodore Leschetitzky in Vienna, at a time when he still dressed and looked like a poor student.[13] In fact, it was Modjeska that made the Vienna studies possible, by organizing for him a benefit concert in Kraków. She later described the pianist as "a polished and genial companion; a man of wide culture; of witty, sometimes biting tongue; brilliant in table-talk; a man wide-awake to all matters of popular interest, who knew and understood the world."[14]

Figure 1: Paderewski as an archangel from "Paderewski Plays for the Victor," marked "drawing by Burne-Jones" and published in January 1912 in The International Studio. *Maja Trochimczyk Collection (the subsequent illustrations are from the same collection unless otherwise indicated).*

---

[13] According to Piber, *Droga do sławy, op. cit.,* 114-116.
[14] Modjeska cited by Henry Finck, *Paderewski, op. cit.,* p. 9.

The moment of inception of Paderewski's angelic image was also a beginning of a life-long friendship between the composer and the actress. In keeping with Modjeska's vision, the role that the handsome Paderewski was to play during his climb to the artistic summit was that of the "archangel." His appearance was a vital aspect of his public persona that embodied the ideals of beauty of the Aestheticism movement. Modjeska had encountered these ideals in the writings of Englishmen, the founders of the Aestheticist movement: Dante Gabriel Rosetti (1828-1882), Matthew Arnold (1822-1888), and Walter Pater (1839-1894).[15] Furthermore, she was aware of the beautified angelic imagery through the Pre-Raphaelite art of Rosetti, Lawrence Alma-Tadema (1836-1912) and Edward Burne-Jones (1833-1898). Rosetti was a writer, poet, and painter, the initiator of the pre-Raphaelite movement. Burne-Jones was a British painter of the Pre-Raphaelite orientation; Sir Lawrence Alma-Tadema was a British painter of classicist orientation. They formed a group of English artists and aesthetes that Modjeska befriended in 1881-1882.[16] These painters idolized and imitated the Italianate styles of Fra Angelico, Botticelli, and Giotto—painting angels and angelic youth on flat, decorative backgrounds. Modjeska personally knew these British artists and writers since 1881 and she frequently mentioned their names in her *Memories.* She confessed, for instance, experiencing "the feeling of veneration" in the presence of the art of Burne-Jones that "satisfied the most exalted desires" of her soul and imagination.[17] It seems that her inclination to rely on the repertoire of Aestheticist concepts in her encounters with the young Paderewski influenced the pianist's choice of his public "persona."

---

[15] Walter Pater (1839-1894), *The Renaissance: Studies in Art and Poetry* (London: Macmillan., 1920, first published in 1873 as *Studies in the History of Renaissance*; second version of 1877 under the current title; reprinted in 1888, 1900-1, 1910, 1920). Matthew Arnold (1822-1888), *Culture and Anarchy* (1869), a collection of essays first published in the *Cornhill Magazine* in 1867-68, reprinted with a new preface in 1875; new edition, Robert H. Super, *Culture and Anarchy with Friendship's Garland and Some Literary Essays*, volume V of *The Complete Works of Matthew Arnold* (The University of Michigan Press, 1965).

[16] See Modjeska, *Memories*, 428-433.

[17] *Ibidem*, 431.

Paderewski took Modjeska's lessons and exhortations to heart; he grew out his hair, changed his style of clothing (after the death of his first wife favoring dark jackets with white shirts and neckties), and became a living embodiment of an image of an inspired, spiritual and sensuous artist. Thus transformed, he embarked upon his musical conquest of Europe and America. The phenomenon of "the immortal Paderewski"—a charismatic virtuoso surrounded by the adulation of crowds of his female listeners—emerged in Western Europe during the young pianist's British tours in 1890. In May and June that year, Paderewski gave his first London concerts. He was advertised as the astoundingly successful "Lion of Paris" (a title ascribed to him during his Parisian debut in March 1888, but disdained in London). Yet, he was not warmly welcomed by the skeptical British press. George Bernard Shaw, called him a "harmonious blacksmith" who enthusiastically pounded on the piano, completely wrecking the instrument.[18]

Playing the piano with skill and passion was only one element of Paderewski's appeal. His looks were as important. In 1890, the pianist sat for a series of portraits, including two by the most influential members of the British Pre-Raphaelite and Aestheticism movements and Modjeska's friends, Edward Burne-Jones (See Figure 1 above) and Sir Lawrence Alma-Tadema (See Figure 2 in Essay 4). According to an anecdote cited in *The Paderewski Memoirs*,[19] Burne-Jones drew an image of Paderewski from memory, after accidentally seeing the young pianist on a London street. Following the angelic trope, the painter described the stunningly beautiful stranger as "an Archangel with a splendid halo of golden hair treading the London pavements" and was delighted to capture his appearance on paper. The long, curly hair, featured prominently in the drawing, endowed Paderewski with an unusual quality. The representation of his face in a profile, facing away from the spectator, and looking wistful, poetic, was another part of

---

[18] Shaw's critical concert review in *The World,* 16 June 1890.

[19] The anecdote is cited as being well-known to British aristocrats and the Burne-Jones circle, but not necessarily true; Paderewski replaces it with a more mundane account of their first encounter; see *The Paderewski Memoirs,* by Paderewski and Mary Lawton (New York: Charles Scribner's Sons, 1938), 176-77.

Paderewski's public image as an "archangel" that—as I will show—formed the cornerstone of his marketing to female audiences.

The 1890 silver-point drawing by Burne-Jones presented a profile pose similar to that from a photograph of Paderewski often used for promotion during his concert tours at that time. Copies of this drawing repeatedly appeared in Paderewski's literature including, for instance, an advertisement entitled "Paderewski plays for the Victor," issued in *The International Studio* in January 1912 in New York (Figure 1). The young pianist's talent as a model posing for the camera is obvious when viewing two portraits reproduced in a 1895 issue of a British music monthly, *The Strand*: one photo dating from 1887 (Figure 3) and one taken eight years later (Figure 4). In the original portrait, the eager young man, shown, typically from his left profile, is dressed in a wrinkled, checkered, grey wool suit and a white shirt. He appears to look with admiration on a young woman on the opposite page; she stands by the piano and languorously picks notes on the keyboard, lost in reverie (Figure 2). The elegant's woman's image, of significance for the Paderewski cult among his female devotees, is based on a painting "Harmony" by R. Poetzelberger and, in September 1906 was adapted for the cover of *The Etude* (Figure 8). It embodies the significance of piano music in enclosed interiors of Victorian homes and the female psyche. I will return to this image later.

Paderewski assumed the mysterious left-profile pose in the 1880s and used it through the mid-1910s. Postcards were printed in large numbers and the profile image appeared in many concert programs as well. His mass of curly hair was the most striking feature, also apparent in the drawing from life by H. M. Paget, reproduced in a London weekly, *The Graphic* on 17 December 1892 (see Figure 1 in Essay 4). This image captures Paderewski in action, at the piano; he is depicted with the long, tousled hair and the famous left-side profile, seen from within the stage. Interestingly, in a typical concert hall his audience would have seen his right-side profile instead.

NEXT PAGE. Fig. 2: "Harmony" by R. Poetzelberger reproduced in The Strand Musical Magazine, *vol. 2, no. 9 (September 1895), pp. 162-163.*

Fig. 3: Paderewski photograph from 1895 by Hugo Gorlitz, in The Strand Musical Magazine, *vol. 2, no. 9 (September 1895), p. 165.*

From the painting by R. Poeterlberger.

That, equally handsome, side is captured in another portrait, from 1903, by Davis Sanford (Figure 4). The portrait shows the pianist with his back turned away from the viewer; he appears lost in thought, with downcast eyes—an angelic, mysterious presence. This iconic image was copied into drawings throughout the next decade: a variant appeared in an ad for The Aeolian Company placed in the *Century Life of America* (January 1914) and a cameo adorned James Huneker's article bemoaning the decline of inspiration among pianist after Paderewski, published in the *New York Times* (March 1917).[20] Another, related photograph from a Davis Sanford portraiture session appeared in *The Ladies Home Journal* in March 1910. It showed Paderewski sitting in the same pose and holding a white page of music or a letter. This picture accompanied Paderewski's own article on "Poetic Piano Playing." A distant echo of Vermeer's *Girl Reading a Letter*, perhaps?

---

[20] The Aeolian Company ad features a left profile of Paderewski looking down, and two pages of hand-written testimonials about the quality of piano roll recordings by this company. The article by James Huneker, "The Grand Manner Has Vanished from Pianists" (*The New York Times*, 11 March 1917) is illustrated with portraits of: Paderewski, Eugen d'Albert, Vladimir de Pachman, Josef Hofmann, and Sophie Menter.

Figure 4: Paderewski's portrait by Davis Sanford, 1903.

It should be emphasized that not all of Paderewski's portraits as an "archangel" display his profile. The musician faces the viewer in the widely reproduced portrait by Alma Tadema, set in a luxurious interior with golden tapestries that match the "halo" of Paderewski's hair (Figure 2 in Essay 4). References to the pianist's hair as an ethereal aureole or a dazzling golden halo recur in numerous accounts of his public appearances. During the virtuoso's first American concert tour in 1891-92, Helena Modjeska reported from New York to her friend Emilia Szierzputowska in Warsaw: "Paderewski plays here with an enormous success. Women are crazy about him. Critics praise him without limits. The only two things they criticize are his performance of Beethoven and his too large of a mess of hair. One of my friends calls him a chrysanthemum, which is an accurate description of his head. I attended one of his concerts, he truly plays like an angel."[21] As Modjeska had predicted in 1884, Paderewski's "poetic face combined with his genius" made him famous.

His hair is prominent in later remembrances of the pianist, for instance in an endearing anecdote about the virtuoso's encounter with a precocious five-year-old girl at his home in Riond-Bosson near Morges, Switzerland (published in 1922). During the 1908 visit, the girl "tousled the famous Paderewski's auburn locks and remarked: 'I love your hair!' Paderewski laughed and kissed her."[22] It seems that the love of his hair was so widespread among the female folk, that it became the predominant theme of his caricatures. A humorous image from the *New York Herald* showed the virtuoso from his famous left profile, playing the piano in a "recital cage, or the female kiss-fender" with a full box marked "my hair - help yourself."[23] Apparently, such an enclosure was intended to put an end to frequent incidents in which Paderewski's admirers approached him to snip his locks with scissors. Another widely disseminated caricature appeared during the Chicago World Fair on 15 May 1893. A rosy-cheeked long-haired Paderewski turns around on a piano stool to play, with a blur of multiple arms, all the pianos at once. This was the proposed "Peaceful Solution" for the next world fair where the manufacturers' competing claims for Paderewski's attention and services would be speedily resolved.

The lasting popularity of Paderewski's angelic image with youthful face framed by an aureole of hair may be seen in a colorful interpretation of the Burne-Jones portrait pattern, the profile of the young man with "flaming hair" that graced the cover of *The Etude* Magazine in February 1915, in an issue dedicated to *The Music and Musicians of Poland* (Figure 5).[24]

---

[21] Letter of 1891 cited from Józef Szczublewski, *Żywot Modrzejewskiej* (Warsaw, 1975), 533.

[22] An anonymous account of a 1908 meeting, published in *The Record Digest* (September 1922), p. 13.

[23] New York Public Library – Paderewski collection; the caricature is published on the back cover of Zamojski's biography of the composer.

[24] Joseph A. Herter discusses "*The Etude's* 1915 Musical Salute to Poland," with a description of its contents and biographical information about the

THE ETUDE

Presser's Musical Magazine

FEBRUARY
1915

PRICE 15¢
$1.50 PER YEAR

PADEREWSKI

THE MUSIC AND MUSICIANS OF POLAND

Figure 5: The cover of The Etude Magazine, *February 1915, with an idealized portrait of the "immortally young" Paderewski, with reddish-golden hair, modeled on the Burne-Jones profile.*

Such youthful sweetness! Alas, the image was more than a bit outdated: in 1915, Paderewski was fifty-five, not twenty years old. His face was marked by mature worries, and the abundant "golden aureole" was replaced by graying hair and a receding hairline (Figure 6). For many years, to keep his image intact, Paderewski dyed his hair, with his wife Helena serving as the hairdresser. Only during World War I, he emerged as a white-haired statesman; this image is discussed in the final portion of this paper.

---

authors in *Polish Music Newsletter* 7: 11 (November 2001), online.

Figure 6: A 1915 photograph of Paderewski. From the Cover of Selected Pieces from the Concert Programmes of I.J. Paderewski, *Edwin Ashdown Ltd, London..*

2. The Aestheticism of the Gilded Age

The Polish actress, Helena Modjeska, played a significant role in initiating Paderewski's American career not only through coaching him and advising on artistic matters, but also through a direct intervention. The pianist's American biographer Henry T. Finck observed that "the famous Polish actress, Mme. Modjeska, was perhaps the first to recognize his rare gifts."[25] She supported him financially by contributing from her own funds to the revenue of Paderewski's 1884 benefit that raised funds for his study in Vienna. In 1890, she had a hand in his transformation into an

---

[25] Henry T. Finck, *Paderewski and His Art* (New York: Wittingham and Atterton, 1892), 9.

"archangel at the keyboard" by helping him find a personal style and a stage image. She introduced the virtuoso to Pre-Raphaelite British painters that portrayed him as an angel. At the outset of the pianist's 1891 American tour, Modjeska introduced him to several influential members of artistic society of New York, including her long-time personal friend, a writer, editor and poet, Richard Watson Gilder (1844-1909), the editor of *The Century Illustrated Monthly Magazine*[26] and one of the leaders of the American Aestheticism movement.

Paderewski's involvement with Aestheticism is closely related to his friendship with Modjeska and with visits to the Gilders' artistic salon. They held an open house on Friday evenings, welcoming guests that ranged from literary and artistic figures to the pillars of the industrial society. The artist Will H. Low remembered that "everyone who came to New York in those days bearing a passport of intellectual worth" found the way to the Gilders.[27] Paderewski was a frequent guest at their salons and held fascinating conversations with the gracious hosts and other visitors.[28] Here,

---

[26] For more information about Gilder see Herbert F. Smith, in *Dictionary of Literary Biography, Volume 64: American Literary Critics and Scholars, 1850-1880*, John W. Rathburn, Monica M. Grecu, eds. (The Gale Group, 1988), 71-77. See also Herbert F. Smith, *Richard Watson Gilder* (New York: Twayne Publishers, 1970). R. W. Gilder, *The Poems of Richard Watson Gilder* (Boston, New York: Houghton Mifflin, 1908); *Five Books of Song* (New York: The Century Co., 1894); *The Fire Divine* (New York: The Century Co., 1907). A good source of information about *The Century* magazine and Gilder's role in its "golden age" is the study by Arthur John, *The Best Years of the Century: Richard Watson Gilder, Scribner's Monthly, and the Century Magazine, 1870-1909* (Urbana: University of Illinois Press, 1981).

[27] Low's statement in a recollection of his daughter from 1957; cited from Susan B. Hobbs, *The Art of Thomas Wilmer Dewing: Beauty Reconfigured* (The Brooklyn Museum in association with the Smithsonian Institution, 1996), 7.

[28] Paderewski may have encountered these ideas already in Europe where he socialized with the artistic and aristocratic elite; his personal circle included the intellectual and artistically minded Romanian Princess Raoulka de Brancovan, his lover and confidante whom he abandoned to marry Helena Górska, known as Baroness de Rosen (see Piber, *op. cit.*, 187-90, 538-542).

the Polish virtuoso met numerous musicians (Adele Aus der Ohe), writers (Mark Twain), poets (Walt Wightman), artists (Maria Oakley Dewing and Thomas Dewing), industrialists (Andrew Carnegie, John Rockefeller), publishers (Charles Scribner), and opinion-makers.

The pianist used this contact to his best advantage. His appearances on concert stages during the American tour of 1891-92 were accompanied by an extensive and well-orchestrated publicity campaign, including a series of articles in Gilder's periodical. In March 1892, *The Century Magazine* issued three texts dedicated to Paderewski: a biographic essay by a pianist and editor, Fanny Morris Smith,[29] an essay of music criticism by pianist William Mason,[30] and a poem by Gilder himself. These texts were repeatedly cited and reprinted in local press in cities visited by Paderewski during his tours.

William Mason's 1892 "Paderewski: A Critical Study" provided a general appreciation of the performing style of this "inspired and phenomenal pianist."[31] According to Mason (p. 578), Paderewski's distinction at the keyboard stemmed from his unique personality and virtuosity:

> He mirrors his Slavonic nature in his interpretations, with its fine and exquisite appreciation of all gradations of tonal effects. His marvelously musical touch, a great, mellow, and tender voice, chameleon-like, takes on the color of his dominant mood. He is a thoroughly earnest and at the same time an affectionate player, and too much stress cannot be laid on the humanisms of his style,

---

[29] Fanny Morris Smith was a pianist and music writer/editor; she served as Paderewski's co-editor on the board of *The Century Library of Music* (1900-1905), assisting in the publication of the twenty illustrated volumes of music and essays. She also wrote several articles about music, for instance, "What Poet is Most Akin to Chopin?" which appeared in vol. 18 of *The Century Library of Music*, along with articles on Paderewski (New York: Century Co., 1902), 585-590.

[30] William Mason (1829-1908) was a pianist and writer; a son of composer Lowell Mason, he penned *Memories of A Musical Life* (1901).

[31] William Mason, "Paderewski: A Critical Study," *The Century Illustrated Monthly Magazine* (March 1892), reprinted in and cited from Ignacy Jan Paderewski, et al., eds., *The Century Library of Music* 18 (New York: Century Co., 1902), 577-584.

which is so intensely sympathetic and so eclectic that it embraces all schools. His never-failing warmth of touch and his vivid appreciation of tone gradations and values result in wonderfully beautiful effects. In addition to these qualities, his magnetic individuality puts him at once in sympathy with his hearers, and this magnetism is felt and acknowledged even by those who do not entirely and uniformly approve of all of his readings and interpretations of the great composers.

Mason reviewed Paderewski's interpretations of Bach, Beethoven, and Chopin, in all areas finding him superior to his predecessors. In an ongoing collaboration, the pianist reciprocated the endorsement that he received from Mason, by offering a testimonial for ads promoting his friend's piano school that appeared in *The Etude* and other music periodicals. Another music critic, whose article welcomed the pianist to America in 1892, Fanny Morris Smith, went on to collaborate with Paderewski as an associate editor of a 20-volume series, *The Century Library of Music,* published a decade later (1900). Her own contribution to that series revealed a thoroughly Aestheticist mind-set and a focus on the idea of the correspondence of the arts.[32]

The famed virtuoso arrived in the U.S. in November 1891; within one month Richard Watson Gilder wrote a poem *How Paderewski Plays* (dated 18 December 1891), thus setting the "inspired" tone for the pianist's American reception.[33] The poem was published in March 1892 and later reprinted in *A Book of Music* of 1906, a collection of Gilder's poetry inspired solely by music and dance.[34] Known primarily as an outstanding editor of *The Century* magazine, Gilder was one of the pillars of the turn-of-the-century

---

[32] In one article, she compared Chopin to various English-language poets, arriving at a conclusion that he was most akin to Keats. See Fanny Morris Smith, "What Poet is Most Akin to Chopin," In *The Century Library of Music*, ed. Ignacy Jan Paderewski, Fanny Morris Smith and Barnard Boekelman, vol. 18 (New York: Century Co., 1902): 585-590.

[33] Paderewski's sponsor, the piano maker Steinway and Sons, has issued several promotional brochures, with his portraits, biographical notes, and a selection of extensive excerpts from his reviews, for instance from London and Paris during the first American tour. Later, Paderewski's promotional literature also included program notes with information about his repertoire by the influential music critic, Henry E. Krehbiel.

[34] Richard Watson Gilder, *A Book of Music* (New York: The Century., 1906).

literary world, associated with the Aestheticism movement. He published numerous volumes of poems, often dealing with other arts, like painting, acting, and music. Gilder believed in poetry's capabilities to express hidden emotions and impressions of its author in a perfectly crafted form. As a poet, he is associated with Aestheticism and the "genteel" tradition, the representatives of which avoided erotic or stark subjects, attempting to edify, rather than shock, or bewilder their readers. Music, the "wordless art," was the poet's supreme challenge. Gilder had an opportunity to hear Paderewski during the pianist's first American tour and described his impression in a letter to his wife:[35]

> His genius is altogether individual and if the individuality appeals, fascinating. It appealed to me immensely. He is not sublime, but most intensely poetic; his touch is delicacy itself in the tender parts—fairy-like; almost sharp, certainly charmingly crisp and at times powerful; there is a quiet alertness, like some queer new animal sure of his prey.

The writer perceived Paderewski's performance style as filled with striking displays of virtuosity, instinctive power, and intensity of expression. Gilder's poetic response to the Polish virtuoso's mastery of the piano in *How Paderewski Plays* juxtaposes a range of synaesthetic comparisons of music to natural phenomena, replete with romantic, enchanting imagery:

> If melody were tears and tears were starry gleams
> That shone in evening's amethystine dreams;
> Ah, yes, if notes were stars, each star a different hue,
> Trembling to earth in dew;
> Or, of the boreal pulsings, rose and white,
> Made majestic music in the night;
> ... If every stroke of light and sound were excess of beauty;
> If human syllables could e'er refashion
> that fierce electric passion;
> If ever art could image (as were the poet's duty)
> The grieving, and the rapture, and the thunder
> Of that keen hour of wonder,

---

[35] Richard Watson Gilder's letter to his wife, Helena de Kay Gilder, of 21 November 1891 after the first American concert of Paderewski. Cited from Rosamond Gilder, ed., *Letters of Richard Watson Gilder* (New York: Houghton Mifflin), 215.

That light as if of heaven, that blackness as of hell, —
How Paderewski Plays, then might I dare to tell.

The romantic and sensuous intensity of this poem is well balanced with its elaborate form; it is a perfect aesthetic artifact. Irregular phrase length piques the interest of listeners, or readers awaiting the unexpected resolution; the verse seems written to be read aloud or recited. The poem was widely reprinted in Paderewski's concert programs and certain expressions which were apparently inspired by Gilder's vivid imagery recurred in reviews of the pianist's concerts throughout his tour. The poet and the reviewers used the elevated synaesthetic language of the *correspondence of the arts*, expressing the beauty of music in terms of majesties of nature, the spectacles of starlight and rainbow colors (stars, sky, aurora borealis, etc.).

Interestingly, similar "cosmic" terms also appeared in Paderewski's discussion of the essence of music in a speech celebrating the 100th anniversary of Chopin's birth in 1910. Here, Paderewski focused on the "cosmic" quality of music that was, as he said, "the only Art that actually lives." His listeners encountered a cornucopia of colors, textures, sounds, and images, from atoms to planets:[36]

> If music be the most accessible of all the Arts, it is not because she is cosmopolitan, but because she is of her very nature cosmic. Music is the only Art that actually lives. Her elements, vibration, palpitation, are the elements of Life itself. Where Life is she is also, stealthy, inaudible, unrecognised, yet mighty. She is mingled with the flow of rushing waters, with the breath of the wind, with the murmur of forests; she lives in the earth's seismic heavings, in the mighty motion of the planets, in the hidden conflicts of inflexible atoms; she is in all the lights, in all the colours that dazzle or soothe our eyes; she is in the blood of our arteries, in every pain, passion, or ecstasy that shakes our hearts. She is everywhere, soaring beyond and above the range of human speech unto unearthly spheres of divine emotion.

---

[36] Ignacy Jan Paderewski, "Chopin: A Discourse," trans. Laurence Alma-Tadema (London: W. Adlington, 1911); *Polish Music Journal* 4:1 (Summer 2001). The speech was given at the opening of the Chopin Centenary Festival in Lwów, Galicia (Austrian-occupied Poland) on 23 October 1910.

Paderewski's vision of music as the essence of the "life-force" inhabiting "unearthly spheres of divine emotion" as expressed in his 1910 article has antecedents in Gilder's poem. This connection places the pianist in the midst of the Aesthetic movement. Two British critics and writers, Matthew Arnold (1822-1888) and Walter Pater (1839-1894) provided the philosophical foundation and inspiration to American artists who pursued the aesthetics of art for art's sake. The main traits of Aestheticism include: the belief that the full meaning of human life is only found in the pursuit of perfection, beauty and intelligence, and the belief that such inwardness of perfection-seekers places them at odds with the modern world of "machinery" of the material civilization. In his writings, Walter Pater selected models of beauty and intelligence from the Italian Renaissance, especially the art of Botticelli and Leonardo da Vinci. According to Pater, the interaction of poetic imagery, harmony of color and shape, and the immaterial, sonorous beauty was the prime condition of the arts. Moreover, art was seen as a refuge from the pressures of modern industrial world, a locus of escape into an internal realm of emotion and beauty. In *Studies in the History of Renaissance* (1873), Pater wrote:[37]

> Great passions may give us a quickened sense of life, ecstasy and sorrow of love, the various forms of enthusiastic activity, disinterested or otherwise, which comes naturally to many of us. Only be sure it is passion - that it does yield you this fruit of a quickened, multiplied consciousness. Of such wisdom, the poetic passion, the desire of beauty, the love of art for its own sake, has most. For art comes to you proposing frankly to give nothing but the highest quality to your moments as they pass, and simply for those moments' sake.

Pater noted that three forms of art—painting, music and poetry—were particularly important in romantic and modern times. Only into these three related arts "may be translated every delicacy of thought and feeling incidental to a consciousness brooding with delight over itself" (p. 183). The highest rank was assigned to music, for, as Pater stated,

---

[37] Walter Pater, *The Renaissance: Studies in Art and Poetry*, cited from the 1920 edition, 212-213.

all art constantly aspires towards the condition of music. For while in other kinds of art, it is possible to distinguish the matter from the form, and the understanding can always make this distinction, yet it is the constant effort of art to obliterate it.

When thinking about the sense and value of human life, Pater posed a question (p. 210):

> How can we pass most swiftly from point to point, and be present always at the focus where the greatest number of vital forces unite in their purest energy? To burn always with this hard gem-like flame, to maintain this ecstasy, is success in life.

For Pater, and for the Aesthetes in general, the purpose of art was to put "a happy world of its own creation in place of the meaner world of common days" (p. 186). Where could one better experience the "happy world" of art as a refuge from the commonplace than in a concert hall? What could create better conditions allowing the seeker of beauty to withdraw into the internal realm of great passions than a piano recital, without the operatic distractions of costume and plot? While engrossed in the music, the listeners could feel the "vital forces" united in their "purest energy," "the poetic passion;" they could fully and intently experience "moments as they pass." It appears that listening to a great concert constituted a perfect realization of the Aesthetes' quest for individual fulfillment—experienced in ecstasy, in which the listeners were consumed by the "hard, gem-like flames" of intense emotions.

Publications in *The Scribner's Monthly* and *The Century Magazine*, edited by Gilder, ensured a wide exposure for the Aesthetic ideals in America.[38] Copies of texts by both authors were owned, read and cited by the protagonists in the American Aesthetic movement. These books could be found in the libraries of Richard and Helena Gilder and their friends, including, besides Modjeska and Paderewski,[39] also American artists, such as Maria Oakey Dewing

---

[38] Gilder was assistant editor of *Scribner's Monthly* since 1870 and the editor of *The Century Illustrated Monthly Magazine* since 1881; the latter one was a transformation of the former.

[39] These books are included in his personal book collection donated to the Jagiellonian University in Kraków, and preserved in the Paderewski Center, as confirmed by its staff.

(1845-1927) and Thomas Wilmer Dewing (1851-1938), two American painters, inspired by the pre-Raphaelite ideology.[40] These encounters provide yet another node in the rich and complex nexus of relationships connecting Paderewski to American Aestheticism. The pianist's conversations with Maria Oakey Dewing (1845-1927) and Thomas Wilmer Dewing (1851-1938), frequent guests at the Gilders (through the friendship between Maria Dewing and Helena Gilder), were likely to include discussions of the art and ideas of Edward Burne-Jones and Lawrence Alma-Tadema, who had befriended Modjeska in 1881, portrayed Paderewski in 1890, and inspired the Dewings.[41] In his paintings, Thomas Dewing initially adopted an approach to Aestheticism modeled on British patterns. The vaguely allegoric landscape of the *Summer* of 1890, for instance, with its graceful row of ladies dancing to the music of the harp, reveals an inspiration with the symbolic imagery of Alma-Tadema, often featuring beautiful, youthful women placed in enigmatic poses in classical gardens. Gilder celebrated this painting in another poem, but a more interesting connection—from the point of view of "publicity"—arises from its use by the Steinway, the same piano maker that organized Paderewski's American tours. The pianist's exclusive contract with Steinway and Sons tied him to this instrument for a major portion of his career. Paderewski's exclusive contract with Steinway and Sons proved lucrative both to the pianist and the piano maker: his tours were sponsored by Steinway and the phenomenal virtuoso provided the company with free advertising. The symbiotic connection between the company and

---

[40] Dewing was one of the most highly respected American painters at the turn of the century, the favorite painter of Charles Freer, founder of the Freer gallery at the Smithsonian Institution. Since 1920s, his rarefied imagery of sophisticated young women in evening gowns, seemed too old-fashioned and his reputation suffered. His art has been recently rediscovered by the Brooklyn Museum that organized a monographic exposition in 1996. Susan B. Hobbs, *The Art of Thomas Wilmer Dewing: Beauty Reconfigured* (Brooklyn Museum in association with the Smithsonian Institution, 1996); Jennifer A. Martin, "The Rediscovery of Maria Oakey Dewing," *Feminist Art Journal* 5 (summer 1976), 24-27, 45.
[41] See Susan B. Hobbs, *The Art of Thomas Wilmer Dewing: Beauty Reconfigured* (The Brooklyn Museum in association with the Smithsonian Institution, 1996.

the pianist was not always made public, especially at the outset of his American concertizing. He found the Steinway keyboard to be hard on the hands, and tried to switch to Weber piano, for the 1907-08 season. But then he returned to Steinway. His concert programs usually contained ads by Steinway; music journals and newspapers were filled with Steinway adverts featuring images of and endorsements by Paderewski. In addition, Steinway issued a variety of leaflets and brochures with Paderewski's likeness and signature,[42] e.g., *Paderewski: Steinway Progress An Appreciation. Promotional brochure for Steinway pianos* (New York: Steinway & Sons, 1923) that included a copy of Paderewski's handwritten letter, dated 4 May 1914.

Paderewski, Aestheticism, Dewing and Steinway met in an unusual artefact: the Steinway piano no. 100,000, the first instrument made by the company for the White House in 1903. This is an ornate *objet d'art*, adorned with wood carvings and decorated with the image of Dewing's graceful dancers from the painting *Summer*[43] discussed above. Paderewski played this beautified piano during his White House concerts. Indeed, the painter and the pianist belonged to the same artistic and intellectual sphere of Aestheticism and shared its ideals. Their patrons, though, were different: while Dewing painted slender, elegant ladies of leisure and grace to be admired by his (male) industrialist supporters who purchased the paintings, Paderewski played for the ladies themselves.[44]

---

[42] An example of the first category is "Steinway, the Instrument of the Immortals," an advertisement for Steinway pianos with an image of 'Paderewski Plays the Minuet,'" (*The Musician*, July 1923). An example of the second *is Paderewski: Steinway Progress An Appreciation*, a brochure for Steinway pianos (New York: Steinway & Sons, 1923), with a copy of a handwritten letter by the pianist, dated 1914.

[43] This information was provided by Margaret Wolejsza from Steinway and Sons Co., e-mail of 28 October 2002.

[44] His chief benefactor was Charles Freer, the founder of Freer Gallery at the Smithsonian Institution, Washington, D.C. My search for the connections between Paderewski and the American Aesthetic movement has been inspired by repeated visits to this museum and a personal discovery of the art of Thomas Dewing.

MATINEE SCENE AT CARNEGIE HALL WHEN PADEREWSKI FINISHED.

Figure 7: "Matinee Scene at Carnegie Hall, When Paderewski Finished," a drawing from the New York Herald, *17 November 1895. Paderewski Archive, Archiwum Akt Nowych, Warsaw, Poland.*

3. The Cult of Paderewski and his Female Audience

From the outset of his Western career, as Modjeska had predicted, women crowded Paderewski recitals, eager for a glimpse of his "immortal" beauty. At the end of Paderewski's first American tour, the *Chicago Times* thus described his listeners: "young and old, rich and poor, musicians with degrees and those who cannot distinguish a sonata from a gigue, and whom music does not concern even a bit. The greatest majority, of course, consists of women."[45] In this context, Modjeska noted with satisfaction the

---

[45] *Chicago Times,* 13 March 1892, copy in Paderewski Archive, Archiwum Akt Nowych, Warsaw.

emergence of a Paderewski cult in 1891: "his personality is of a kind that it attracts crowds, mostly of the feminine kind. American girls and ladies simply are crazy about him . . ."[46] Similarly, the *New York Daily Tribune* noted that at the final concert of his first American tour, held at Carnegie Hall on 26 March 1892, the cult of Paderewski reached a new stage: "It became a crazied fashion, not responding either to reason, to common sense, nor to the sense of Justice." *The New York Times* reported from the Carnegie Hall recital of 9 November 1895 that "women were turned towards him in positions of such zealous devotion that it could be assumed that fanatics listen to a sermon of a prophet of a new religion."[47] (See Figure 7). In contrast, male reviews of his concerts described him as "not a handsome man" (*The New York Times*, 18 November 1891) or as "slim, pale and sick-looking man" (during the tour of 1893, *The New York Herald*).

The Paderewski cult or "craze" initiated in the U.S. in 1891-92, reached its apex during the third American tour of the pianist, in 1895-1896, only to continue, practically undiminished, until World War I. *The New York Times* claimed that Paderewski's Boston audience during a recital of 1893 included at least 500 young female fans, the so-called "Paderewski girls," among three thousand people. These young enthusiasts of Paderewski were also called "matinee girls," since they preferred to attend daytime recitals, while audiences of evening events had a larger share of male listeners.[48] The press (i.e., the male music critics) often referred to them in derogatory terms and ridiculed their youthful enthusiasm for the Polish musician. After a concert on 12 December 1899 at Carnegie Hall, Alan Dale reported in *The Journal* that the audience was filled with young women: "I was in a mass of girls... feeling completely embarrassed and entirely out of place." Apparently, the growing frenzy sometimes put the object of all this devotion in danger. The Polish periodical *Scena i Sztuka* reported

---

[46] Helena Modjeska's letter to Maria Chłapowska, *Korespondencja Heleny Modrzejewskiej in Karola Chłapowskiego*, vol. 3, p. 165; Piber, *op. cit.*, 225.

[47] The *New York Times* (Sunday, 10 November 1895); Performing Arts Division, New York Public Library.

[48] This term was used in *Springfield News*, warning that Paderewski would be protected from the "matinee girls" and their affections by his new wife that he brought from Poland (*Springfield News*, 7 December 1899).

in April 1908 that after Paderewski's recital in San Francisco on 1 March 1908, the virtuoso was virtually mobbed by his enthusiastic female admirers:[49]

> During the concert in San Francisco, Paderewski was so ardently admired by his audience, that ladies and misses—filled with delight—threw themselves upon the artist to congratulate him and shake his hand. In the crowd, Paderewski lost his breath and nearly fainted. He was liberated with the greatest difficulty. After being taken to the hotel, he suffered a nervous breakdown, following which he had to rest for several days.

The San Francisco program included works by Paderewski (Variations and Fugue in E-flat minor), Beethoven (Sonata in E-flat major Op. 27 No. 1), and Chopin (Two Nocturnes Op.15; the whole Op. 10 of his Etudes, and Scherzo in B-flat minor Op. 31). Three arrangements of Schubert's songs by Liszt, and a sentimental miniature by Paderewski's friend, Zygmunt Stojowski (*Chant d'amour*) complemented the concert that ended, as most Paderewski recitals, with the "tonal typhoons"[50] of one of Liszt's *Hungarian Rhapsodies* (this time, no. 13). The scope of the program and its sheer size could make one swoon and faint; no wonder that mass hysteria of female listeners occurred at this, and many other recitals given by Paderewski.

Who were these ardent female fans? On the basis of usually negative newspaper reports (their patronizing tone borders on ridicule with a dash of resentment), the "Paderewski girls" could be described as young, single women, devoted to music as performers and listeners, educated and well-read, independent financially and personally, with disposable income that they would freely spend on furthering their education and interests. These insatiable Paderewski devotees attended all the recitals of the object of their affection, stalked his hotels, and cried at his departure for Europe. In one satirical image a crowd of female admirers surrounds Paderewski arriving from Europe on an oceanliner. His face is seen under a garland of "welcome" and the

---

[49] Report from Paderewski's recital in San Francisco, 1 March 1908, in *Scena i Sztuka* [Stage and Art] 15 (11 April 1908).
[50] Expression borrowed from a review of Paderewski's concert in *The New York Herald* of 7 November 1907.

caption names this occasion "The Revival of the Paderewski Craze."[51] Each of his female admirers "loved" him individually, and each experienced his music, to paraphrase Walter Pater, as "the individual in her isolation, each mind keeping as a solitary prisoner its own dream of a world."[52]

By so intently pursuing the enjoyment of music, the "Paderewski girls" strove to accomplish the only true success in life prescribed by Aestheticism, that is, a personal fulfillment through the full intensity of unique passions, or the experience of the preciousness of the moment, best projected and discovered through music. As Pater wrote, art "comes to you proposing frankly to give nothing but the highest quality to your moments as they pass, and simply for those moments' sake" (pp. 212-213). This is a life of "being," not "having," nor "doing." The "vita contemplativa" was an ideal presented to, and embraced by, women who constituted the majority of Paderewski's listeners.

The cover of a 1906 issue of *The Etude* magazine portrays such a potential "Paderewski" girl in a beautiful gown, seen from the back, standing at the piano in the interior of her home, with one hand absentmindedly picking up some notes on the keyboard (Figure 8). I previously discussed its "parent" image from the 1895 issue of British journal, *The Strand,* where Paderewski's portrait is strategically placed to make him a voyeur, watching the day-dreaming young lady at the piano (see Figures 2 and 3 above). The striking pose of the elegant young woman indicates the interior focus of her mind as well as a withdrawal from social interactions into the inner world of music, in accordance with the teachings of Matthew Arnold ("the idea of perfection as an *inward* condition of the mind and spirit") and Walter Pater ("a consciousness brooding with delight over itself").[53]

---

[51] This image, dated Saturday, 7 January 1893, is in a press clipping from an unknown newspaper. Paderewski Collection, Polish Music Center, USC. Andrzej Piber's monograph documents numerous instances of Paderewski being harassed by his female fans and being upset about it.

[52] Walter Pater, *The Renaissance*, 208.

[53] Arnold, *Culture and Anarchy*, 8; Pater, *The Renaissance*, 183.

Figure 8: The Cover of The Etude, *with a version of "Harmony," a trompe-l'oeil image within image (the cover is on the piano), September 1906.*

The pose and setting of this introspective "piano girl" resembles a model portrayed by Thomas Wilmer Dewing in *The Spinet* (1901-02, held at the National Museum of American Art, Smithsonian Institution, Washington D.C.). In this painting, the beautiful, aristocratic woman reveals the beauty of her body in a low-cut, long evening gown seen from the back. She is seated in front of her instrument in a claustrophobic, decorative interior filled with rich golden hues, glowing in dim, artificial light. The most striking part of her body, her bare shoulders, and the anonymity of her face, transforms her into an alluring object of male contemplation and desire.[54]

---

[54] The model was the painter's mistress, single mother and suffragette Lucia Fuller. For a discussion of various meanings associated with

The representations of a young lady from on cover of *The Etude* of 1906 (modeled on the painting of "Harmony" in *The Strand*, 1895) and Dewing's musician at the spinet (1902) have seventeen-century antecedents in the charming young women playing musical instruments in Johannes Vermeer's old Dutch interiors: *A Lady Standing at a Virginal, Concert, The Music Lesson*, and *Woman with a Lute*. The similarities of these images emphasize the domestic isolation of women in the claustrophobic (or simply intimate) enclosures of their music-filled homes, where the instrument was the only "window" into the outside world. The "Dewing girl" (as the models were dubbed in the press) was a slender, sophisticated young woman in an evening gown listening to music, playing, or daydreaming over books or letters in sparse, airless interiors. Even if there was more than one woman in the picture, they were all alone. Dewing painted such singular, refined women from 1890s until the end of his career.[55] His subjects, elegant and enigmatic, lost in moods of vague expectations, were categorized by contemporaneous critics as belonging to "a certain type of female character" that is easily recognizable though "not precisely discreet" to describe.[56] For Dewing's critics, the "worldly" allure of these unattached women was somewhat morally dubious.[57]

Similarly suspect to traditionalists must have been the freedom and independence enjoyed by female crowds of Paderewski's admirers who had the time to pursue their own interests and

---

Dewing's feminine models see essays by Susan B. Hobbs ("Beauty into Art: The Life of Thomas Wilmer Dewing") and Barbara Dayer Gallati ("Beauty Unmasked: Ironic Meaning in Dewing's Art") in Hobbs, *The Art of Thomas Wilmer Dewing: Beauty Reconfigured*, op. cit., pp. 1-50 and 51-82 respectively. Information about *The Spinet* comes from p. 164.

[55] Particularly significant examples are in paintings: *Brocart de Venise* (1904-5; Washington University Gallery of Art, St. Louis); *The Letter* (1907, The Toledo Museum of Art), and *Lady in Grey* (1911-12, Museum of Art, Rhode Island School of Design, Providence).

[56] Expressions cited after Susan B. Hobbs, from an 1898 anonymous report from Dewing's exhibition at the St. Botolph's Club in Boston; see Hobbs, *Dewing*, 68.

[57] Barbara Gallati discusses the irony inherent in Dewing's choice to paint his current mistresses, often models or painters themselves who could be recognized by his male friends, but were seen as anonymous symbols of female beauty by the general public; Gallati, "Beauty Unmasked," 60-70.

traveled alone to his recitals. In contrast to the passive and withdrawn ladies from the paintings, however, their real-life counterparts acted as female voyeurs and transformed the pianist—not without his complicity—into the object of their fantasies and a focus of their dreams. In the Paderewski cult, the traditional gender dynamic between the admired object (woman in the painting) and the admiring subject (the male spectator) was reversed. The pianist, the "archangel," was worshipped for his ethereal beauty and for his ability to transcend the physical location of the recital and transport the listeners into the internal worlds of emotions triggered by music. Paderewski constructed both the image and the setting for his musical messages of "every pain, passion, or ecstasy that soars in our hearts."[58]

Just like the women painted by Dewing, Paderewski—as depicted in promotional literature at the outset of his career—was pale and slender, enigmatic and elegant, distant and alluring. But he was not just an image; he was also its creator. Similarly to Dewing, who gradually purged his canvases from all non-essential objects, dissolving backgrounds into undistinguished haze, and placing one sophisticated beauty at the center of the painting, Paderewski refined his form of self-presentation. He appeared alone on the stage. In the limited and limiting space of the concert hall, revered silence surrounded the "tonal fireworks" and "murmurs" of the music.[59] Only when darkness and aural separation tuned out all details of the outside world and the listener's immediate surround-ings, could the "magic and moonlight" of the music begin.[60] Entering into the interior space of emotion required an attenuation of stimuli received in the exterior space of experience.

A personal response to Paderewski's music is found in an account written by a female listener, Nellie Cameron Bates, who called herself a "country girl" and attended his recital in 1914.[61] Her

---

[58] Paderewski, "Chopin: A Discourse." *Polish Music Journal* 4:1 (2001).

[59] Cited from Gilder's poem and Nossig's essay on Paderewski.

[60] Cited from Olin Downes's review of Paderewski recital in New York (*The New York Times*, 7 November 1907).

[61] Nellie R. Cameron Bates, "A Country Girl at a Paderewski Concert," (*Musician* 19 of February 1914), p. 125-126. Paderewski toured the U.S. between October 1913 and April 1914. It is possible that Bates attended a concert in late November or December 1913. He performed at the

report comes from a later phase in Paderewski's tours, just prior to the outbreak of World War I, but reflects the subjective response of one member of his female audience that might be seen to typify the Paderewski cult begun twenty years earlier (p. 126):

> There was music to see as well as hear! Oh! The poetry and grace of the swiftly flying supple hands and the ever-moving feet! Sometimes his arms were lifted as high as his head; sometimes they glided on the surface of the keys like foam on the waves, but always with absolute ease and precision. And the music! You soon forgot to note the amazing technic, the endless variety of tone quality, the kaleidoscopic change of effects. You felt only that a great soul was speaking to you and drawing you close to the heart of life. He was opening God's great book of human life for you and letting you read the pathos, the grandeur, the terror, the hope, the joy, the love which lie deep in the heart of this life of ours. You heard that song which has pulsed for so many years - old, old as the world and yet, forever new.

The words of Nellie Cameron Bates echo sentiments from Paderewski reviews, emphasizing the emotional fulfillment and spiritual illumination awaiting the devoted listeners at their Master's recitals. Bates wrote in first person, describing the music, heard in a public recital as communicating intimately and directly with her inner self, "drawing her to the heart of life." This immediacy of an individual experience suspended the awareness of the external world and transformed attending a piano recital into a quasi-religious occasion. Bates's description of her state of mind during the concert (and the preceding narrative of traveling to this concert as if it were a pilgrimage) is a document of Paderewski cult that had spawned forms of cultural expression virtually unchanged since its inception in 1891 until World War I. The angelic image was a key ingredient here, coupled with a reinterpretation of a piano recital as a "quasi-sacred" ritual.

National Theatre in Washington, D.C.; Carnegie Hall in New York, Symphony Hall in Boston, and Carnegie Music Hall in Pittsburgh. The latter concert on 16 December seems a likely candidate for this report.

4. How Paderewski Played

By 1895, the Paderewski recital assumed its final form, virtually unchanged throughout the remainder of the composer's career. A lone spotlight highlighted the golden hair of the pianist at the center of the stage; the concert hall was shrouded in darkness and emptied of sensory stimuli other than the sound of Paderewski's piano, heard in hushed silence.[62] Playing alone, in a semi-darkness of lowered lights, the pianist centered all the attention on himself. In *The Paderewski Memoirs* he bemoaned the inattentive audiences: "It is agonizing to play when nobody seems to listen, and many times in the beginning of my career I have had that humiliating experience."[63] In this context, it is interesting to note that a report from Paderewski's 1895 concerts in Paris mentions the "brilliance of electric light" as a characteristic trait of his recital there. A reviewer of a Paris recital published in Poland wrote about Paderewski's personal, improvisatory performance style that made works by other composers seem to be his own and lead the listeners to forgetting their surroundings and the "pianist on the stage in coattails, in the glare of electric lights."[64] In America, this brilliance gave way to a mysterious darkness.[65]

In *The Paderewski Memoirs*, the pianist mentioned this "sacred atmosphere" that he created while giving recitals in the home of Mrs. Bliss of Santa Barbara, whose "love and appreciation of music were very rare. To play in her house was an experience unlike anything else I found—it was like celebrating a Mass. The atmosphere of silence was like that of a temple. It was beautiful and inspiring" (p. 210). Clearly, Paderewski enjoyed performing for audiences whose love for music and concentration on his artistry was palpable through their silence.

---

[62] Małgorzata Perkowska, *Diariusz Koncertowy Paderewskiego* (Kraków: PWM, 1990), Andrzej Piber, *op. cit.*, chapters 5, 8, 11, and *The Paderewski Memoirs, op. cit.*, chapters 9 to 12.

[63] Paderewski, *op. cit.*, 230.

[64] Quotation from *Niwa* 10 (15 May 1895) after Piber, *op. cit.*, 236.

[65] Philip Hale noted in *Literary Digest* (31 December 1899) the unusual darkness in concert halls where lightning would be centered only on the pianist during his recitals.

The pianist shared this need for capturing a complete attention of his audiences with his great theatrical mentor, Helena Modjeska.[66] Similarities between the approach to performing embraced by both Modjeska and Paderewski extended to include the artistic expression of elevated emotional states and the sublimation of sensuous passion. As an actress, Modjeska was praised for "having the power of infusing life into her creation, and of exciting sympathy in their behalf."[67] She believed that, on the stage, she should "play as one can only play for life or death" and achieve such an "intensity of the situation" that would bring about a full emotional involvement and concentration of all members of the audience (pp. 137, 161). A complete "communion" with her audiences, with bated breath following her every word and gesture was one of the hallmarks of her appearances. When describing her Warsaw debut of 1868, Modjeska noted that the audience

> was immediately hushed into silence. And what a deep silence it was! Such listening is never known in America. Polish audiences go to the theatre really to enjoy a performance and therefore they listen and look in an almost reverent manner, so as not to lose one intonation, one delicate shading of the voice, nor one slight gesture, one passing expression of the face.[68]

The same traits (i.e., Modjeska's "dead silence" p. 137, or "hushed silence" p. 161) became the fundamental characteristics of Paderewski's performing style. The audience listened in near darkness, in rapt attention, without distractions. The pianist overwhelmed and exhausted his listeners by mammoth programs of twelve to seventeen pieces—up to three hours of music, including as many as five to seven encores.[69] Reviewers pointed out that his concerts would often consist of two recitals, one in the program, and one played afterwards. The pianist indulged his audience and kept playing; according to anecdotal accounts, the requests for additional encores were stopped only when porters carried Paderewski's piano out of the hall.

---

[66] Modjeska, *Memories, op. cit.*, 161.
[67] *The Century Magazine* 27: 11 (November 1883): 25-26; cited from p. 26.
[68] Modjeska, *Memories, op. cit.*, 161.
[69] Some of Paderewski's concert programs at the Research Collection NYPL, Performing Arts Division, include pencil annotations with several encore titles.

During his recitals, the pianist also revealed his playful side by capriciously changing the program (depending on his mood), by arriving late, or by interrupting performances in response to the slightest disturbances in the concert hall. Praised for his personal charisma, Paderewski knew how to direct his emotional energy towards those who seemed indifferent and distracted; he would conquer them with his pianistic technique and seduce them with his musicality and magnetic charisma. Of course, there were few such absent-minded listeners in attendance at his recitals; the attendees were mostly his faithful, of one heart and mind. The pianist offered the following description of his audiences in *The Paderewski Memoirs*:[70]

> I think that an audience is like a colossal collective individual, and primitive to the excess. It is never guided by reasoning, but always by intuition, by feeling and instinct. Audiences, no matter how large (the larger the more so), feel just like a collective personality; they always feel whether the one to whom they show their sentiment loves them or not. I have always loved them, and I love them still—the thousands I have played for through the long years.

The pianist's selection of repertoire contributed to the creation of his beautified image as an otherworldly creature of mystical powers, an object for female affection and admiration. The recitals always included several pieces by virtuoso pianist-composers, Chopin and Liszt; of the latter, Paderewski favored transcriptions of songs by Chopin and Schubert (both virtuosic and sentimental) and Hungarian Rhapsodies that provided thunderous conclusions to his recitals, eliciting outbursts of unfettered enthusiasm from the audiences.[71] Since his listeners were mostly female pianists at various stages of advancement, he had to show his "pianistic" side

---

[70] Paderewski, *Memoirs, op. cit.,* 277.

[71] Liszt's *Hungarian Rhapsody* no. 10 is among Paderewski's most acclaimed recordings, praised for instance by Lidia Kozubek in "An Attempt at Defining Ignacy Jan Paderewski's Performing Style," (www.chopin.org/2001_f/PADEREWSKI.htm; translated by Slawomir Dobrzanski). The interpretations have been preserved on Welte-Mignon piano rolls (recorded in November 1906, released on EMI 67 27 0448 1, "Franz Liszt auf Welte Mignon") and on a 78' record, recorded in Camden in June 1922; released on Pearl's GEMM CD 9943 "The Art of Paderewski. Volume II." Both recordings show Paderewski at his best.

in the difficult repertoire of Bach and Beethoven; his interpretations of Beethoven were sometimes controversial.[72]

During the American tours prior to World War I, Paderewski often performed Beethoven's Piano Sonatas Op. 53, 57, and 111.[73] Beethoven was Paderewski's favorite composer since his youth; the pianist professed admiration for the "sublimity and passion" of this universal and lofty composer, especially for the late sonatas, Op. 109 and 111. In an article entitled "Musical Opinion" and published in *The Musical Digest* (October 1933, p. 9), Paderewski stated:[74]

> The full force of music—the sublimity and passion of that art which the longest lifetime is all too ephemeral adequately to serve—was not revealed to me until, when I was twelve, I heard in Warsaw a performance of Beethoven's Fifth Symphony. Some sixty years have passed and the composer whom, of all, I still play with unmitigated satisfaction is Beethoven. Beethoven is universal. He is consistently lofty. Playing Beethoven, I feel that he is the soul of music and that he contains the germs of all later musicians.   I hear Schumann, Mendelssohn, and even Chopin lying implicit in Beethoven.

Nonetheless, it was the romantic "Moonlight Sonata" in C-sharp minor, Op. 27, No. 2 that became his signature Beethoven showpiece in the later years. Alas, the quality of his interpretations of this Sonata decreased in time so much so that by the late 1930s, when the film of the same title was made, including a twenty-minute Paderewski recital with the Sonata as its centerpiece, it fell

---

[72] See William Mason's defense of Paderewski's Beethoven in the 1892 article cited above. In 1892 the *Chicago Evening Post* (17 February 1892) criticized Paderewski's interpretation of the Waldstein Sonata Op. 53, one of his most frequent recital selections. This criticism remained a lone voice; Paderewski's interpretations of Beethoven were praised in the majority of subsequent reviews.

[73] It should suffice to say that Paderewski's interpretations of Beethoven's Sonata Op. 111 was praised by *San Francisco News Letter* (22 February 1896), the Toronto's *Mail and Express* (2 May 1900), and, most importantly, after a performance during the Beethoven Festival in Bonn in 1901 (the positive reaction is cited in Paderewski's *Memoirs, op. cit.,* 419). For further details about critical appraisal of Paderewski's Beethoven performances see Piber, *Droga do sławy, op. cit., passim.*

[74] He talked about Beethoven's Op. 109 in this article; he mentioned Op. 111 in 1895 (interview for *Sunday Advertiser*, 3 November 1895).

to the level of a beginner or an amateur, with the aging virtuoso unable to maintain the steady rhythm of triplets in the accompaniment, and often hitting wrong notes.[75]

In November 1907, Olin Downes (1886-1955), the music critic of *The New York Times,* thus described a Paderewski recital held on November 6, with a program including Paderewski, Beethoven, Chopin, and Liszt:[76]

> A Paderewski recital—seance might be a better word—is an occasion that requires no signboard to identify. The crowded stage, the roped-in piano, the scurrying ushers, the excited twittering of the ladies, the matinee miss and her confidential friend, the whole rows of female colleges—for is not the mighty one meat and drink and bon-bons to them?—and finally, on the pianist's appearance, that species of hushed applause that voices the general spirit of reverential suspense and expectation—all these things combine to impart an atmosphere of rare novelty peculiar to the occasion.

"Why?"—asked Downes. The answer was: "personality. That vital spark that made possible a Paganini and a Liszt, that has enabled this Pole to enthrall and subjugate his audiences until whatever he does, they cry 'Ave imperator!'" The critic also pointed out that during the solo recital one could hear "Paderewski of the golden, melting tone, of magic and moonlight, of Oriental languor and volcanic impetuousness."

Another reviewer of the same recital was even more enthusiastic than Downes: "Paderewski was in fine fettle and from beginning to end he held the huge audience captive with the manifold charms of his wondrous art. He filled the almost breathless air with tonal typhoons, and again with tones soft and silky as plush."[77] The synaesthetic imagery of "melting tones," "moonlight," and music that was "soft and silky as plush," had its sources in, besides the

---

[75] The 1937 British film *The Moonlight Sonata,* directed by Lothar Mendes, is a story of survivors of a plane crash, guests of a Swedish baroness, also hosting Paderewski who helps a young couple find love. The 78-year old Paderewski plays himself, giving a full scale piano recital in the film.

[76] "Paderewski Delights Music Lover" in *The New York Times* (7 November 1907), review by Olin Downes. NYPL, Performing Arts Division.

[77] From *The Journal,* November 8, 1907, Zygmunt Stojowski Collection, USC Polish Music Center.

florid style favored in that period, Paderewski's artistry as a performer and his famous "touch" noted and described by his attentive listeners. Writer Alfred Nossig (the librettist of Paderewski's only opera *Manru* of 1901), in an article published in 1902, noted the astounding expressive range of his interpretations and the richness of tone colors, as well as his ability to "seize, warm, and transport" his audiences, as well as to "electrify and enchain the listeners."[78]

The standard Paderewski recitals prior to World War I were rounded up by a variety of encore-type miniatures, often associated with the subject of love. His repertoire featured a variety of love-themed compositions, starting from the two seminal excerpts from Wagner's apotheosis of eternal love, *Tristan und Isolde*: *The Prelude* (transcribed by Paderewski's student, Ernest Schelling) and *Isolde's Liebestod* (arranged by Liszt).[79] When heard now, these staples of overwrought romanticism, recorded in the 1930s by the 70-year-old pianist, well past the summit of his career, sound quite horrid under his fingers.[80] Yet, with their flowing melodies, passionate themes of ecstasy and

---

[78] I discuss Paderewski's collaboration with Nossig in my article, "*Manru* Paderewskiego" [Paderewski's *Manru*]. *Przeglad Polski [Nowy Dziennik]*, 26 June 2005, pp. 1-2. Further details are in my article, "Searching for Poland's Soul," *op. cit.* Nossig was active as a sculptor, journalist, and a playwright writing in German. *Manru* was his only finished libretto. The majority of his writings dealt not with art, but with social and political issues of Polish Jewry, though he published a monograph on Paderewski (*I.J. Paderewski*; Leipzig: H. Seemann Nachfolger, 1901).

[79] For a study of American reception of Wagner's *Tristan und Isolde* see Joseph Horowitz, *Wagner Nights: An American History* (Berkeley and Los Angeles: University of California Press, 1994), 106-124. For Polish reception of Wagnerian music and ideas at the end of the 19th century, see Magdalena Dziadek, "Polish Reception of Wagner's Music and Ideas," in *A Romantic Century in Polish Music*, ed. Maja Trochimczyk (Los Angeles: Moonrise Press, 2009), pp. 123-149.

[80] The Gemm 9943 CD (Pearl) includes recordings of both pieces, both of strikingly bad quality. The Prelude to *Tristan und Isolde* is in a piano transcription by Ernst Schelling, recorded in New York in October 1930, released on Victor 7324; the Liszt's arrangement of Wagner's *Liebestod* from *Tristan und Isolde* fares even worse; it is recorded from a live performance on short-wave radio broadcast in September 1938.

eternal love-to-death, and ambiguous sequences of unsolved dissonances, these works, suffused with love symbolism, continued to be appealing to Paderewski's predominantly female audiences.

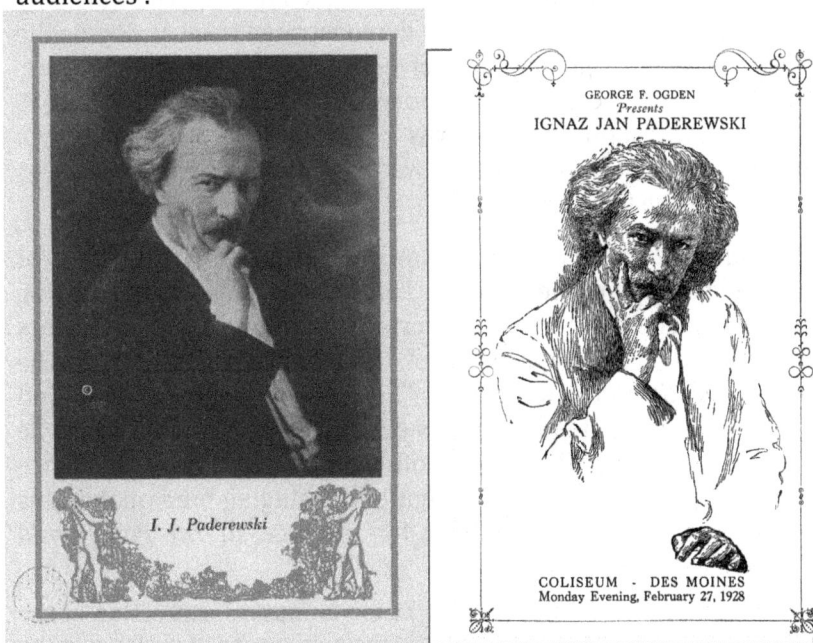

Figure 9: Two concert programs with the same image of a "thoughtful" pianist. L: undated. R: Concert of 27 February 1928, Des Moines, Iowa. Paderewski Archives at Archiwum Akt Nowych, Warszawa.

Another genre associated with romance was the nocturne. During the 1908 San Francisco recital that ended with crowd hysteria described above (hardly the only incident of this kind during his career), Paderewski performed two nocturnes by Chopin. During his tours until World War I, the majority of recitals included at least one nocturne. Paderewski's earliest piano-roll recording of 1905 was a Chopin Nocturne, in G major, Op. 37, No. 2.[81] Significantly, the very first work published in the U.S. during his American appearances of 1891-92 belonged to the same genre: it was the

---

[81] Recorded on Welte-Mignon piano rolls in 1905. Released on "Berühmte Pianisten der Jahrhundertwende spielen Chopin" by Teldec 2292 43 586-2, along with the Etude in D major, Op. 10, No. 3.

Nocturne in B-flat major Op. 16, issued by G. Schirmer in 1892.[82] The prominence of this genre in Paderewski's concert repertoire deserves consideration in the light of the topical significance of the nocturne as both "feminine" and relating to love. In "The Harmony of the Tea Table," Jeffrey Kallberg demonstrated to what degree the nocturne was popularly conceived of as a "feminine" genre, functioning in a context of gendered aesthetics.[83] According to Kallberg, the piano nocturne was "a kind of love poem sung by a man to a woman," yet the genre was simultaneously perceived "as a mirror of the feminine spirit."

The *cantabile* sound quality was one of the main characteristics of Paderewski's piano technique. Throughout his career, starting from the earliest American concerts in Buffalo in 1892, reviewers emphasized his "singing tone." On 18 February 1892, the *Milwaukee Sentinel* wrote that "his use of pedals is free and continuous; it creates marvelous effects. With their assistance he sings at the piano..." Paderewski often emphasized the significance of pedaling in the accomplishment of the singing tone quality; his remarks on this subject appear, for instance, in *The Paderewski Memoirs* where he states: [84]

> The pedal is the strongest factor in musical expression at the piano, because first of all it is the only means of prolonging the sound. The piano is a percussion instrument, you know, and the only way of making it appear prolonged is the pedal... Whenever learning a new piece, one must learn also the proper effect of the pedaling. Each new piece requires a new pedaling, adaptable to the character of the music.

Characteristically for the constant mixture of the artistic and commercial considerations, the attention to tone color and its impact is firmly linked in *The Memoirs* with Paderewski's support for his main sponsor, the Steinway Pianos. There, he claimed that the Steinway pianos "are the greatest pianos in the world... The quality of the tone of the Steinway is supreme . . . a Steinway, with its beautiful tone, is always singing, no matter who plays it" (p. 249). The long-lasting resonance of the piano with the pedal may

---

[82] The other option was the publication of Gavotte in E-minor, Op. 2.
[83] Kallberg, "The Harmony of the Tea Table," *op. cit.*, 32-40.
[84] Paderewski, *Memoirs, op. cit.*, 329.

be linked to the inwardness of emotional experience and a contemplative mood associated with the fantasy of perfect love. Here we see the confluence of aesthetic and commercial considerations that characterized the Paderewski cult from its outset, with its interlocking aspects of image, sound quality, repertoire, concert setting, audience's devotion, and publicity.

Simultaneously, his concerts served to fulfill the social goal of displaying affluence, thanks to Paderewski's uniformly high and ever increasing ticket prices that indirectly assured his audiences that they received a product of the highest quality and value. Between 16 November 1891 and 30 April 1892, during his first American tour sponsored by Steinway and Sons with a contract for 80 concerts, Paderewski gave 107 concerts to ever increasing and more enthusiastic audiences. During the second tour (22 December 1892 to 6 May 1893), Paderewski appeared at 66 concerts and recitals earning about 178,000 dollars. During the third American tour, begun in New York on 23 October 1895 and completed in New York on 18 April 1896, Paderewski earned a gross of 223,106 dollars and netted 178,500 dollars.

The three tours jointly consisted of 259 concerts spanning the entire country; the greatest number of recitals was given on the East Coast. The virtuoso earned ever growing profits from ticket prices and sales of his music. His tickets were as high-priced as those for the opera, without discounts, though they were freely given to the needy devotees—partly to fan the flames of ever-spreading adulation. The virtuoso described America as the "promised land" for all European artists: "A land of fantastic and fabulous legend, with money and appreciation flowing out to meet the artist from the great and lively and generous American public."[85]

The cult of Paderewski remained firmly entrenched even after the locale of music distribution changed from the concert hall to the home. With the advent of recording technology, women could stay at home and listen to Paderewski in the comfort of their own living rooms, instead of attending public concerts. The virtual reality of recordings brought the pianist into the intimacy of their private

---

[85] Cited from Paderewski and Lawton, *Memoirs*, 188

space. As vividly shown in a 1925 advertising for a new model of Victrola gramophone (published in the *Pictorial Review*, September 1925, see Figure 10), the virtuoso waited at the imaginary piano to play for his female fans, when they wanted, what they wanted. All they had to do was to play a recording.

Figure 10: "Waiting to play for you," Ad for Victrola: Victor Talking Machine Company, Pictorial Review, September 1925.

Of course, they also had to be able to afford buying the recordings and the newest models of the gramophone that replaced piano rolls as the most ubiquitous music reproduction medium. Women, who appeared in the world of Paderewski marketing, whether playing the piano or starting the gramophone to hear him play, were well-dressed in the fashions of their time and enjoyed their musical entertainment as an attribute of wealth and leisure. Art historian Susan B. Hobbs pointed to this aspect as an essential factor of the Aestheticism of the Gilded Age. Culture thrived against a background of new affluence and an intensity of social changes brought about by the explosion of productivity and inventiveness in the industry. The richest owners of railroads, car companies, banks, or oil monopolies became art patrons sponsoring the turn toward "pure beauty" and contemplation as an antidote to the frantic pace of their business lives. According to Hobbs, "for these industrialists, art was a realm removed from daily life. Society divided the workplace from culture, and particularized gender roles separated worldly males from aestheticized females" whose beauty was painted by Dewing and others.[86] We could stretch her thesis, to say that the industrialists' wives, daughters, mistresses, and their children's teachers, however, found their aesthetic and emotional fulfillment in attending Paderewski concerts.

The music "soaring beyond and above the range of human speech unto unearthly spheres of divine emotion"—to cite Paderewski again—was emotionally satisfying for those fancying themselves "in love" with the ideal, angelic man. Paderewski played sentimental pieces to charm his female audiences, with the unexpected result of being censured by the male music critics who expressed impatience with his tendency to engage in "crowd-pleasing" sentimentality. After his Boston recital on 27 December 1899, for instance, the reviewer for *The Herald* beseeched the composer to play for musicians and not only for his "hysterical admirers" and to distance himself from sentimentalism and from seeking applause at all costs. After the same concert, Phillip Hale, the reviewer of *The Journal*, tartly observed that Paderewski tended to focus on being admired and sacrificed artistic standards for applause.[87] Indeed, the musician liked the adulation received from his female fans. In the *Memoirs*, he wrote wistfully:[88]

> Ah, there are so many beautiful things to remember, revealing the eager youth and the enthusiasm of youth, and it prevailed for

---

[86] Susan Hobbs, *Dewing, op. cit.*, 24.
[87] *The Herald* (December 1899). *The Journal* (28 December 1899). Press clippings in the Performing Arts Division, New York Public Library
[88] Paderewski and Lawton, *The Paderewski Memoirs, op. cit.*, 277.

many years. I met that spirit again and again, particularly in the West. I often think about it now, and their eagerness and devotion.

While examining the idealization of Paderewski's image as a mysterious epitome of beauty, an object of female gaze and admiration, we noted the various elements of his portraiture: the perfect embodiment of both sweetness and light, or Arnoldian beauty and intelligence in an image of youth, beauty, mystery and ambiguity, angelic perfection and human vulnerability. Strikingly non-conventional, Paderewski's appearance in his promotional materials emphasized the attitude of evasion and the lack of confrontational power—through the obvious preference for the downturned eyes, the left-side profile... The pianist firmly controlled all aspects of his public presentation and participated in the creation of this image. He formatted of his recitals to magnify the impact on his female listeners, and selected works with the direct appeal to their hearts. Matthew Arnold stated in *Culture and Anarchy*: "Greatness is a spiritual condition worthy to excite love, interest, and admiration; and the outward proof of possessing greatness is that we excite love, interest, and admiration."[89] With those words, we could summarize Paderewski's greatness.

5. The Change of Image—A Polish Statesman

While Paderewski's image dramatically changed in time, his "greatness" continued to attract love and admiration, albeit among a different crowd. The "Polish" image of Paderewski as a "new Chopin," first articulated by Dr. Tytus Chałubinski back in 1880s, was best captured in a late 19th-century postcard issued by a painters' collective in Krakow.[90] The postcard depicts a crowd of ancient royal ghosts emerging in an eerie light from the piano, while the red-headed "archangel" Paderewski plays on.

The cult of Paderewski as a potential national savior was widespread among Polish emigres. In 1888, during his concerts in

---

[89] Matthew Arnold, *Culture and Anarchy*, 18

[90] See the image in Essay No. 1. This postcard was first reproduced in "Paderewski in Poetry," *Polish Music Journal* 4, no. 1 (2001), and also on the cover of the paperback edition of Halina Goldberg's *The Age of Chopin* (Indiana University Press, 2004).

Belgium, Henryk Merzbach, the president of the Polish Charitable Society of Brussels addressed the "new Chopin" with an exhortation to "play for us and let the nation resurrect"[91] (see Essay 1). The idea caught on among Polish emigres in America, especially during World War I. Since 1915, Paderewski transformed his American recitals into patriotic occasions, giving over 350 passionate speeches on behalf of Poland's independence and the plight of Polish widows and orphans—the innocent victims of the war, who were the intended beneficiaries of his charitable activities.[92] He stimulated the interest and helped unite the American Polonia—divided into a multitude of small and weak organizations. More importantly, as a friend of President Woodrow Wilson, Paderewski helped add the Polish cause to the list of America's postulates for the peace treaty, and, in this way, secure the granting of Poland's independence.

For his role in the "resurrection" of Poland, Paderewski was rewarded with the title of the President of the Council of Ministers and Minister of Foreign Affairs of the newly independent country. Alas, he served only for a year (January to December 1919). He retained the title of "President" for his lifetime and, in a 1928 tribute, during celebrations of the tenth anniversary of Poland's independence, this was all that mattered.[93] As the Princeton professor and editor of the *New York Times*, poet John Huston Finley (1863-1940) wrote for this occasion:[94]

> As ancient Orpheus trod the aisles of hell
> To rescue from its thrall Eurydice,
> So you for Poland. But though Orpheus failed
> You won. Polonia Restituta lives.

---

[91] Henryk Mierzbach, poem welcoming Paderewski to Brussels, on his first European tour; *Dziennik Poznański*, (no. 289, 16 December 1889) cited after Piber, *op. cit.*, 166, transl. Maja Trochimczyk.

[92] Józef Orłowski, *Ignacy Jan Paderewski i Odbudowa Polski* (Chicago: The Stanek Press, 1940).

[93] See Orłowski, *op. cit.*; Henryk Przybylski, *Paderewski: Między muzyką a polityką* [Paderewski: Between music and politics] (Katowice: Unia, 1992). *To Ignace Jan Paderewski: Artist, Patriot, Humanitarian / 1918-1928* (New York: Kościuszko Foundation, 1928).

[94] I discuss this poem in Essay No. 1 above: "Paderewski in Poetry: Master of Harmonies or Poland's Savior?"

The same sentiments had been expressed back in 1916, but merely as a hope for the distant future, in a "Tribute to Paderewski" by one of his female admirers, Henryetta Teresa Beckert. The poem was inserted into her portrait with a picture of Paderewski in hand:[95]

> You are a Genius, born of love
> Of your Nation, love of your People —
> Your life is eternal - you are immortal
> In strains of labor, you lead us to a miracle —
> Under your guidance we have to win
> Because we are Poles, we are your Nation.

Beckert made a transition from one audience—women enchanted with an "archangel at the piano"—to another, his patriotic compatriots honoring Paderewski as their public representative. Accordingly, the image of the "hero" was also transformed in the process. No longer turning his head in diffidence, lost in dreams, Paderewski became a statesman filled with masculine power and gravitas. In this new image (Figures 9 and 11), surrounded by the attributes of power, frowning, he sternly faces the viewer. Even his musical representations, after his presidency, depict him as imbued with the seriousness and focus of a government leader. Such a portrait graced the cover of *The Etude* in May 1931 (Figure 6 in Essay 4); unlike the 1915 youthful fiction, the portrait showed Paderewski as he actually looked like at that time.

Artur Szyk (1894-1951) drew Paderewski in a similar mode, in a 1939 postcard with bilingual captions, issued in Poland as a part of a series of "Pictures from the Glorious Days of the Polish American Fraternity." Here, the elegant and serious Paderewski, dressed in his official finery, holds up a declaration of allegiance of American Poles who profess to remain "supremely loyal and grateful" to their new country "in time of war, in time of peace." An image of the 1914 Grunwald Memorial that Paderewski funded in Krakow to commemorate the 400th anniversary of the victory of Polish-Lithuanian armies over the Teutonic Knights, reminds the spectators who their war-time enemy was. The virile, serious, and focused leader is fully

---

[95] Cited from Orlowski, *op. cit.*, p. 90. Beckert came from a Silesian noble family, with musical talents and an intense interest in Paderewski.

grounded in this world; somewhat weary and worried, he has full confidence in his societal role and responsibilities.

Figure 11: Paderewski in a portrait by Artur Szyk, "Pictures from the Glorious Days of the Polish American Fraternity." Postcard issued by Drukarnia Narodowa, Kraków, 1939.

While Paderewski's white-haired "statesman" images appeared in photographs and adverts, such as posters for his 1937 film, *The Moonlight Sonata*, the "archangel" image did not entirely disappear. Myths do not die. Three years after publishing Paderewski's "statesman" portrait, *The Etude* returned to the idealized, red-haired, young "archangel," on the cover of the July 1934 issue (Figure 5 in Essay 6). It may be of interest, that the pianist's famous reddish-gold hair was also immortalized in popular music. In 1895, Charles Mills Gayley, professor of English and Classics at the

University of California at Berkeley, penned a song celebrating the athletic achievements of Cal, UC Berkeley sports teams. The Cal marching band plays *The Golden Bear* until today, boosting the team spirit with praise for their "Golden Bear" mascot, and keeping alive the memory of Paderewski's hair:

> Oh, he has a very patient air, patient air,
> He wears a Paderewski hair, 'rewski hair,
> He's the center rush of the heavens I swear,
> Our silent, sturdy Golden Bear.

It is easy to note how much did Paderewski's image changed over the course of his career, when comparing Szyk's image with those of the Aestheticists discussed earlier. In the late nineteenth century Paderewski was idolized as an Archangel by his foreign audiences, while being cast as "the new Chopin" by his Polish compatriots at home and abroad.[96] By the outbreak of World War I, the cult of "the greatest pianist of our times"[97] was almost independent from his musicianship; it was a phenomenon of its own.[98]

During and after the war, the pianist transformed into a statesman; he maintained a politician's polished professional appearance and a ruling-class gravitas even after leaving office and returning to the concert stage. He continued performing and touring the world until the outbreak of World War II, appealing to his faithful devotees, including daughters and granddaughters of his original female admirers from the 1890s.[99]

In the interwar period, his image went a transformation among the musicians, the general public, and Polish Americans, the latter of whom viewed him primarily as a politician and an elder statesman—Mr. President.[100] The subject of Paderewski's image,

---

[96] The expression comes from a 1888 poem by Henryk Merzbach, *op. cit.*.
[97] Expression from an article by William Mason, *op. cit.*.
[98] *The New York Daily Tribune* (27 March 1892), New York Public Library, Performing Arts Division, Lincoln Center, Paderewski Files.
[99] The issue of Paderewski's chances of a successful return to the concert stage was discussed prior to his first American concerts after the hiatus of five years; see Charles Rosebault, "Paderewski Restored to Music Lovers," *The New York Times Magazine* (19 November 1922).
[100] I discuss the transformation of Paderewski's images in the interwar

role and achievements as a politician, however, is better left for another occasion.

Grief Over War Stays Hand of Polish Genius

Figure 12: Paderewski caricature about World War I, interrupting his career as a concert pianist, 1916.

---

period in "Celebrity in Decline: Paderewski's Musical and Political sReception in America 1919-1939" ("Muzyczna i polityczna recepcja Paderewskiego w Ameryce 1919-1939,") at the 3rd "Topos narodowy" conference in Warsaw, November 16-17, 2009, published in Polish in *Topos narodowy w muzyce polskiej międzywojnia*, eds. Wojciech Nowik and Katarzyna Szymanska-Stułka (Warsaw: Uniwersytet Muzyczny Fryderyka Chopina, 2013).

Essay 3.
A Paderewski Album from Brighton, England, 1890-1914

Maja Trochimczyk[1]

The meteoric rise to fame of the Polish pianist and composer Ignacy Jan Paderewski (1860-1941) was accompanied by the phenomenon of the "Paderewski girl"—i.e., a single, educated, music-loving young woman, who followed her idol to concerts around the country (see Essay 2). One such "Paderewski girl" was Miss Michell from England, of whom little is known, except that she lived in Brighton and collected all things "Paderewski" in a large album of press clippings and autographs, starting in 1890. I came into possession of this album via eBay in 2011. Its sellers had purchased it in bulk with other old books at an estate auction in the U.K. and had no information about the album or its author. This unique artefact will be called the *Brighton Album*.

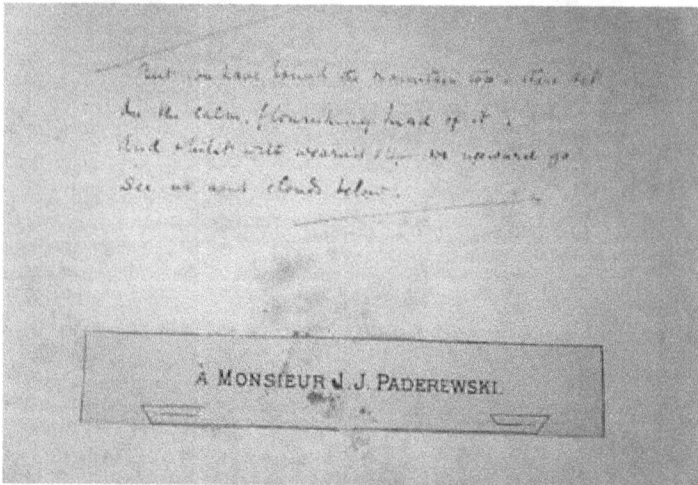

Figure 1: Dedication. the Brighton Album, *1890. Maja Trochimczyk Collection (subsequent illustrations mostly from the same source).*

---

[1] This essay is an expanded version of "Following Paderewski: An Album of Autographs and Clippings from Brighton, England, 1890-1911," paper presented at the 74th Annual Meeting of the Polish American Historical Association, Denver, Colorado (January 6, 2017).

The album begins with a dedication to "Monsieur I. J. Paderewski" and a poetic quotation: "But you have found the mountain top — there sit / On the calm, flourishing head of it; / And whilst with wearied steps we upward go, / See us and clouds below." I will return to this quote and its ramifications at the end of this study. The large, cloth-covered book (12.5 x 17 inches) consists of 123 numbered pages, preceded by a handwritten index, with large red and black letter tabs, two to three letters per page. The author filled 90 pages with tightly assembled press clippings, concert programs, and tickets, starting from articles about Paderewski's 1890 concerts in Paris and London.

Figure 2: A signed portrait of Paderewski. The Brighton Album

The album contains four loose items inserted between pages: three concert programs from 1911-1914, and torn pages from a magazine article about Paderewski. The items mainly originate in the years 1890-94, with detailed documentation of the pianist's concert tours in England, including fifty concerts that Michell personally attended, as demonstrated in the array of tickets glued into the album's pages. The following four years, 1895-98, are represented by sporadic items, such as programs and reviews from about one concert per year.

There are three items with the pianist's autographs: two cards, and one portrait. The majority of his photographs appear to have been clipped from periodicals, concert flyers, or ads. Surprisingly, there are no typical concert souvenirs such as signed promotional photos, that are abundant, even today, on eBay. This absence of signed photographs from concert promoters, along with the existence of blank spots in the book, marked by glue stains (for instance around the Paderewski portrait reproduced above), indicates that such signed photos could have been present, but were removed afterwards, perhaps to be sold separately.

Among hundreds of news clippings from England and America (in English only) there are announcements about Paderewski's tours and travels, sailing to and from America, and arrivals in England before giving concerts. The densely assembled clippings also preserve information about planned concert programs and their dates, concert previews and reviews, as well as biographical articles, and interviews. Unfortunately, some of these reports do not contain the name of the newspaper, nor the date of its publication, which limits their usefulness. However, among the most important articles listed in the index we may find:

- Henry T. Finck, "Mr. Paderewski in America," *The Forum* (June 1893): 416-427 (seven pages cut from the journal, affixed on pages 52-53)
- Dr. H. H. Haas, "The Paderewski Piano Recitals" and "Paderewski Piano Compositions," *New York Musical Preview* (affixed on pages 22-23)
- A. L., "Paderewski, the Pianist," *New York Musical Preview* (affixed on pp. 50-51)
- William Mason, "Personality in Piano Playing," *The Century Magazine* (30 November 1891), affixed on page 34
- Fanny Morris Smith, "Paderewski: A Critical Study," *The Century Magazine* (1892), affixed on page 35

Michell also collected several interviews with Paderewski or about him; the most unusual of these contained a chart of revenue from a series of his concerts, and a summary of his first American tour ("The Piano King in America: An Unconventional Interview in London," 1891, on page 27).

The range of topics of press reports is quite extensive, from analytical studies of Paderewski's music to anecdotal stories about his dog, luxurious rail carriage, ways of travel, hair, habits, his temperament, and eccentricity. Their range encompasses even a "Phrenological Character Sketch" by J. Millott Severn (*The Popular Phrenology*, January 1903). There are multiple reports about Paderewski's concert tours in America, his performances in Germany, France and specific towns in England, Wales, Scotland, and Ireland. The reports note his appearances at Bournemouth, Bristol, Bradford, Birmingham, Cheltenham, Clifton, Dublin, Edinburgh, Hampstead, Leeds, Liverpool, London, Oxford, Plymouth, Sheffield, to mention just a few of the English, Scottish and Irish cities the pianist visited on his tours. The index identifies 11 pages dedicated to Paderewski's concerts in Brighton itself.

The Brighton Album contains copies of 36 programs from 1890 to 1898, glued into the book's pages and additional three programs from 1911 and 1914, loosely inserted in the back. The final of these concerts on 15 June 1914 was given at the Queen's Hall by the London Symphony Orchestra, conducted by Arthur Nikisch. No wonder it was the end: World War I erupted on 28 July 1914 and Paderewski stopped giving concerts, dedicating his time, energy, and attention to the struggle for Poland's independence.

Fifty concert tickets from events attended by Ms. Mitchell were assembled in decorative patterns on three different pages, with 35 tickets, 14 tickets, and one ticket respectively (See Figures 9 and 10). It took a lot of time to track and assemble this incredibly detailed record of Paderewski early concert career, from his English debut through the first set of tours in the U.K. and America. What does this effort say about its author? Obviously, it was someone with a passion for music, and more specifically, a fascination with Paderewski.

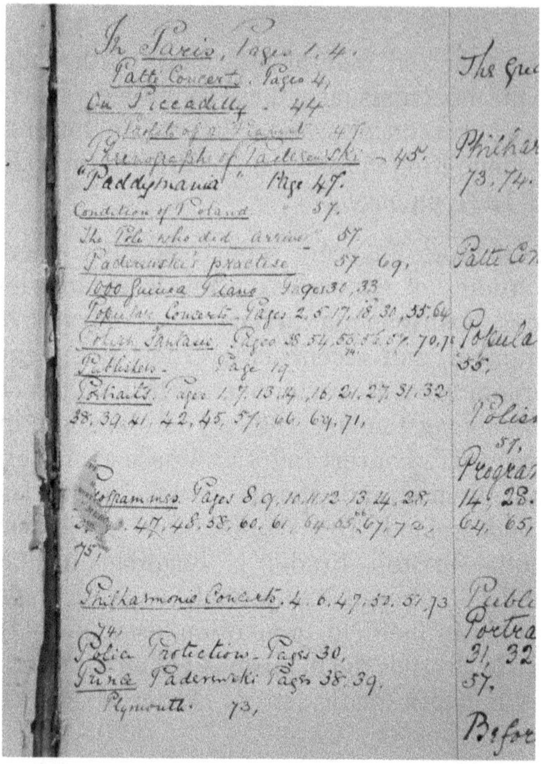

Figure 3: Fragment of handwritten index in the Brighton Album.

In order to make information contained in *The Brighton Album* easier to find, Michell created a handwritten index with topics and page numbers, referring to various Paderewski compositions as well as subjects discussed by music critics and reviewers. The Index documents 18 references to Paderewski's portraits, 21 copies of concert programs, eight performances of the Polish Fantasia, seven Philharmonic concerts, three articles about Paderewski's pianos, two about his practice habits, one story about "the condition of Poland" (p. 57) and one on "Paddymania" (p. 47)- the phenomenon of cultish worship of the pianist by his female admirers. Michell may have been considered a prime example of such "Paddymania" herself!

The volume includes two letters with her last name, and one torn telegram with her address, but no other personal information. The E-Bay seller, Ellen Speer from Knightsbridge, Sussex, stated in an email of 29 December 2016 that they bought this item with quite a number of other books from an old country house near Woodchurch, in Kent — some fifteen miles or so from our address in East Sussex. The whole contents of the property was being sold by a lady who was acting in the capacity of an Executor. Unfortunately, we did not learn very much from her concerning the family who had owned the property.

Luckily, some clues about the identity of *The Brighton Album's* author may be found within its pages. There are two letters that identify her by last name. The first letter to Miss Michell, dated 2 April 1892 (Figure 4), is from staff at the Offices of Sebastian & Pierre Erard, the makers of Paderewski's pianos and sponsors of his British tours: "Dear Miss Michell, I have not been able to confirm the movements of our mutual friend..."

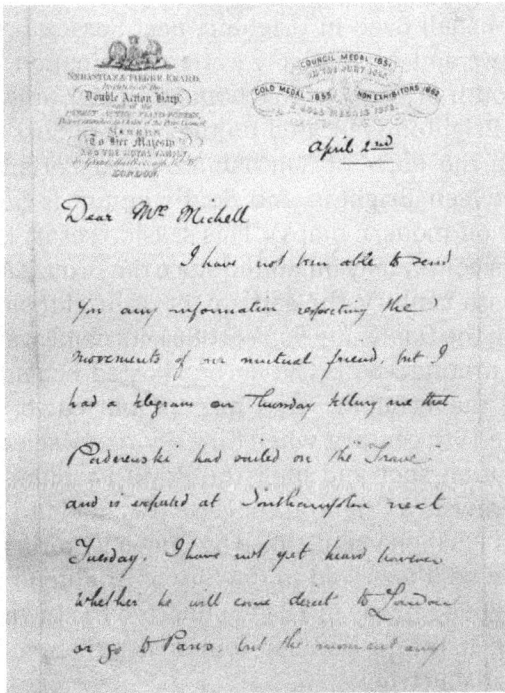

Figure 4. A letter to Miss Michell about Paderewski's schedule.

However, as the Erard employe assures her, a telegram was received that Paderewski had sailed on the "Traue," returning from America from his first triumphant tour of 107 concerts across the continent. The pianist was scheduled to arrive in Southampton the following Tuesday, but it was not clear whether he'd go to London or Paris. The note was unsigned.

The second note was sent on 2 December 1892 from the office of Concert Direction Daniel Mayer in London. "Dear Miss Michell," writes Mayer, "the photo & letter I gave Mr. Paderewski myself as I went to see him in Paris, on his birthday. He was much delighted & touched by the kind affection..." Clearly, Michell was reaching out to her idol and trying to get a more personal response. The Album she assembled does not contain any proof of receiving any reply from Paderewski; this letter itself indicates that the pianist distanced himself from yet another persistent fan. At least this missive allowed us to identify the last name of the Album's author. In continued search for clues, I noticed that the index includes a reference to "Madelaine Michell" on page W-X. Why place Mitchell under the letter X? Could it be the author? I do think so.

Madelaine Michell lived in Brighton, East Sussex, a fashionable seaside resort and a popular vacation destination, located 47 miles due south of London. Her home was at 7 Stillwood Place. The City of Brighton is located on the coast of Sussex, England, not far from the Ports of Southampton and Portsmouth.[2] The distance between Brighton and Southampton is 55 miles (63 miles by car on modern maps). This seaside resort is in an area that has been continually inhabited since the Bronze Age. Already in the eleventh century, the settlement of Brighthelmstone was mentioned in the *Domesday Book* (1086); its name was shortened to Brighton around 1660. The harbor hosted boats traveling to France and the economy was maritime-oriented, before the middle of the 19th century, when King George IV selected it as his favorite vacation spot and built the Royal Pavilion,[3] where the first of Paderewski's Brighton concerts was held in 1890 (Figure 5). The Royal Pavilion was disliked by Queen Victoria who needed more privacy, so it was sold to the City of Brighton in 1845. The construction of a railway in 1841 connected the town to London, transforming it into a popular tourist destination for seaside weekends and day trips.

---

[2] Nicholas Antram and Richard Morrice, *Brighton and Hove. Pevsner Architectural Guides* (London: Yale University Press, 2008); Anthon Seldon, *Brave New City: Brighton & Hove Past, Present, Future* (Lewes: Pomegranate Press, 2002).
[3] Information from "The Royal Pavilion, East Sussex," in *A History of England in 100 Places from Stonehenge to the Gherkin* by John Julius Norwich (London: John Murray, 2011), 315-317.

Brighton was one of Paderewski's preferred sites to perform right before leaving for and right after returning from America. He traveled to New York on ocean liners from the nearby harbor of Southampton. This partly explains his frequent appearances in Brighton: he commenced and concluded his American tours in the fall and the spring respectively, from/to the shores of Britain.

In addition to attending Paderewski's concert in town, Michell frequently traveled from Brighton to his recitals in nearby cities, including over 20 solo and symphonic concerts in London; held in the St. James's Hall, Queen's Hall, Crystal Palace, and other locations. Chronologically, the earliest item in the Album is a press clipping, published in the *Brighton Gazette* on 31 May 1890, reporting on Paderewski's concert at St. James's Hall in London. The reviewer described the recital as

> ...a display of M. Paderewski's remarkable power of interpreting, as it would seem, every style of music with equal ability. He possesses in a high degree the art of making the instrument 'speak' and of eliciting from it that sympathetic thrill of human passion which is sometimes thought of to be an attribute of stringed instruments only. His touch is clear and delicate at the extreme, in the loudest as well as the softest passages, and even when he plays fortissimo he never seems to be using much muscular effort.

Figure 5. The Royal Pavilion in 2011, By Qmin. Wikimedia Commons.

The first two of Paderewski's Brighton concerts, one noted in the Album only with press clippings, and one documented with a program and a set of reviews, took place at the Royal Pavilion's

Music Room in June 1890 and on 18 October 1890. Neither of these two concerts was previously recorded by scholars in Paderewski's concert calendar.

The solo recital at the Royal Pavilion held on 18 October 1890 featured a massive number of pieces, starting from Beethoven's Sonata Op. 111, followed by three shorter compositions by Schubert, Henselt, and Brahms; three works by Schumann; four by Chopin (Sonata in B minor, a Nocturne, Scherzo in C-sharp minor and a Waltz); and two miniatures by Paderewski himself (Melodie and the ever-present Minuet). The evening ended with the 20-minutes-long *Fantasia "Don Giovanni"* by Franz Liszt based on themes from Mozart's opera of the same title.

The audience was enthusiastic. One reviewer (in an unidentified press clipping) stated: "His playing may justly be characterized as sensational, it is marked by splendid contrasts; he astonishes by his fire and fury but is also fully at his ease in portraying graceful light and shade." Other, equally positive, critics went on to note his "striking individuality," a "delicious tone and superb touch." Frank Mott Harrison's review in the *Brighton Guardian* (22 October 1890) highlighted Paderewski's interpretations of individual pieces and ended with praise for the young pianist's rendering of Liszt's Fantasia that

> ...displayed to the fullest extent the extraordinary prowess of mechanical pianism with his marvelous execution; thick and rich tone; exquisite taste and expression; intellectual and artistic reading. Paderewski may justly claim a foremost position in the front rank of executants.

After the first two concerts, in subsequent appearances in the seaside town, due to huge crowds flocking to attend Paderewski's recitals and the fact that the Royal Pavilion was too small to accommodate such extensive audiences, his concerts moved to The Dome. In *The Brighton Album*, Michell documented eight concerts held at The Dome in six years, by gluing in programs, some of which included notes on program changes and encores. She meticulously affixed tickets, news clippings, and reviews.

The Dome concert hall was built in 1815 in Indo-Saracenic style by John Nash and served as a part of royal barracks. Bought by the City of Brighton in 1850, it was again used as a cavalry barracks from 1856 to 1864.[4] Its interior was remodeled by architect Philip Lockwood at a cost of 10,000, before reopening on 24 June 1867 as a concert and assembly hall, spacious enough to hold over 2,500 people.[5] A 16-foot diameter gas chandelier was fitted as its grand centerpiece amidst opulent decorations. The Dome had an organ, orchestral stage, and circular parterre, surrounded by elegant private boxes (Figure 6). Actually, this spacious concert hall was repeatedly remodeled later, and it is still in use today, mostly for popular music. The Dome's website mentions concerts by Jimmi Hendrix and five appearances by David Bowie among its highlights. The venue hosted ABBA's victory in the 1974 Eurovision Song Contest (*Waterloo*). The innovative rock group Pink Floyd regularly performed at the venue, appearing eight times between 1966 and 1972. They famously debuted their classic album *The Dark Side of the Moon* live at the Brighton Dome in January 1972.

Figure 6: The interior of the Dome with the Brighton Symphony Orchestra, established in 1925; Photo from 1928, Wikimedia Commons.

Appropriately for such illustrious followers, Paderewski's first concert at The Dome on 1 December 1890 could be described as a huge variety show, consisting of 20 numbers divided into two

---

[4] Lily Johnston, "Everything you need to know about the Brighton Dome," Brighton Journal (15 May 2020).

[5] Details about the history and modern use of the Brighton Dome are from its website: https://brightondome.org/whats-on/.

parts. The pianist played two sets of compositions, sandwiched between performances by singers and an orchestra. Then, on 26 May 1891, he appeared with a French cellist Jean Gerardy (1877-1929). However, by 31 October 1891 (Figure 7), the celebrity pianist was able to fill the hall by himself. He organized the program into four blocks of music, marked with brackets in the program and consisting of 1) Beethoven's Variations and Sonata Op. 53 in C major, 2) Felix Mendelsohn's *Variations sérieuses*, Robert Schumann's *Papillons,* and Chopin's Sonata in B minor, Op. 58, "that contains the Funeral March," 3) Chopin's Nocturne, Valse and two Etudes followed by Franz Liszt's *Au bord d'une source* (from *Années de Pèlerinage*) and his *Etude de Concert,* plus an Etude by Anton Rubinstein; 4) Paderewski's Nocturne, *Valse (Mein lebt nur einmal)* by Strauss-Tausig, and *Rhapsodie Espagnole* by Liszt, for the melodious and rousing finale. This massive program is notable for the inclusion of Mendelssohn and ending with a Spanish, rather than a Hungarian Rhapsody by Liszt. Reviewers commented on high ticket prices of his solo recitals and observed full attendance—there were between 2,500 and 3,000 listeners at each concert.

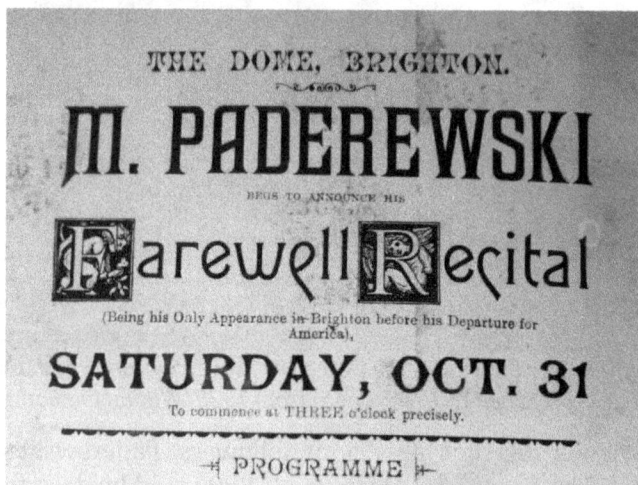

Figure 7: Fragment of program of Paderewski's first solo recital in Brighton, held on 31 October 1891.

The Paderewski's recital at the Brighton Dome held on 10 December 1892 was exceedingly well documented, with seven reviews, and two news briefs announcing the virtuoso pianist's imminent departure for America. The program consisted of a

Handel's Suite, Prelude and Fugue in G minor by Bach-Liszt, a Sonata by Weber, a set of pieces by Chopin (Barcarole, Mazurka, Waltz, Preludes, and Etudes), Paderewski's Nocturne and a Liszt's *Hungarian Rhapsody*. The reviews noted that there were over 2,500 people in the audience of this "superb" recital, that ticket prices were very high, and that Paderewski performed on a "thousand-guinea Erard Piano..." Let's enjoy some phrases: "He rendered the program in his usual brilliant style"... "his performances were marvelous in every particular"... "M. Paderewski held his hearers engrossed and delighted by his consummate manipulative dexterity, by the exquisite beauty of his touch, his wonderful power of subtle tone gradation, that constitutes such a notable feature of his playing..."

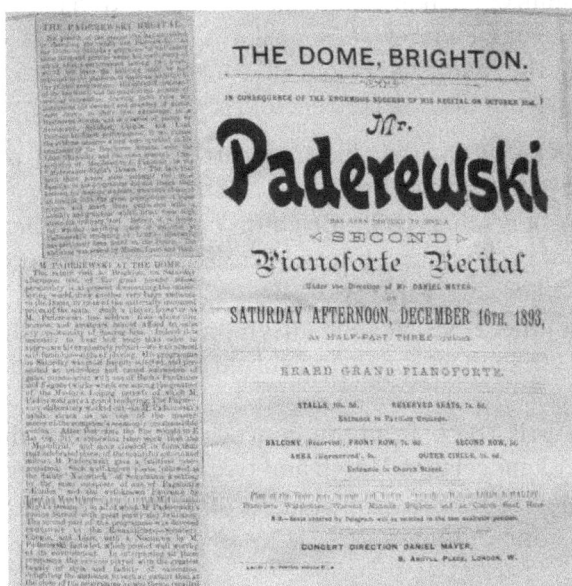

Figure 8: Fragment of program of 16 December 1893, The Dome.

The eight concerts attended by Michell in six years at The Dome were as follows:

- 1 December 1890: a 20-item, two-part concert with orchestra and other musicians
- 26 May 1891: two soloists' concert with Jean Garady, a French cellist
- 31 October 1891: the first solo recital, noted as the final appearance before Paderewski's departure for America
- 10 December 1892: a solo recital

- *21 October 1893: a solo recital*
- *16 December 1893: a solo recital*
- 12 October 1895: a solo recital
- *6 December 1898: the last Brighton concert in the Album*

I compared items in the Brighton Album with the list of Paderewski's concerts in that city that was previously assembled by Malgorzata Perkowska in *Diariusz Koncertowy Paderewskiego ("Diariusz").*[6] Of the 10 concerts listed above at the Royal Pavilion and at the Dome, only four had extant programs, preserved in archives. Three of these concerts, attended by Michell, are marked in italics in the list above. The other six events she documented were not previously known. This indicates the historical value of Michell's meticulous preservation of programs and tickets from Paderewski's performances. In addition, the majority of the pianist's Brighton concerts are listed in the *Diariusz* as part of his U.K. concert tours:

- December 1892: the last concert before the pianist's departure for the second American concert tour
- October-December 1893: Brighton concert on 16 December as part of a 23-concert tour in October, with eleven concerts in December
- January-June 1895: A June Brighton concert; a tour of 12 concerts in January, seven in February, nine in April, and four in June
- March-April 1897: Brighton concert on 27 March during a tour of 13 concerts in March and two concerts in April
- December 1898: Brighton concert on 6 December, as part of a seven-concert tour

Consequently, we can add two more concerts at the Dome, in June 1895 and March 1897, neither attended by Michell, to the list of Paderewski's concert appearances in Brighton before 1900. What happened later? When reviewing the concerts listed by Perkowska in the period not covered by *The Brighton Album*, we notice that the virtuoso always performed at the Dome and that the concerts continued to be a part of his U.K. tours.

---

[6] Malgorzata Perkowska. *Diariusz koncertowy Ignacego Jana Paderewskiego* [Paderewski's Concert Calendar], (Krakow PWM, 1990).

- March 1907: a tour of 11 concerts in March including Brighton, followed by two concerts in June in London
- June 1912: U.K. concerts in three cities, including Brighton
- April 1937: U.K. tour of six cities, including Brighton
- October 1938: U.K. tour of seven cities, including Brighton

The 16 Brighton appearances (10 documented by Michell and six additional ones from Perkowska's *Diariusz*) were usually coupled with recitals in other smallish cities, such as neighboring Portsmouth, Wolverhampton, Huddersfield, and Middleborough (1893); Bournemouth, Leamington, Maidstone, and Ipswich (1895); Ryde, Derby, Salisbury and Warrington (1897); Harrogate and Sheffield (1912); Newcastle-on-Thyme, and Cheltenham (1938). Furthermore, a handwritten note in the index of *The Brighton Album* adds another U.K. concert tour to Paderewski's performance history. As Michell wrote, in April 1894, Paderewski gave concerts in Nottingham (on the 16th), Plymouth (19th), Exeter (20th), Torquay (21st), Bath (23rd), Eastbourne (25th), Turnbridge Wells (26th), St. Leonard's (27th), Folkestone (28th), and Oxford (30th). On 2 May 1894, the virtuoso played with orchestra at the Queen's Hall in London; the tour ended on 4 May at Newcastle. None of these concert dates have been previously recorded by scholars. Their discovery illuminates challenges faced by the pianist's biographers and difficulties in accurately documenting all his activities. He simply did too much.

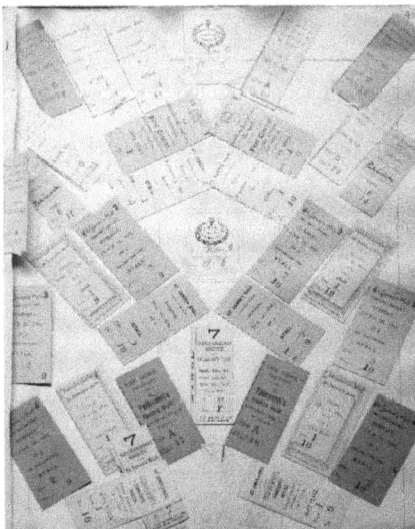

Figure 9: Paderewski concert tickets, p. 49 of The Brighton Album.

Prior to Paderewski's second American concert tour in 1893, the celebrated pianist gave a solo recital at the Brighton Dome on 21 October 1893. The rich program consisted of: Bach's Chromatic Fantasy, Beethoven's Sonata, Op. 31, Schumann's Sonata, Op. 11, five pieces by Chopin with the Ballade No. 2, in F major, and the Polonaise in F-sharp minor, Op. 44, followed by Chant de Voyageur and Intermezzo Polacco by Paderewski himself. That was not the end: the program continued with Rubinstein's Valse-Caprice, and Liszt's *Hungarian Rhapsodie* No. 1. Plus, as Michell noted in pencil on her copy of the program, the pianist added a Chopin's Nocturne and Liszt's *Rhapsodie* No. 10 as an encore. Again, the (unnamed) music critics in Brighton were enthusiastic, noting that "seldom has the Dome been so crowded..." and observing that "sheer admiration reigned supreme"... "His brilliant playing was met with great appreciation..." Given Michell fascination with the pianist, whose concerts she faithfully attended since 1890, and her apparent knowledge of piano repertoire, it is possible to assume that at least one of these anonymous reviews was a fruit of her labor. At that time, women still preferred to hide their identity when seeking publication and sent their work to print either anonymously or under a male pseudonym.

Figure 10: Page with a program from Hampstead and tickets, in
The Brighton Album.

The author of a review entitled "Pianoforte Recital at Brighton" was particularly impressed with Paderewski's rendition of the Schumann's Sonata: "The pianist's touch was sympathetic, his brilliant execution worthy the warmest praise, and his splendid contrasts of delicacy, refinement, sparkling brightness, bold vigorous phrasing, fully in accord with the spirit of the composer." The reviewer also greatly enjoyed performances of Chopin that showed a "delicacy of touch and poetic feeling" while "the pianist displayed rare versatility in the brilliant and expressive rendering of the various morceaux." Another reviewer was virtually transported into the "great beyond," especially by Chopin's Nocturne:[7]

> It is impossible to express what one felt in the centre of these performances..... Here were thoughts too definite, too heart-stirring for words.... With every bar of that Nocturne familiar to us for years, we never seemed to realise its beauty until Paderewski played it.

Many of Michell's concert programs contain handwritten annotations about repertoire changes, replacement or deletion of works, and encores performed by Paderewski. The attentive listener faithfully recorded details of each recital, as if she were to write a review. On 15 June 1892, at the St. James Hall in London, Paderewski gave a mammoth recital, starting with the Chromatic Fantasia and Fugue by J. S. Bach and a Rondo by Mozart, followed by Beethoven Sonata in C-minor, Op. 111, an Impromptu by Franz Schubert, an Etude by Paganini-Schumann, and three miniatures by Chopin—a Prelude, Etude and Waltz. After his own Nocturne, the vibrant Rhapsody No. 12 by Liszt provided the grand finale, enriched by two encores—an excerpt from Liszt's Piano Concerto No. 2 and Chopin's brief Waltz in D-flat Major, Op. 64, No. 1, known as the "Minute Waltz." In her copy of the program, Michell identified these encores, after checking off each performed piece, one by one.

On 31 October 1891, Paderewski held a "Farewell Recital" in Brighton (Figure 8) before embarking on his first American tour. On 20 December 1893, Paderewski's final appearance in England prior to his travel to New York for the second American tour took

---

[7] Anonymous review entitled "M. Paderewski at the Dome," press clipping in *The Brighton Album*, p. 59.

place at the Hampstead Conservatoire, using an Erard piano. A note in the program explained that "this will be Mr. Paderewski LAST APPEARANCE prior to his Departure from England." Madelaine Michell did not follow him to America; instead, she collected reviews and reports, poems and interviews from the press and created a mosaic of press clippings, marked "America" on the top of each page of this section of her Album. Michel attended 50 Paderewski recitals in England and seems not to have minded hearing the same compositions over and over again. Was her focus just on what she heard? Before addressing this issue, let us unveil another aspect of her hidden identity.

Figure 10: Michell's-of-arms, inside front cover of The Brighton Album.

The inside front cover of *The Brighton Album* (Figure 10) contains a coat of arms with three swans "argent" (silver-colored) separated by a chevron, with another swan in the crest, and a Latin inscription beneath, "Moriens Modulor" ("I die singing"). This appears to be a coat of arms of Madeleine Michell, adding a personal motto of the "Swan Song" to the family coat of arms. The latter appears, as the three-swans pattern without the motto, carved on a 1610 tombstone monument of Roger Ayshford

(1534-1610) and his wife Elizabeth Michell (d. 1608) who lived at the turn of the 16th and 17th centuries. Lady Michell was the daughter of Lord Richard Michell of Sommerset.[8] Further research reveals that the ancestor of the Michell family, Lord Thomas Michell, was the owner of Wembdon Manor before 1428; a series of his successors could be named, though their direct connection to "our" Miss Michell is hard to establish, except general kinship, of the same last name and family crest.[9]

Figure 11: Coat-of-arms of Henry Francis Lyte, Wikimedia Commons.

Furthermore, we may further expand the illustrious background of Madeleine Michell, by observing a similar coat of arms on an "Ex Libris" of an Anglican clergyman and poet Henry Francis Lyte (1793-1847, see Figure 11). Here, a swan in the crest stands on a

---

[8] Information from Wikimedia Commons a photo of the monument: https://upload.wikimedia.org/wikipedia/commons/5/59/AyshfordM onument1610Burlescombe.jpg.

[9] A. P. Baggs and M. C. Siraut, 'Wembdon: Manors and other estates', in *A History of the County of Somerset: Volume 6*, ed. R W Dunning and C R Elrington (London, 1992), pp. 325-330.

trumpet, three swans argent are in-between the chevron, and the ribbon below bears a Latin motto: "Laetitia et Spe Immortalitatis" ("Joy and Hope of Immortality"). Lyte became a clergyman in 1815 and published several books of devotional poems and texts of well-known Anglican hymns, such as "Abide with me," written in 1847. Why is it relevant? While many noble families could use variants of the same coat-of-arms, the pattern with three-swans-with-chevron and one more swan on top is rare enough to be of interest and broaden the ancestral context of Madeleine Michell. Given this noble background, it is hard to believe that a scion of such an illustrious family would willingly transform herself into a silly exemplar of "Paddymania" that swept the world at the end of the 19th century. Or, perhaps, the "Paddymania" was not so silly and indicated a broader cultural phenomenon, that so far evaded the attention of cultural historians?

"Moriens Modulor"—"I die singing"—writes Madelaine Michell on her coat-of-arms. What does it mean? The "Swan Song"! Carmen Cygni. According to an ancient Greek legend,[10] widely disseminated by Western poets, swans are silent but die singing, suddenly reveling their magical, fluted voices that astound their listeners. In English literature we may find references to such dying-singing swans by Chaucer, William Shakespeare (Othello), Orlando Gibbons (madrigal *The Silver Swan*), and Alfred Lord Tennyson *(The Dying Swan)*, to mention just a few. In its most obvious cultural connotation, the "Swan Song" refers to the last, supremely beautiful work of an artist, created just before death. On a deeper, hidden ("occult") level, the phenomenon of "dying-while-singing" points to the joyous, not sorrowful, transition through death out of the valley of tears, that is the material, mortal world, into the glorious, spiritual sphere of immortality. At yet another, more esoteric level, only when an individual "dies singing," does she leave behind trivial preoccupations with the physical world for the sake of entering the spiritual domain of secret knowledge and higher levels of existence. It appears that the conduit to this transition from the material to the spiritual is through music, and particularly the music brought to life by

---

[10] Geoffrey W. Arnott, *Birds in the Ancient World from A to Z* (New York: Routledge, 2007), 182–184.

Paderewski during his piano recitals. Here, Madelaine Michell's motto of "I die singing" acquires a depth of significance.

Let me expand on the notion of exalted and sublime feelings engendered by Paderewski's performances. This idea seems to permeate the entire Brighton Album. Following the Dedication, at the beginning of the volume, Michell glued in a handwritten, untitled appreciation by F.M.C. (Figure 13):

> To Paderewski is given the transcendent genius that turns the very stones along life's way to precious gems of thought; whose gift is to find speech in dumb things, and eloquence in the ideal half of the living world; to whom sorrow is a melody and joy sweet music; to whom the humblest efforts of a humble life can furnish an immortal lyric; and in whom one thought of the divine can inspire a sublime hymn.

The pianist, a "transcendent genius" has the power to transform the quotidian into the sacred; with divine inspiration, in the process of spiritual alchemy, he creates "sweet music," "immortal lyric," and "sublime hymn" out of the dross elements and sorrows of life. These sentiments are echoed in another fascinating, hand-written poem in the Brighton Album. Entitled *Lines to Monsieur Paderewski on Hearing Him Play at the Brighton Pavilion*, it is signed with initials, "M.E.A." Apparently it was written in response to virtuoso's recital of October 1890, the first attended by Michell. In this impassioned poem, his gift of music-making, the magic of his hands on the keyboard, is seen as being "guided by a God-touched heart!" The results "sate our souls with melody / The outcome of divinest art." The enchanted listeners, while barely able to see the "marvelous movements on the keys," experience a richness of emotional and sensuous impressions: "Our mind felt storms and sudden calms / And swish of wind among the trees." But the secret is hidden elsewhere: the music, the poet notices, contains "a flash / Divine which told of hidden fires / From Heaven's altars to foretell / To men the sound of angels' lyres." Finally, a revelation emerges about the role of the musician in the grand scheme of things. Paderewski is not just a virtuoso pianist whose technical skills the listeners admire, and whose musicality touches their emotions with sorrow and joy, passion and drama. Instead, he bears a higher mission. He is "sent by God in mercy here / To raise us, free us from the sordid chains

/ Of earthly care and sorrow..." In conclusion of the third stanza, the poet praises the virtuoso pianist:

> Thou carriest the message to all hearts
> A vital spark to kindle into life
> The finer instincts of our human kind
> And strengthen, help us, in our earthly strife!

Clearly, the purpose of performing classical music is not just artistic, or aesthetic. Far more important is the fact that the art of sound has a spiritual function of raising human thoughts and emotions to the level of divine inspiration. This is, perhaps, what New Age aficionados these days would call "raising the vibration" for the purpose of "spiritual ascension."[11] After all, "following Paderewski" to a multitude of his concerts and listening to the music with intense attention and utter delight meant being true to oneself, even if the choices based on that truth result in being stigmatized or rejected as an unhinged "Paddymaniac," by society that adhered to narrow social norms of propriety and prudence.

In this light, it is worthwhile to revisit the Album's *Dedication*. The quote paraphrases a fragment from "The Motto," a poem written in the 17th century by Abraham Cowley (1618-1667):

> But you have climbed the mountain top-there sit
> On the calm, flourishing head of it;
> And whilst with wearied steps we upward go,
> See Us and Clouds below.

The transformed version (with "found" instead of "climbed") comes from Chapter XII of Night & Morning, a phenomenally popular novel by British writer, Edward Bulwer-Lytton (1803-1873). Published in multiple editions throughout the second half

---

[11] There are many "gurus" in the ascension movement, e.g., David Wilcox, *The Ascension Mysteries. Revealing the Cosmic Battle between Good and Evil* (New York Penguin Random House, 2017). Earlier predecessors include "RA" a mysterious cosmic being, channeled by Carla Rueckert in four volumes of *The Ra Material: The Law of One, Books I-IV* by James A. McCarty Don Elkins, Carla Rueckert (Whitford Press, 1984). and most notably the teaching of Ascended Masters imparted by Godfre Ray King (pseudonym of Ray Ballard, the founder of the St. Germain Foundation and the I AM Activity), *Unveiled Mysteries* (Chicago: St. Germain Press, 1935), and *The Magic Presence* (reprint, 1989).

of the nineteenth century, it appeared in 1841, 1848, 1850, 1859, 1869, 1873, 1878, 1891, and more.[12] The novel's concerns itself with social justice, moral choices, and class distinctions; on the surface it has little to do with spiritual enlightenment, however, the underlying notion does.

Cowley's original poem starts with a Latin motto, "Tentanda via est..." (the path must be taken") and a question: "What shall I do to be forever known, / And make the age to come my own?" The poet rejects Gold and Fame for the sake of Love that alone ensures reaching the mountain's top: "But you have climbed the mountain's top..." Please note, in the Bulwer-Lytton version of this line, the replacement of "climbed"—that is conquering something already known, by "found"—that is discovering the unknown. In mainstream Christian traditions of Catholic and Anglican churches, the spiritual "summit" is to be climbed, since the revelation is already known and the secret has been revealed and described in the Bible—the Gospels, the Apostolic Letters, or the *Apocalypsis*. The faithful have to exert their efforts, follow the known path, and imitate Christ to reach the summit via the way of humility, self-sacrifice and unerring quest for Divine Love.[13]

Figure 12: A Paderewski souvenir—a music fragment from Fantaisie Polonaise, *Op. 19, with Paderewski's signature.*

---

[12] Information about multiple editions of this novel is gleaned from Worldcat.org, the catalogue of world libraries.

[13] See, for instance, *The Imitation of Christ* by Thomas a Kempis, written in the 15th century, phenomenally popular in Christian spiritual circles; in 2025, WorldCat.org lists over 5,000 different editions of this classic.

In contrast, the spiritual revelation or enlightenment "found" on the summit in the version by Bulwer-Lytton is hidden and must be individually discovered by each seeker, following a path of coded messages that they perceive and decipher on their own. It appears that one of the keys unlocking the hidden domains of revelation and giving the seeker access to the Divine is classical music.

Paderewski, by being addressed in the quote in Dedication as "you" who already "found" the secret and is seated, alone, on the mountaintop, the virtuoso musician is transformed into a spiritual Master. Through musical talent, strength of character, and pristine moral values, he ascended and calmly rests on the peak, while his audiences must still climb up to his level... In this interpretation, the pianist's performances bring to the listeners messages from the divine realm of peace and enlightenment. He is the Teacher, Master, Divine Messenger. In a word: an Archangel (as discussed in Essay 2).

Thus, we can conclude that the "Paddymaniacs," obsessively following Paderewski from city to city, from concert to concert, were not acting out of juvenile infatuation and romantic fasci-nation with the charismatic celebrity. Instead, they engaged in a quest for spiritual enlightenment, wherein the seekers of spiri-tual, esoteric knowledge followed the Master in ascension via the Divine path of music. The concert hall was a Temple. Seen in this light, the cult of Paderewski had a spiritual dimension: the purpose was not selfish, emotional gratification with imaginary romance. It was the raising the human spirit to the level of the Divine, taking the music route straight to Heaven. The musician was the listeners' Master, Guide, and Guru, leading his faithful adherents on this sacred quest.

These types of sentiments were expressed in reference to Paderewski's music-making on both sides of the Atlantic (see Essay 4). In 1891, in New York, Richard Watson Gilder wrote a poem "How Paderewski Plays" that Michell cut out and posted on a separate page, by itself, accompanied by a photo of Paderewski piano. I discussed this poem and its superlative language focusing on mystical correspondence of the senses, synaesthesia, and the cosmic ascension imagery in my previous studies (Essays 1 and 2). At that time, I thought that such exalted sentiments were rare and considered the topic of this poem unique. Subsequently, I found many similar poems in the Paderewski Archive in Warsaw, all inspired by the search for the infinite and immortal through listening to romantic piano music.

In the Lines... by M.E.A, the spiritual role of a Messenger of Divine Revelation is assigned to Paderewski, sent to Earth to "kindle finer instincts and strengthen human kind." Apparently, thanks to its spiritual Dedication, the entire Brighton Album elevates the charismatic and inspired pianist to the level of a Spiritual Master, a benevolent, enlightened being that had already "found" the summit and now looks down from his mountaintop onto the followers, attempting to ascend to the peak. This image far transcends the idolization of the various pop stars that decades later followed the "long-haired-idol" Paderewski by giving concerts to crowds gathered at the Brighton Dome. They, alas, shifted the focus of their audiences from divine inspiration and revelation to worshiping the musicians themselves. However, a century earlier, instead of adoring the virtuoso, Michell and the poet she cites sought enlightenment through listening to music. Paderewski's career and concert tours, so meticulously documented by Michell, deserved her attention specifically because his recitals were apparitions of a "musician, sent by God, to raise us, free us..." and to carry the divine "message to all hearts."

To place this observation in a broader context, let us return to the identity of Lord Bulwer-Lytton, whose version of the Cowley quote serves as the *Dedication* to *The Brighton Album*. Bulwer-Lytton, besides being the inventor of science fiction, revealed in his writings a range of eclectic interests in the occult and spiritual enlightenment. His novel *Vril: The Power of the Coming Race* (1871) portrays spiritually, technologically, and morally superior civilization thriving inside the Earth, what is otherwise known as the kingdom of Shambhala or Agartha. The novel *Zanoni* (1842) depicts a model for the subsequent charitable, generous, and immortal Masters, to whose ranks Paderewski seemed to have been raised. Zanoni features references to occult knowledge of the Rosicrucians, the search for immortality, and other esoteric topics.[14] The main character became immortal in Babylonian times, but returned to Earth during the French Revolution, sacrificing his life on the guillotine for the sake of love.

Helena P. Blavatsky (1831-1891), the founder of the Theosophy movement, was inspired by these two novels in developing her concept of Masters or "Mahatmas"—that were later called Ascended Masters, the immortal teachers of humanity.[15] Annie Besant (1847-1933) who converted to Theosophy in 1889, spread these ideas in England, where the movement soon accumulated tens of thousands of adherents. Blavatsky's emphasis on altruism and self-sacrificing work for the welfare of others was exemplified in the life of many spiritual Masters that she identified and wrote about in two volumes of The Secret Doctrine (1888), and other books.

She also highly valued classical music as a tool for spiritual enlightenment, and herself had musical background. Before World War I, in the period that the Brighton Album was assembled, some Theosophists were composers or musicians (Helena Blavatsky, Edmond Bailly, Cyril Scott, and Benjamin Britten). Other composers sought inspiration in certain aspects of Theosophy, occult or esoteric beliefs (Richard Wagner, Alexander Scriabin, Gustave Holst, Luigi Russolo, and Eric Satie).[16] Did these beliefs also provide the conceptual framework

---

[14] H. T. Edge, "The Occult Novels of Bulwer-Lytton," *The Theosophical Forum* (July 1938). Reprinted on the website of the Theosophical Society, reviewed in November 2025.

[15] The term "Ascended Masters" was introduced by Baird T. Spalding in 1924 in *Life and Teachings of the Masters of the Far East* (DeVorss and Co.). It was popularized by Godfre Ray King (Guy Ballard) the founder of the St. Germain Foundation, especially in *Unveiled Mysteries* (1935).

[16] Names of composers and information about about music and Theosophy found in "Music, Theosophy, And," in the *Theosophy World Encyclopedia*, www.theosophy.world/encyclopedia/music-theosophy-and; see also "Theosophy and Music," in *Theosophy and Art* (7 Nov. 2019). theosophyart.org/2019/11/07/theosophy-and-music. For general context, see Joscelyn Godwin, *Harmonies of Heaven and Earth. The Spiritual Dimension of Music from Antiquity to the Avant-Garde* (London: Thames & Hudson, 1987); Joscelyn Godwin, *The Theosophical Enlightenment* (Albany: State University of New York Press, 1994).

for Madeleine Michell in her focus on Paderewski? Without any biographical knowledge, we cannot ascertain that she belonged to Theosophical groups, nor that she was directly inspired by any particular Theosophical writings. Nonetheless, the commonality of values and characteristics assigned to Paderewski by her in key elements in the Brighton Album dedicated to the great pianist and similar values and traits assigned to Great Masters in Theosophy give us something to think about and explore.

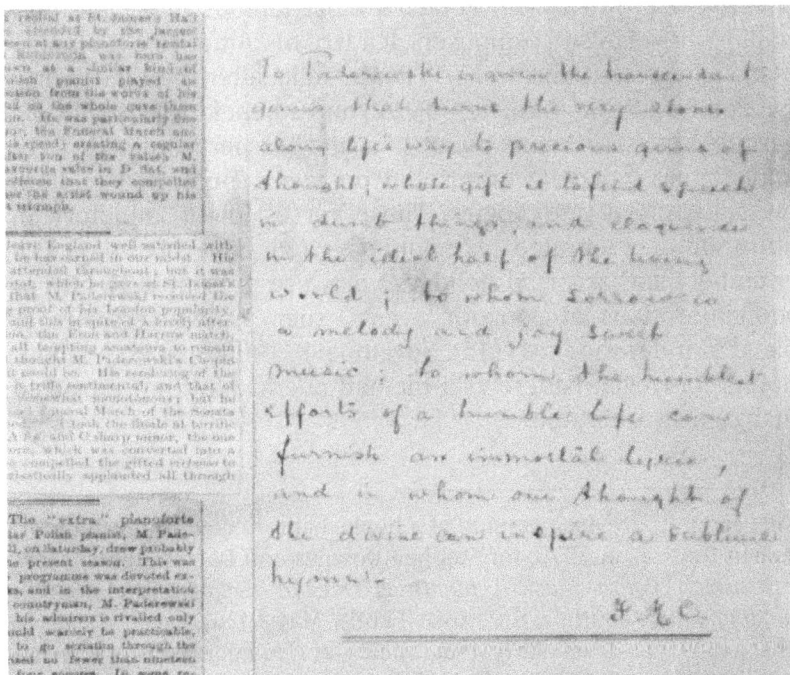

Figure 13. Manuscript of an appreciation by F.M.C. on p. 7 in The Brighton Album.

Essay 4.
Virtuoso, Seraph, Patriot, Immortal:
Poetic Portraits of Paderewski

Maja Trochimczyk[1]

It is not surprising that so many poets wrote tributes to Ignacy Jan Paderewski (1860-1941), Poland's most famous musician after Chopin[2]—a pianist, composer, leader of American Polonia,[3] Poland's representative to Paris Peace Talks after the First World War, Poland's Prime-Minister (1919) and a benefactor of multiple charitable causes. Poems about him and his performances were handwritten, typed in, or printed on flyers, published in both newspapers and anthologies. These verses, often laudatory in nature, often celebrated his name-days (31 July), birthdays (18 November) and assorted holidays,[4] or were presented to him as commemorations of patriotic events, such as anniversaries of Poland's independence (11 November). Unlike poetry about Chopin,[5] however, Paderewski-themed poems have not attracted much critical attention.[6]

---

[1] This essay is a revised version of a book chapter commissioned by Dr. Stephen Downes in 2023, for Stephen Downes and Daniel Elphick, eds., *Constructing Polish Musical Identities Outside Poland Since 1880 – Sounding 'Polish'* (Suffolk, UK: Boydell Press, May 2026).

[2] His most recent scholarly biographies are Małgorzata Perkowska-Waszek, *Paderewski i jego twórczość* (Kraków: PWM, 2010, in Polish) and Adam Zamoyski's *Paderewski* (New York: Atheneum, 1982, in English).

[3] Mieczysław B. Biskupski, "Paderewski as Leader of American Polonia, 1914-1918," *Polish American Studies* 43:1 (1986).

[4] Helena Paderewska, *Paderewski: The Struggle for Polish Independence (1910–1920)*, Ilias Chrissochoidis, ed. (Stanford: Stanford U. Press, 2015).

[5] Maja Trochimczyk, *Chopin with Cherries: A Tribute in Verse* (Los Angeles: Moonrise Press, 2010), "Chopin in Polish American Poetry: Lost Country, Found Beauty," *Polish American Studies* 67: 2 (2011); Irena Poniatowska, *Chopin w poezji* (Warsaw: NIFC, 2020).

[6] Maja Trochimczyk, "Paderewski in Poetry: Master of Harmonies or Poland's Savior?," *Polish Music Journal* 4:1 (2001), with an Appendix of poems and speeches from the Celebration of the 10th Anniversary of

The main focus of this essay will rest on selections from a set of sixty-six poems located in the Archiwum Akt Nowych (AAN, Archive of Modern Records) in Warsaw, Poland.[7] This poetry collection is a part of the Archiwum Ignacego Jana Paderewskiego 1880-1940 (Ignace Jan Paderewski Archive 1880-1940, henceforth "Paderewski Archive") that was donated to the AAN after Paderewski"s death. These documents included hundreds of poems in Polish, English, French, German and Italian. The poems are dated between 1882 and 1940, with penciled-in pagination on manuscripts, typewritten or typeset pages. They were organized alphabetically by the poet's last name. Of the English-language poems, thirty-one were by female poets, twenty-six by male poets, and nine anonymous. There are 40 poems from this collection in the present volume, accompanied by 12 more from diverse sources, especially *To Ignace Jan Paderewski: Artist, Patriot, Humanitarian* (1928), containing tributes to the architect of Poland's independence, written by numerous poets, activists and politicians on the occasion of the tenth anniversary of the country's regained sovereignty.[8]

These American, British, Scottish, Irish and Australian poets, writing in English, created a diversity of labels for the pianist. He was a "great master" (Ester Jacoby Merrill) "sent by God" (M.E.A.), the "enchanter of a human soul" (Mary Francis Crosby), the "magician of thousand themes" (Josephine), "master, the interpreter, the giant soul" (Lucia Clark Markham), or "master, genius" (A. F. Bates). Yet, he was also described as "a lonely tragic figure" (Jessica H. Lowell), "scarred seraph" (Elva V. Williams), a "son of a martyred race" (Robert Underwood Johnson), "the most loyal son of Poland" (Ben P. Keith), a "dauntless fighter for Poland's right" (Adolphe de Castro), and "this Great Genius – Soul of Poland"

Poland's Independence, reprinted from *To Paderewski: Artist, Patriot, Humanitarian* (New York: The Kosciuszko Foundation, 1928).

[7] The Archiwum Ignacego Jana Paderewskiego 1860-1940 (Paderewski Archive) in the Archiwum Akt Nowych (Archive of Modern Records) in Warsaw consists of 5,275 items from 1861-1941. Poems studied in this essay are in the folder signature 2/100/0/8/3763, *Wiersze dedykowane I. J. Paderewskiemu* (Poems dedicated to I. J. Paderewski).

[8] *To Ignace Jan Paderewski: Artist, Patriot, Humanitarian* (New York: The Kościuszko Foundation, 1928).

(William Kimberly Palmer). At the end of Paderewski's virtuoso career, the praise heaped upon him became even more extravagant, as he was raised to the rank of an "Immortal" (Palmer and James H. Cousins) and a "great Master of the Harmonies" (Charles Phillips). Poets claimed that "this man so great and true" (Josephine Rita Sargeant), was "superb, this uncrowned sovereign" (Juliet C. Olin). He was "piano's greatest bard" (Will George Butler), but also the "poet, dreaming dreams impearled" (Ernest Powell), "the master of sublimity" (Windsor V. Richberg), and the "way-shower, prophet, winged king" (Dorothy Hull Beatty).

Figure 1: M. Paderewski at the Pianoforte, giving his last recital at St. James Hall, before leaving for America. Drawing by H. M. Paget, The Graphic, *Saturday, 17 December 1892.*

These labels followed the stages of Paderewski's career, as known in the English-language world: a young, charismatic virtuoso on tour since 1890 through the outbreak of the First World War in

1914; a passionate patriot, giving hundreds of concerts and lectures to raise funds and support for the Polish cause, first for the war victims then for the country's independence (1914-1918); a diplomat and politician, the new country's President of the Council of Ministers and the Minister of Foreign Affairs in 1919; and, again, a master pianist, but also a celebrated philanthropist, and someone who selflessly liberated his country, a "modern immortal" raised high above the common crowd (after his return to the concert stages in 1922, on tour through the late 1930s).[9]

Poems sent to Paderewski may be divided into several groups of distinct yet related subject matter. The majority are portraits of the idealized Paderewski, with his last name in the title (and occasionally added qualifiers). Seven poems bear the title *Paderewski*, by Myrtle E. Cone, Ina Coolbrith, Dorothy Dudley, Jessica H. Lowell, Kate Slaughter McKinney, Josephine Rita Sargeant, and Elisabeth Tousey. Additional two poems add to the titles the pianist's given names: verse by E. A. Paulenton and Procter. Some poetic portraits feature superlative complements in their titles: *The Maestro* (Juliet C. Olin), *Great Master* (Ester Jacoby Merrill), *Genius* (Dorothy Hull Beatty), or the *Immortal* (William Kimberly Palmer). Another set of eleven poems addresses the virtuoso directly, *To Paderewski*: two anonymous poems plus verse by Mary Francis Crosby, John Huston Finley, Ernest Powell, and Elva W. Williams. Here, too, additional qualifiers occur: "Patriot" (Robert Underwood Johnson) or "Sovereign—Pianist" (two sonnets by A. F. Bates).

The majority of poems are penned by Paderewski's listeners, filled with admiration for the virtuoso pianist after hearing his interpretations of great classics. They sometimes name the specific location and recital in the title (*Lines to Monsieur Paderewski on Hearing Him Play at the Brighton Pavilion* signed by M.E.A. in 1890, *Paderewski Plays at Lausanne Cathedral* by James H. Cousins in 1928).[10] At other times, the location and date is given in the poem's

---

[9] Charles Phillips, *Paderewski: The Story of a Modern Immortal* (New York: McMillan, 1933).
[10] The first poem is in the *Brighton Album* discussed in Essay No.3, the second on p. 21 in AAN Paderewski Archive. Due to large number of quotation marks in poetic quotes, the titles of poems will be spelled in italics.

introductory note: a sonnet was "written on hearing a concert given by Paderewski" by Alice Averill Johnson.[11] Jessica H. Lowell penned *Paderewski* after attending his recital during "the dedication of Beechwood Playhouse, Scarborough, N.Y. January 12, 1917."[12] Poets described the virtuoso's mysterious appearance on the stage and expressed their shifting impressions, emotions, and visions, aroused by a particular composition, resounding from under his fingers. For instance, two poems praise the pianist's renditions of sonatas by Ludwig van Beethoven: *Paderewski Plays the Moonlight Sonata* (Arthur Bryant) and *Sonata Appassionata* (Lucia Clark Markham).[13] Finally, poets sought to capture in the most general terms the magical, uplifting, and spiritual experiences of hearing Paderewski in concert: *Impressions of a Paderewski Recital* (Anonymous), *Lines to an Artist [1] (I.J.P.) on His Playing* (A.B.), *When Paderewski Plays* (two poems, by Flora Fain Crist and Windsor V. Richberg) and *How Paderewski Plays* (Richard Watson Gilder).

A separate category may be assigned to poems, often humorous, about quotidian matters: his hair that a bird wishes to nest in (Grantland Rice), the demise of the pianist's dog (Jean Hennepin Render), or the virtuoso's concert travels (*When 'Padi' Comes to Town* by George W. Hootman).[14] These rhymed ditties belong in the artistic sphere of a caricature, ridiculing the pianist for the sake of readers' amusement. Finally, the selected poem in the present volume feature a sample of poems sent to Paderewski that were not about him, but about topics their authors wished to share with the great musician: the all-encompassing, divine essence of music (Berton Bellis), the meaning of Chopin's *Berceuse* (William Struthers) or the suffering and resurrection of the oppressed Poland (Adolphe de Castro and Anthony Zaleski).[15] These authors

---

[11] Alice Averill Johnson, *A Sonnet,* typescript written in Elizabeth, New Jersey, n.d., AAN Poems, p. 61. See also anonymous *Impressions of a Paderewski Recital*, typescript of 1925, AAN Poems, p. 304.

[12] Jessica H. Lowell, *Paderewski,* AAN Poems, p. 103.

[13] In AAN Paderewski Poems, Bryant's is on p. 6, Markham's on p. 115.

[14] In AAN Paderewski Poems: Rice, *When Paderewski Came to Town*, p. 175; Render, *To Paderewski's Dog,* p. 175, George W. Hootman, p. 57.

[15] In AAN Paderewski Poems: *I Am Music* by Bellis, p. 4; *The Last Pure Chords of a Chopin "Berceuse"* by Struthers, p. 197, *Polonia Resurgata* by

took time to type, dedicate, and send their work to the Maestro. Such poems provide a context for Paderewski-themed verse.

In terms of form, poems are mostly rhymed and in stanzas: some have two short stanzas (Myrtle E. Cone, Sara Groenevelt, Halka, Ernest Powell), some—three four-line stanzas (Kate Slaughter McKinney, Dorothy Hull Beatty), and some are longer ballads (anonymous *A Scotch Tribute* and creations of Will George Butler and Elizabeth Tousey). There is a sizeable number of sonnets, penned by A. F. Bates (probably Katharine Lee Bates), Arthur Bryant, Ina Coolbrith, Alice May Moir, and Elva W. Williams. Poets use diverse variants of rhyme and meter, but rarely free verse.

In this body of poems, Paderewski and his music are considered from several distinct points of view:

1. Paderewski, the *virtuoso* musician of incomparable technique, profound musicality, and broad repertoire of Chopin, Beethoven, Liszt, Schubert and Schumann.
2. Paderewski, the consummate *musician* whose vast range of sonorities and emotions evoke in listeners colorful visions of nature, mythical scenes, or cosmic beauty.
3. Paderewski, the *archangel*, or *seraph*, bringing to Earth divine beauty to enchant and uplift his audiences through the shifting energies of sound.
4. Paderewski, the tireless *patriot* whose personal sacrifices and efforts restored Poland's independence.
5. Paderewski, the *immortal* whose performances are not just musical, but spiritual, as they open the gates of Heaven and lead the faithful listeners into enlightenment.

First, the *virtuoso pianist*—greatly appreciated by poets with extensive musical training and musicality, though not necessarily with particular literary talents. Elizabeth Tousey's ballad, for instance, painstakingly enumerates Paderewski's career stages, favorite composers, and even the years of work that earned him success:

> He played in Paris and New York, / Berlin and many cities more,
> The great pianist was the talk / Of music lovers the world o'er.

---

de Castro, p. 11, and *Poland's Resurrection* by Zaleski, pages 280-282.

Interpretation is his field —/ Bach, Beethoven, Schumann, Liszt
Their divinest treasures yield / To his skill of hand and wrist.

"How easy," was the comment made / Of one of Chopin's preludes given, / "Yes, easy" Paderewski said, / "After seven years I've striven."

Poets mentioned Paderewski's performances of Chopin and Beethoven. A. F. Bates wrote a pair of sonnets *To Paderewski— Sovereign—Pianist.* Apparently, the poet's name with initials was a pseudonym of Katharine Lee Bates (1859-1929), the celebrated author of *America, the Beautiful,* one of the most beloved patriotic songs of the U.S. Bates was a graduate and later a professor of English literature at Wellesley College in Massachusetts. She published over 20 books of poetry, essays, and research studies.[16] Her two Paderewski sonnets display her erudition and her mastery of form and meter. The first sonnet is dedicated to the purely musical aspects of the pianist's performances, the second is a consideration of their spiritual dimensions. In the former, the poet delights the reader with the sonnet's intricate flow and her knowledge of the complex relationship between a composer and a performer that brings to life their written compositions:

I bow to thee, incomparable Pole
Thou art a flawless glass wherein we scan
The melancholy which we call Chopin,
Beethoven passionate, tumultuous soul
They cannot die, no bells for them shall knoll.

The second sonnet by Bates seeks to answer the question about the source of such performative magic, wherein Paderewski's interpretations of Chopin transcend angelic music of "far heaven:"

Let me not call on angels for thy peer,
Cry out to some far heaven, vainly scan
The firmament to match thy clear
Soul-sounding deep-sea music; let Chopin
Be thy great harp and Israfel shall fear
Thy mastery, he, a seraph, thou a man.

---

[16] Melinda M. Ponder, *Katharine Lee Bates: From Sea to Shining Sea* (Chicago: Windy City Publishers, 2017)

A daughter of a Congressional minister, Bates was steeped in Christian tradition, but whether the views on music's spirituality expressed in this sonnet go beyond the dogma remains uncertain. What we may be sure about is the heavenly pairing of Paderewski with Chopin that utterly delights the listener.

In a report from Paderewski's recital at the Lausanne Cathedral in 1928, Irish-Indian poet, writer, and philosopher James H. Cousins lists composers whose work the pianist played: "He talks through Schumann's beauty, Chopin's tears, /Beethoven's quiet and the storm of Liszt..." Overall, Fryderyk Chopin's name appears in seven English-language poems about Paderewski, though for some poets, like Dorothy Dudley, Chopin is merely a sign of suffering "Polishness," not pure musicality. Ludwig van Beethoven caught the attention of six poets; besides Bates and Cousins, he was mentioned by Bryant, Butler, Markham, and Tousey. These "mentions" encompass two poems inspired by Beethoven's Piano Sonatas: "Moonlight" in C-sharp minor, Op. 27, No. 2—admired by Arthur Bryant and "Appassionata" in F minor, Op. 57 that caught the attention of Lucia Clark Markham. Franz Liszt, whose rousing Hungarian Rhapsodies often served as the grand finales or encores at Paderewski's recitals, was mentioned three times (Butler, Cousins, Tousey). Franz Schubert delighted Bates and Cousins, while Robert Schumann was noticed by Cousins and Tousey.

Of Paderewski's compositions, The Minuet in G major, Op. 14, No. 1 was listed twice, by Butler and Tousey. The latter, in her didactic tour through the virtuoso's own works mentioned the Polish Fantasy in G-sharp minor, Op. 19 (1891-93); a Fugue and Variations (either Variations and Fugue in A minor, Op. 11, or in E-flat minor, Op. 23), the piano cycle Voyager (i.e., *Chants du voyageur*, Op. 8 of 1882) and the opera *Manru* (1901). The inclusion of such copious detail does not make for a great poem, nor is it an indication of the poet's affinity for the musical gifts of the pianist-composer. For this, we must turn to a poem that mention his "tired, orchestral hands" and explores the most fanciful vocabulary in a portrayal of the most unique musical experience. Here's the conclusion of Elva W. Williams's *To Paderewski. A Sonnet*:

> Hush, what frenzy those learned hands do phrase,
> That fecundates the circumambient air,
> With absinthian, voluptuous despair,

Then, — onward the delirious fancy strays,
In labyrinth of loveliness delays,
In misty lands obscure, a region where
Exquisiteness is orthodox, — not rare.
Wan face above the black piano raised.

Williams' sonnet is unparalleled in the richness of its language, yet visions of Paderewski's masterly hands bringing miracles of sound into the concert hall are not rare: such images are evoked by 15 poets. Here, Williams herself led the way: "from this ebon wood, this sonant loom, / Your hands pluck out such precious, poised, complaint." Josephine Rita Sargeant (*Paderewski,* 1923) expresses a bewilderment with the magical power of the virtuoso's hands and a delight to hear "From the instrument beloved,/ Guided by his master's hand, / Delicate, forceful tones, / Obeying his commands." Windsor V. Richberg (*When Paderewski Plays,* 1934) focuses on the sonorous outcome of the pianist's actions: "His hand he raises from the key / To guide the wafted melody, / And from the taut, vibrating string / Ethereal voices call and sing." Finally, in another take at describing what happens *When Paderewski Plays*, Will George Butler cites an extravagant quotation from a music critic Henry Krehbiel of the *Chicago Tribune* in his description of beauteous sonorities brought into the concert hall by the Maestro:

> The concert grand beneath his spell / Responds to every thrill
> Vibrating in the master's hand, / Commanded by his will.

> His tones of beauty sensuous, / Flow rich in melodies,
> *Ecstatic halleluiahs and / In harping symphonies.*

After ascertaining how the music is made, poets move on to describing the sonorous beauty that often leads them on flight of fancy, so instead of listening they are imagining scenes of a "knight in silver plume bedecked" on a black steed (Mary Francis Crosby, *To Paderewski*) or visualizing the serenity of a countryside, as in the continuation of her poem:

> The simple country in the joyous time of spring,
> The happy glades with apple blossoms gleam,
> A summers night when e'ven the heavens sing.

Crosby's undated poem, *To Paderewski*, expresses her longing to hear him play and conjures up an array of fanciful images evoked during the concert, as if the Maestro performed descriptive, program music.[17] Yet, she does not miss the spiritual aspects of music, when she considers the secret of the pianist's allure: "What mystic charm thou hast with thee / Thou enchanter of a human soul." Similarly to Crosby, poet Myrtle E. Cone from Sioux Falls, North Dakota (*Paderewski*), responds to the pianist's recital in Minneapolis with impressions of sunlight, spring rain, snow-capped mountains, and a tender lullaby.[18] She perceives the charms of all seasons while listening to the virtuoso's recital:

> Sunlight dancing on the leaves,
> Spring rain dripping from the eaves,
> Snow-capped mountains towering heights,
> A mother's tender lullaby —
> When Paderewski plays.

The range of natural sounds associated with music heard during a piano recital by Ms. Cone encompasses "A brooklet tinkling on its way, / The mighty ocean's surge and sway..." All that is delightful in nature ("jewels flashing in the sun") is contained in sounds of the piano. In yet another example of poets' tendency to visualize the music, after hearing the pianist in Montgomery, Alabama, in January 1924, Kate Slaughter McKinney (1859 –1939) observes: "His face — the home of sorrow / His heart — Heaven's half, / And when his hands caress the keys / I hear a dryad laugh."[19] Today, we tend to think that here is a certain childishness and immaturity in using visual and synaesthetic language when describing abstract music. But more than a century ago, such youthful exuberance was common among amateur poets, enamored of Paderewski and zealously frequenting his concerts.

George Warren Hootman's humorous ditty *When 'Padi' Comes to Town* (written in 1920s) speculates what "the people sit and marvel" about when "He comes in regal fashion / This king in music

---

[17] Mary Francis Crosby, *To Paderewski*, signed typescript, no date, AAN Poems, p. 23.

[18] Myrtle E. Cone, *Paderewski*, poem in a newsprint clipping dated Minneapolis May 6, glued onto p. 13 of AAN Poems, with handwritten note, addressed in North Dakota, dated 15 April 1924.

[19] Kate Slaughter McKinney, *Paderewski*, manuscript on letterhead, AAN Poems, p. 116. She wrote under a pseudonym Katydid, published four books and in 1931 became Poet Laureate of Alabama. F. E. Willard, and M. A. R. Livermore, *A Woman of the Century* (Buffalo, 1893), 488.

grand."[20] Apparently, as he observes, the content of Paderewski's recitals is primarily spiritual. The audiences enjoy "The melodies of heaven / That come pouring out of him"—while angels are jealous of their blessings. At the end, the poet pauses to wonder why "This music wizard leads me / From the earth up to the sky."

Figure 2:. Portrait of Paderewski by Laurence Alma-Tadema, ca. 1892

For some reason, women were particularly susceptible to perceiving this heavenly content of Paderewski's recitals. As Hootman quipped: "It is said of Paderewski / When his charming music flows / That it hypnotizes women." Myrtle E. Cone, for instance, envisioned a clear path of spiritual ascension through music. In my earlier study of "an Archangel at the piano" (Essay 2), I focused on this phenomenon of female adulation, cultivated and amplified with Paderewski's golden-haired, "angelic" image—developed with the assistance of Polish actress, Helena Modjeska, 1840-1909), and her British and American friends. To recap: At the outset of his tours, Paderewski was portrayed by painters Edward Burne-Jones and Lawrence Alma Tadema in London as an other-

[20] Poem written by George Warren Hootman in the 1920s in Salinas, Kansas, but typed on 19 April 1931, AAN Poems, p. 57.

worldly *archangel*.[21] He was later described as such by American poets Ina Coolbrith, Sara Groenevelt, and Richard Watson Gilder. The most popular of the images was by the pre-Raphaelite Burne-Jones, showing the pianist in profile, with a storm of golden-red hair—the halo of an "Archangel," as the artist called his model.[22]

Richard Watson Gilder (1844-1909),[23] a friend of actress Helena Modjeska, and Paderewski's New York host during his first years of concert tours in America,[24] described the Pole's pianistic talents in *How Paderewski Plays* (1891). In this extended simile, Gilder brings up a range of synaesthetic comparisons of music with natural and cosmic phenomena, from dew drops and storm-clouds to aurora borealis. An astounding assemblage of similes ends with a peculiar conclusion, that "the great master" might have been a medium, channeling

> some disembodied spirit which had rushed
> From silence into singing; and had crushed
> Into one startled hour a life's felicity,
> And highest bliss of knowledge—that all life, grief, wrong,
> Turn at the last to beauty and to song!

After the "sweet singer of California," Ina Coolbrith (1841-1928), a poet active in the San Francisco Bay Area,[25] heard the virtuoso

---

[21] Edward Burne-Jones (1833-1898) and Sir Lawrence Alma-Tadema (1836-1912) were among British artists that Modjeska befriended in 1881-1882; they painted "angelic" portraits of Paderewski in 1890. See Modjeska, *Memories*, 428-433.

[22] See Paderewski's portraits in Essay 2. The anecdote of Burne-Jones's random street encounter with an "Archangel" was countered in Paderewski's memoirs, *The Paderewski Memoirs*, by Paderewski and Mary Lawton (New York, 1938), 176-77.

[23] Herbert F. Smith, *Richard Watson Gilder* (New York, 1970). Arthur John, *The Best Years of the Century: Richard Watson Gilder, Scribner's Monthly, and the Century Magazine, 1870-1909* (Urbana, 1981).

[24] Adam Zamoyski, *Paderewski, op. cit.*, 101, 104; Richard Watson Gilder, *Letters*, Rosamond Gilder, ed. (New York, 1916), 216.

[25] Ina Coolbrith, *Paderewski*, printed poem with a handwritten dedication dated 8 April 1900, AAN Poems, p. 15. See Edward Jewitt Wheeler, and Frank Crane, "American Poets of To-Day: Ina Coolbrith," *Current Opinion* 28:1 (April 1900), 16–17.

(presumably in San Francisco in 1900), she captured the performance's impact in her poem, *Paderewski*:

> So here — from what great star, divinely crowned? —
>> Rapt in whose ecstasy of perfect sound
>> Each ivory key becomes a living thing
> Aeolian murmurs of a mystic dream
> The gathering tempest mighty thunder-roll
>> A sob, a shivering sight, just breathed, and mute
>> Strife, triumph, rapture, peace of Heaven supreme —
> All, all are his, the Master's...

For Coolbrith, Paderewski was a messenger sent forth by "The stars that sang in Time's awakening" to continue the musical mission of "David with his magic string" and become "twin soul of Israfel"—the Islamic Archangel of music that played the trumpet at the Last Judgement. Coolbrith did not shy away from such displays of erudition. After all, she was the Oakland City Librarian, and the first Poet Laureate of California.[26]

A similar, romanticized language permeated *To Paderewski*, penned in 1892 by Sara Groenevelt (1842-1899), a pianist who studied at the Leipzig Conservatory of Music in Germany and performed Ignaz Moscheles's Piano Concerto with the composer conducting the Gewandhous. Groenevelt was a poet and prolific writer, publishing under various male pseudonyms. Paderewski's 1892 New York concert inspired her somewhat plodding rhyme: "Thy fingers skilled upon the heartstrings play / While smiles and tears their changeful mood obey, /The soul's impassioned language they translate / And its weird poesy articulate."[27]

Like Groenevelt, the majority of Paderewski's female fans were trained pianists, including Madeleine Michell of Brighton, U.K. who attended dozens of Paderewski's English concerts and assembled

---

[26] Coolbrith may have met Modjeska who debuted in San Francisco in 1877, prior to writing her tribute to Paderewski. Both Coolbrith and Modjeska were included in Rockwell D. Hunt, "Great Women of California," *The Historical Society of Southern California Quarterly* 31:3 (1949), 197-211 and in his 104 profiles of eminent Californians, *California's Stately Hall of Fame* (Stockton, 1950).

[27] *To Paderewski* was written in cursive after 3 February 1892 concert; AAN Poems, pp. 48-49.

a massive album of souvenirs, clippings, reviews, concert tickets into a detailed documentation of his U.K. concert tours of 1890-98 (see Essay 3). The album includes *Lines to Monsieur Paderewski, after his Performance at the Brighton Pavilion*, by an unknown "M.E.A," who was delighted with the exquisite musicianship of the Polish pianist: "And this the human hand can do, / When guided by a God-touched heart! / Could sate our souls with melody / The outcome of divinest art." In the midst of emotional turmoil evoked in the music, she noticed "a flash Divine" of "hidden fires from Heaven's altars" and "the sound of angels' lyres." Then, she observed that the musician was "Sent by God in mercy here / To raise us, free us from the sordid chains / Of earthly care and sorrow." The poet concluded that the real purpose of playing classical music was to lead audiences on their spiritual ascent.

It is not hard to find more instances of such elevated language in other poems, raising Paderewski to the level of a spiritual master or a divine messenger. Arthur Bryer wrote in a brief reflection, *Lines to an Artist (I. J. P.) On his Playing*, that both the pianist and his performances give the listeners "A brief glimpse of heaven / ... / An ideal world dawning..."[28]

Writing on 2 March 1897, Rosa Lenkoff described dramatic, sonic power of orchestras and storms, concluding that it was not needed by Paderewski, for "God has bestowed upon you a gift great / to harmonize the soul and the thoughts to elevate."[29] On 12 December 1899 in New York, Alice May Moir penned a *Sonnet to Paderewski* where she envisioned the pianist as a "wondrous charmer" whose "mystic, strange" music, "holds us spellbound," and brings the "highest hope," while uplifting the audience to the "gates of joy."[30] For her, the Polish pianist's music-making is truly sublime, raising both the musician and the audience to great spiritual heights. Similarly, in a 1904 poem, Kyra (no last name) expressed her longing to hear Paderewski play and wondered:[31] "Paderewski,

---

[28] A.B. *Lines to an Artist (I. J. P.). On his playing*, manuscript, with penciled name Bryer, 6 November 1928, AAN Poems, p. 7.
[29] Final stanza of Rosa Lenkoff, *To Mr. Paderewski*, Cannes, France, manuscript, AAN Poems, p. 102.
[30] Alice May Moir, *Sonnet to Paderewski*, manuscript, AAN Poems, p. 123.
[31] Kyra, *Paderewski*, written in Sept. 1904, manuscript, AAN Poems, p. 81.

Paderewski / What supreme power is this / That hast endowed thee with such a gift / To make this heavenly music hear exist? / from the heart the soul – God's gift."

PADEREWSKI.
. . . . "The matrons flung their gloves,
Ladies and maids their scarfs and handkerchiefs."
Coriolanus, ii. 1.

Figure 3. A caricature of Paderewski's profile in the crescent moon, with a quotation from Shakespeare's tragedy Coriolanus *Act 2, Scene 1, ca. 1895. From AAN Paderewski Archive, Warsaw, Poland.*

In a farewell note to the pianist, written in Toorak, a rich Victorian suburb of Melbourne, Australia, Josephine & M. wished Paderewski, to "fare thee well" and described the pianist as a "magician of thousand themes" who "weaves the web of golden dreams"—in short, one of God's "minstrels," sent to earth for the edification of its inhabitants.[32] Paderewski played in Melbourne on

---

[32] Josephine, *Paderewski, Fare Thee Well*, manuscript on letterhead, Toorak, Australia, AAN Poems, p. 104.

9 July 1904 and on 10 May 1927; the poem appears to have been created in 1904.

Flora Fain Crist of Atlanta, Georgia,[33] collected a similarly rich assortment of imagery, mostly associated with music through onomatopoeic similarity, in a kind of "mimesis"—where the sounds of the stream, birdsong, "children's merry voices" are followed by the thundering noises of the hunt, "a whirlwind of tempestuous sound," and stillness with one "trinkle of a bell / from some distant hill."

Of interest to our survey of poetic responses to the stage persona and musical talents of Paderewski is the poets' focus on describing—in aesthetic, emotional, and spiritual terms—the impression that his performances made on them. Several poems recounted their authors' concert-going experience in detail, from the pianist's appearance on the stage, through the emotional rollercoaster of sounds and emotions, to frenetic applause and silence afterwards.

This preoccupation with the listener's individual emotional and spiritual experience was a characteristic of poetic responses to Paderewski's music-making outside of Polish and Polonian communities. Unlike their American and British counterparts, Polish emigres and Poles were singularly focused on the patriotic meaning of Paderewski's art, and his role as a dedicated Polish leader (see Essay 1). The awareness of Poland's suffering after the loss of independence in 1795 and a series of failed uprisings in 1830-31, 1848, 1863-4, was widespread in Polish-language poetry about Paderewski, but rare abroad.

Only during the first World War, after Paderewski replaced his regular concerts with lecture-recitals filled with advocacy for Poland's war victims and the country's independence, did his non-Polish audiences became fully aware of these national tragedies. The dramatic breakthrough in the way of portraying the pianist followed Paderewski's transformation of his recitals into patriotic manifestations. Notably, his attachment to the Polish cause seems to have broken Paderewski's Archangel's wings, as noticed by Eva

---

[33] Flora Fain Crist, *When Paderewski Plays*, poem in three stanzas, handwritten, dated 29 Nov. 1923, AAN Poems, pp. 18-19.

W. Williams: "Scarred seraph! Dragoman of ream so quaint, / Forlorn! You must be sweety drunk with gloom."[34] Newly acclaimed not as an archangel but a *patriot,* he turned out to be a charismatic and convincing speaker. Thanks to hundreds of lectures and fundraising events, Paderewski's English-language audiences became aware of the suffering of Poland, dismembered by partitions into Russian, Prussian and Austrian portions for over 115 years. Paderewski played a key role in this public education campaign, as his homeland's "most loyal son" (Ben P. Keith), who did not hesitate to abandon music for the sake of serving the beloved nation.

Adolphe de Castro (1859–1959), a Polish-Jewish-American poet, writer, and rabbi with a colorful career of a journalist, dentist, lawyer, and U.S. Ambassador to Spain, dedicated *Polonia Resurgata* ("Poland, resurrected") to Paderewski, "the dauntless fighter for Poland's right, / In and out of Poland."[35] In Castro's overview of Polish history, the "poor Poland" waited for a "hero to lead her to freedom" while she was still being enslaved and filled with grief. Here, we arrive at the third conceptual sphere associated with the Polish pianist in the English-language poetry, that of the *patriot.* This trope arose from Paderewski's own actions, his bravery and patriotism that resulted in abandoning a thriving music career for the sake of political advocacy.

On 13 April 1916, in Washington, D. C., Paderewski gave a recital at the National Theatre and soon after Robert Underwood Johnson (1853-1937) wrote *To Paderewski, Patriot*[36] where he described the composer as: "Son of a martyred race that long / Has honed its sorrow into song / And taught the world that grief is less / when voiced by Music's loveliness." The four-stanza poem ends with a prayer for the pianist:

> May Heaven send thee, at this hour,
> Such access of supernal power

---

34 Elva W. Williams, *To Paderewski. A Sonnet,* signed typescript, written in San Francisco, AAN Poems, p. 272.

35 Adolphe de Castro, *Polonia Resurgata*, a sonnet, undated, signed manuscript, AAN Poems, p. 11.

36 Józef Orłowski, ed., *Ignacy Jan Paderewski i odbudowa Polski*, 2 vols (Chicago, 1939-1940).

that every note beneath thy hand
May plead for thy distracted land.

Details about Poland's tragic history may be found in a poem by Ben P. Keith of San Francisco, a ten-stanza ballad entitled *Poland* and dedicated to Paderewski, "the most loyal son of Poland" as "a tribute of my admiration of your love and fidelity to poor suffering Poland."[37] The text, in four-line rhymed stanzas, describes the country's suffering under the partitions and the longing of its heroes—who were also heroes of the American Revolution—Tadeusz Kosciuszko (1746-1817) and Count Kazimierz Pułaski (1745-1779) for "The dearest dream of a come true / Their country once more free." The eighth stanza acknowledged the pianist's efforts on behalf of Poland: "They would bless you Paderewski / Artist of world-wide fame / Who has worked for suffering Poland / With heart and soul and brain." In the following stanzas, the poet directly addressed the musician: "You have moved the hearts of thousands / With the magic of your art / And sounded strains of sorrow / Through every listening heart // Until the wrongs to Poland done / Dimmed the eyes with tears."

Figure 4. Selected Pieces from the Concert Programmes of I. J. Paderewski, fragment. London Edwin Ashdown, 1915.

---

[37] Ben P. Keith, *To Ignac Jan Paderewski, the Most Loyal, Son of Poland*, signed typescript, AAN Poems, p. 73.

Paderewski's years of advocacy for Poland's independence were brought to fruition at the Paris Peace Conference ending with the Treaty of Versailles that he signed with a golden pen. His political career was crowned with the paired positions of the new country's President of the Council of Ministers and Minister of Foreign Affairs (January-December 1919). But the patriotic pianist's political career was short-lived. Following resignation, he returned to music, while continually receiving tokens of gratitude for his patriotic service. On 16 May 1928, the Kosciuszko Foundation in New York organized a ceremonial banquet in his honor, on the tenth anniversary of Poland's independence. The musician received a commemorative volume filled with letters of congratulations, speeches, and poems, *To Ignace Jan Paderewski: Artist, Patriot, Humanitarian* (this publication is discussed in Essay 1). Dr. John Huston Finley (1863-1940) filled his two poems for Paderewski with classicist erudition, references to Homer's *Iliad*, Shakespeare's *Troilus and Cressida*. and Greek myth of Orpheus and Euridice. In Finley's celebratory poem (1928), Paderewski/Orpheus was able to lead his Eurydice/Poland to freedom, addressing the pianist-statesman "But though Orpheus failed / You won. Polonia Restituta lives."[38] During the same 1928 celebration, Prof. Charles Phillips (1880-1933) of the University of Notre Dame, the author of Paderewski's biography, *The Story of a Modern Immortal* (1933),[39] recited *Paderewski and Poland*, attributing the country's resurrection to Paderewski's patriotic deeds.[40]

Writing in March 1934, William Kimberly Palmer of Massachusetts followed Phillips' lead, borrowing from Paderewski's biography the adjective "immortal" for the title of his poem seeking to capture the essence of the pianist-statesman's lifetime achievement.[41] Palmer firmly attributed the great Pole's claim of immortality to

---

[38] In Latin, "Polonia Restituta" means "rebuilt" or "restored" Poland; it is also the name of the new country's most important state honor, awarded to individuals that assisted the country on its way to freedom.

[39] Charles Phillips, *Paderewski: The Story of a Modern Immortal* (New York McMillan, 1933).

[40] Charles Phillips: *Poland and Paderewski*, copy of two handwritten pages, in *To Paderewski: Artist, Patriot, Humanitarian* (New York, 1928).

[41] William Kimberly Palmer, *Immortal, Jan Ignace Paderewski*, printed and signed page, AAN Poems, p. 141.

the restoration of Poland's independence: "This Great Genius –Soul of Poland / Did Ably lead his Race." Paderewski was, indeed, "A wonderful composer / A superb artist of renown," who gave up his musical career "to pull the tyrants down." Consequently, he "founded / A nation that will last," though surrounded by enemies, for it is "A people none can overthrow / Since God hath brought them through the woe." Paderewski gave his country a "place /Among the leading nations" and, therefore, he could be assured of centuries of acclaim "as a soul of supreme Grace." In his attribution of Paderewski's "immortality" to his political success, Palmer was a rare exception among American poets.

The theme of Paderewski's patriotic efforts in defense of Poland resurfaced after the outbreak of WWII, when the aging pianist returned to America to again advocate for his "dear unhappy land." On 24 February 1940, the *Montreal Daily Star* published a brief poem by Euphemia L. Morrison, addressing *Jan Ignace Paderewski. President of Poland National Council.*[42] "Music, sweet mistress looks for you in vain / Your country needs you and you take the helm / On perilous, uncharted seas again / exile from home, self-banished from your realm." E.A. Peterson accurately described Paderewski's abandonment of music for patriotic service in January 1940: "The Master touches not 'the harp,' / Since his loved land was overrun. / The stabbing pain was all too sharp, / And sorrow blotted out the sun."[43]

Not every poet admired the unwavering Polish focus of Paderewski, the Patriot. On 12 January 1917, the virtuoso performed for the dedication of Beechwood Playhouse in Scarborough, New York, and his recital was captured in verse (*To Paderewski*) by Jessica H. Lowell.[44] As she observed, the pianist on the stage became a

> ...lonely, tragic figure
> Only as true genius ever is

---

[42] Euphemia L. Morrison, *Jan Ignace Paderewski. President of Poland's National Council,* clipping from the *Montreal Daily Star,* 24 Feb. 1924, AAN Poems, p. 124.

[43] Einar Atair Paulanton (pen name of E.A. Peterson), *Ignace Paderewski (1940),* typescript, 26 Jan. 1940, AAN Poems, p. 145.

[44] Jessica H. Lowell, *Paderewski,* press clipping from *The Club Candle,* 1917, AAN Poems, p. 103.

Tragic with sorrows weightier than his own
Grave — with intense devotion to ideals
A man of men and a musician rare,
Filed with the sacred flame.

Aware of Paderewski's dedication to the suffering Poland, the poet was nonetheless more interested in the aesthetic dimensions of his performance: "In noble and beautiful themes / As broad and as deep as the ocean / He told us ineffable things / Stirred out souls to a lofty emotion / And stilled us to peace." The concert ended with "a finale of meteoric splendor" reverberating in the memory:

But the musical magic he wrought
Held us breathless and spellbound the while
And illumines our memory still
Like a star in a twilight of dreams.

For true music lovers outside of Poland, the country's tragedies were not as significant as the musician's unique artistic and spiritual power. Music-obsessed poets hoped to see Paderewski involvement with the cause of Poland's independence as a passing phase and looked forward to his return to the concert stage. Josephine Rita Sargeant noted in her portrayal of the pianist (*Paderewski*),[45] that in his performances "delicate forceful tones" are "obeying his command" so that, "Music for the soul / calls the world to listen / shows the brother-hood of man." Sargeant observed that when "his country called him /This man so great and true," did not hesitate to abandon his musical career. Yet, at the end, music won: "After duty came the music /Flashing, floating, fair / Ringing out free tones of love/ Filling all the air." Similarly, in a 12-line anonymous poem of 1925, Paderewski was considered both a "star of genius" shining with "Heaven-given light" and the "establisher of Poland free" whom the nations will remember as a "peeress proof of Poland's might." His musical talent was more significant since "millions of his listeners owe a debt of gratitude for the "bliss" he gave them.

On 27 November 1928, a well-known Irish-Indian poet, writer, editor, and intellectual, James Henry Cousins (1873-1956) transcribed his impressions of how *Paderewski Plays at Lausanne*

---

[45] Josephine Rita Sargeant, *Paderewski*, typescript, AAN Poems, p. 182.

Cathedral:[46] "Master, and freeman of the word's free lands / You, with no gesture of the hand that deigns / Suffering, like Chopin for a land in chains, / Laid by your art at Freedom's rough demands." The poet noticed that the angelic appearance of the pianist largely disappeared, yet his empathy for the suffering of Poland remained: "Now, though your hair, no aureole expands, / Of russet fame, the inner fire remains / With man's long sorrow sweetening your strains, / And his sure triumph thundering from your hands." The most important is Cousins' conclusion, reflecting on Paderewski's silver hair, not a sign of advancing old age, but of immortality:

> With eyes unflinching and unwavering tread,
> By paths which only Alpine spirit knows,
> Whose end is in the white accomplished peak
> Where the immortals with immortals speak.

This grand finale of immortality is not accidental element of this poem. Cousins was so taken with the teachings of immortal, spiritual Masters encountered in religious treatises of Theosophy, Hinduism, and Buddhism, that in 1915 he moved to India and dedicated most of oeuvre to exploring spirituality of the East and the tenets of Theosophy, such as the Oneness of all existence and the immortality of human spirit undergoing multiple incarnations on an ascending path of evolution into perfect union with the Divine. On this arduous road, humans are guided by Ascended Masters. Cousin's literary background featured friendships and collaborations (or conflicts) with William Butler Yeats, George William Russell, and James Joyce in Dublin, before he travelled to India, sponsored by Annie Besant (1847-1933), President of the Theosophical Society. There, he wrote 12 books on Eastern spirituality and several volumes of poetry; he converted to Hinduism in 1937.[47] This poem demonstrates that the fascination with Paderewski as a Divine Messenger, an Archangel, or an Immortal did not abate in the interwar period.

Between the two world wars, Paderewski's audiences again had ample chances to attend his recitals and enjoy their emotional,

---

[16] James Henry Cousins, *Paderewski Plays at Lausanne Cathedral*, typescript, AAN Poems, p. 17.

[47] Dilip Kumar Chatterjee, *James Henry Cousins: A Study of His Works in the Light of Theosophical Movement* (South Asia Books, 1994).

aesthetic and spiritual aspects. The pianist's American concert tours resumed in the fall of 1922, with 68 concerts given in that season, 74 concerts between November 1923 and May 1924, 69 concerts in 1925-26; 58 concerts in 1928, and 77 concerts in 1930-31, when he turned 70 years old. His grueling schedule was interrupted with rest periods at his estate near Paso Robles, California and at Riond-Bossond in Switzerland.[48] In 1927, he again toured Australia, and throughout the period gave numerous concerts in England, France, Italy, Spain and other countries.

Figure 5. Cover of The Etude Magazine *with Paderewski, July 1934.*

Ernest Powell, in *To Paderewski—After Years*,[49] recalled hearing the virtuoso in his youth and "after years" while describing the "soulful

---

[48] Marek Żebrowski, *Paderewski w Kalifornii* (Toruń, 2018).
[49] Ernest Powell, *To Paderewski. After Years*, n.d., typescript from

melodies" of Chopin that delighted him then and again: "Gold inwrought with jewels bright / Preludes, etudes, nocturnes, all / let them spare, glimmer, fall" and concludes by imploring the pianist as a "Poet, dreaming dreams impearled" to "Pour out beauty on the word." Paderewski: not a Pole, but the Poet.

An anonymous, white-verse poem of 20 February 1924, *To Paderewski,*[50] brings out yet again a panoply of cosmic, spiritual imagery. What if the pianist is one whose "hands have played with the raiment of God" and, while doing so, he could say that "universes have spun around my fingertips" and, perhaps, also that "moonlight flowed my veins/ And came out in a white song / Ethereal as morning mist!" That's not all, this supernatural being's "soul conceived the sun / And burst in a golden fury triumphant." We are in the same sublime realm that was imagined by Ina Coolbrith and William Watson Gilder in the 1890s. But is the lyrical subject of this original poem Paderewski himself, or is it some "disembodied spirit" that possessed him, as in Gilder's verse? Is this Paderewski transformed into an "Immortal," fully united and integrated, as one with the Cosmic Divine, i.e., is he an Ascended Master? The poem concludes with the words ascribed to its hero: "I shall elude all this / Lifting me upward / Leaving behind the golden glowing light." The otherworldly immortal left for us a light that shines through Paderewski's music.

This *immortal* trope associating the Polish musician with elevated spiritual realms was the most persistent in Paderewski's reception in English-language poetry. Taken as a corpus of works, the poem gathered in the present volume followed the trajectory of a Hegelian trinity, from "thesis" (Paderewski as sublime archangel, prophet or medium appealing to the whole humanity, in the period from 1890 to 1914, the outbreak of the Great War), to "antithesis" (Paderewski as a brave, heroic Polish patriot, saving his sorrowful, beleaguered nation during and immediately after World War I), to "synthesis" (Paderewski as an "immortal" pianist-statesman who melded the love for his homeland with that for all humanity and thus helped them all to "resurrect" or "ascend").

Marshall, Texas. AAN Poems, p. 150.
[50] Anonymous, *To Paderewski*, poem in two stanzas, typescript, AAN Poems, p. 289.

Already in the first period of Paderewski reception (1891 to 1914), A. F. Bates (the second of two sonnets, *To Paderewski—Sovereign—Pianist*) praises the *immortal* musical genius that is "so intense / so faultless, crystal-pure like dew that drips / on a far-mountain side from one flower's lips / the bees have found not."[51] Bewildered by the "sheer suspense betwixt the notes," the poet seeks the source of the Master's magic in the spiritual dimension. This search raises the musician to a level far above the sirens that lured Orpheus with their otherworldly voices, far above even angels in the "far heaven." No need for the perplexed poet to "vainly scan / The firmament to match thy clear / Soul-sounding deep-sea music." The pianist, a mere man, has ascended to the mystical heights of a seraph, the apocalyptic Archangel of Music, Israfel—an entity not from Chrisian but Islamic tradition. It is fascinating to note that another contemporaneous poet, Ina Coolbrith of San Francisco, also named Paderewski "twin of soul with Israfel" in her sonnet.[52] Like Bates, she describes the listeners trajectory from rapture in the "ecstasy of perfect sound" to "Aeolian murmurs of a mystic dream" and, finally, "Strife, triumph, rapture, peace of Heaven supreme—." While neither of these two sonnets is dated, their rhetoric and vocabulary indicate a shared placement in the first period of Paderewski's reception by poets.

Long after the turmoil of the war, on 6 February 1931, after a concert in Montgomery, Alabama, Juliet C. Olin, declared, on behalf of Paderewski's listeners that:[53] "From the thunder of the tempest / To the sky lark in its bliss / From the depths of human agony / To the touch of Cupid's kiss / We will follow him enraptured / Where Elysian billows swell / That burst in glorious anthems / Where the hosts of Eden dwell." Music heard during Paderewski's concert encompasses the power and beauty of nature, and captures the full array of human emotions, from suffering to affection and enchantment. Finally, the poet confirms the spiritual mission of the pianist turned Divine Messenger:

> Ablaze in all his glory,
> Imperial with his peers,

---

[51] A. F. Bates, *To Paderewski—Sovereign—Pianist,* AAN Poems, p. 9.
[52] Ina Coolbrith, Paderewski, AAN Poems, p. 14.
[53] Juliet C. Olin, *The Maestro. To Paderewski*, AAN Poems, p. 128.

Evolving with the ages
And growing with the years,
Superb, this uncrowned sovereign
Attuned to God and man
Comes heralding to mortal ears
The strains from spirit-land

A prolific song composer Will (William) George Butler (1876-1955) heard similar spiritual content in the concert hall and recorded his impressions in *When Paderewski Plays* (1933).[54] While engrossed in the sounds made by the "piano's greatest bard," the poet observes that "across our heartstrings tenderly, emotions freely play" giving rise to "the deepest music of the soul." Not to be outdone, English poet Arthur Bryant concurs: "The music that he makes a message brings —/ We are immortal, in this faith we live." (*Paderewski Plays the Moonlight Sonata*).[55]

The themes of spiritual immortality and ascension to realms of etheric, cosmic beauty continued to intertwine in a poem recounting yet another rapture of an ecstatic listener, Windsor V. Richberg narrating the emotions experienced *When Paderewski Plays* (1934) in Chicago.[56] The pianist has eyes that "pierce as a shaft of light / And see afar, into the night / And on through space among the spheres / Is there the music that he hears?" The appearance of the virtuoso, engrossed in his performance, is briefly noted – his nodding head, his lips that "move as in silent prayer / Speaking to things we cannot see / The master of sublimity." Indeed, cosmic phenomena occur when Paderewski plays and a life "seems to be / Envelop by his ecstasy." The conclusion is inevitable:

The ocean checks its mighty roll
Time stops, the earth becomes a soul

---

[54] Will George Butler, *When Paderewski Plays*, signed typescript with notes, 1933, AAN Poems, p. 8. Butler composed over 200 songs, conducted a military band, and directed music program at Mansfield State Normal School now known as Mansfield State College in Pennsylvania. See Chris McGann, "World-famous composer: Wiliam George Butler," online (2007).

[55] Arthur Bryant, *Paderewski Plays the Moonlight Sonata*, manuscript, AAN Poems, p. 6.

[56] Windsor V. Richberg, *When Paderewski Plays*, manuscript, 26 Oct. 1934, Chicago, AAN Poems, p. 176.

The stars responsive to his theme
Clustered in brilliant silence —gleam
Where he has sought and caught the key
Of a celestial symphony.

Additional heavenly and cosmic associations are found in *Sonata Appasionata*, by Lucia Clark Markham of Lexington, Kentucky after a concert held on 26 January 1923.[57] Markham (1870-1967) was a well-known poet, physician and teacher, active in literary circles of her native Kentucky and Vancouver, Canada. She was the author of poetry volumes *The Path of Gold, Songs of Florida* (1924), *Sonnets to Eve* (1930), and five more books of sonnets. According to Markham, when Paderewski plays Beethoven's Sonata Op. 57 in F-minor the music transports the listeners "Out where the pure notes drift / On lakes of silence through the silvery rift / Of ultimate echoes against heaven's bar." The listener is placed on "the antiphonal towers of God." In the process, all the earthly suffering, the "dark discordant ways" are subsumed and transformed into the "majesty of mellow chords" and "benignant harmony" where "time and pain were nought." With her musical training, Markham is aware that the magic of music has triple sources: the first is the perfection of the grand piano as an instrument; the second refers to the genius of the composer whose music rivals the singing of the Serafim, and the third is

the Master, the Interpreter,
The giant soul who felt the mystic stir
Of ancient memories and the secret sweep
Of dim foreknowledge break beyond the deep
Of all the melodies that leap
From God to man across the chasm of time
And with his touch sublime
Brought this transcendent beauty into birth
All sorrowing, all loveliness, all mirth
Were linked in music's thrall
With All-in-All

"All-in-all" is a phrase from the first Letter to the Corinthians, where Saint Paul writes about the ultimate, all-encompassing presence of God: "so that God may be all in all" (1 Corinthians 15:28). Nonetheless, this reference may also be read in a non-

---

[57] Lucia Clark Markham, *Sonata Appasionata*, typescript, AAN Poems, 115.

Christian, Theosophical, way, as implying the Oneness of the entire living Universe, permeated by and united with the Divine Absolute. The Theosophical Society, established by Helena Blavatsky (1831-1891) in 1875 developed their beliefs from a range of syncretic sources, including the occult traditions of Christian, Hindu, and Buddhist mysticism, Hermetic esoterism, and even the novels by Bulwer-Lytton (see Essay 3). Blavatsky herself was a trained and performing musician: she wrote about the music of the spheres, cosmic vibrations, and interrelationships of music with spirituality. Among the Theosophists, music was understood to have a major impact on an individual's psychological and spiritual development, as claimed in 1892 by Henry Steel Olcott (1832-1907), the co-founder of the Theosophical Society.[58] Discussing their theories of music of the spheres and other mystical-musical themes is beyond the scope of the present study.[59]

It is of interest, though, to observe, that an important forerunner of Theosophy, deeply involved in spiritualism, Edward Bulwer-Lytton (1803-1873) made an obscure appearance in the *Brighton Album* assembled by Madeleine Michell in the late 1890s (see Essay 3). This copious volume starts with a Dedication citing Bulwer-Lytton's words (a paraphrase of a poem by Abraham Cowey): "But you have found the mountain top – there sit / On the calm, flourishing head of it; / And whilst with wearied steps we upward go, / See us and clouds below." This spiritual Master is Paderewski, idealized as an Immortal who ascended way above ordinary mortals, to the realm of the sublime, inspiring others to follow.

It is also fascinating that among the variety of handwritten poems sent to the virtuoso pianist is *The Sphinx* by a forgotten

---

[58] Henry Steel Olcott, "The Influence of Music in Psychic Development," The Theosophist 13:4 (Jan. 1892), 226–29; F. L. Reed, "Music and Theosophy," The Theosophist 13:10 (July 1912), 591–94; G. Lachman, "Concerto for Magic and Mysticism: Esotericism and Western Music," *The Quest* 90:4 (July 2002), 132–37; K. Leland, "Theosophical Music," *The Quest* 99:2 (2011), 61–64.

[59] According to its website, "The Mission of the Theosophical Society is to serve humanity by cultivating an ever-deepening understanding and realization of the Ageless Wisdom, spiritual self-transformation, and the unity of all life." These themes occurred frequently in poems about Paderewski. https://www.ts-adyar.org/mission-objects.

poet Amy Geyer Smith.[60] Initially, I thought the almost illegible poem transforms the pianist himself into a Sphinx of profound wisdom, shrouded in mystery, unapproachable. Since I could not decipher the cursive handwriting, I asked Emma Boyd of the National Library of Scotland for assistance. She transcribed most of it, yet the content remained dubious in too many places, so, with regret, I decided not to add this unusual poem to this collection.

However, I am still perplexed: why send a poem about an ancient Egyptian monument to a modern, virtuoso pianist? In the poet's words, this enormous sculpture is "Imperishable as the red basalt pyramids,/ Whose kings lie in their unfeeling breasts / Coffined and silent?" They await the return of the Spirit of Osiris "on the black / Wings of Death to Hades, to triumph in his / Ghost haunted kingdom." Then, on this "day of days," "in its awful majesty," Osiris "shall rise to give birth, birth the World craves, yet humbles at." Embodied yet again, the immortal will transform the world. Meanwhile, death is "the penalty of man if he but tries to read / Its open pages," while "sits the grey, passionless / Sphinx in stony silence, his sightless eyes / Fixed on the pale East." There, "a fierce flame burns" as "the sun breathes into the shifting sands" and the driest lips "mutter in supplication, / For the gold-hammered heavens."

The Sphinx plays a particularly important role in Theosophical beliefs, as discussed by Annie Besant, in her 1890 lecture, *The Sphinx of Theosophy*.[61] This Guardian of Mysteries, protects the hidden knowledge about the dual nature of human beings, belonging both to the Earth and Heaven. The Sphinx embodies "the four-fold path" to spiritual perfection ("To will, to know, to dare, and to be silent"). The East that the Sphinx faces is also saturated with occult symbolism: the rising sun means enlightenment, the rise of a glorious human spirit, resurrected from its base body... None of this would have pertained to Paderewski had he not been the Great, Spiritual Master in the eyes of the poet....

---

[60] Amy Geyer Smith, The Sphinx, AAN Poems, p. 180.
[61] Annie Besant, The Sphinx of Theosophy, published as a pamphlet in 1890 in New York, see https://archive.org/details/besantthesphinxoftheosophy.

In Theosophy and its successors, such a role has been assigned to Ascended Masters, selected from all cultures and nations as humanity's greatest teachers. It seems, that, for some poets, at least, Paderewski, due to his "immortal genius," also joined their ranks. Masterly interpreted classical music had a potential to lead its listeners on a path of spiritual ascension. That was its true value. Paderewski was the unique "Immortal" individual, an embodiment of prescient wisdom, that made this journey possible.

However, having said that, I owe the readers a disclaimer. Besides the spiritual evolution of James H. Cousins, and clear echoes of the I AM Activity of adherents of the St. Germain Foundation within the poem I Am Music by Berton Bellis,[62] there is scant biographical information about poets that would allow to definitely prove their connections to Theosophy and related spiritual movements. Though my analysis is largely conjectural and contextual, it raises questions. Would an orthodox Christian believer of any denomination cite Israfel, an Islamic Angel of Music and the Last Judgment—as A. F. Bates and Ina Coolbrith did? Probably not. Is every reference to what is "immortal," "eternal," or "heavenly"—Christian? Probably not either, though many such mentions are. For instance, when Ester Jacoby Merrill (O Great Master,) reminds the aging pianist in 1939 that "you will play / The first firm strain of your life's symphony / Upon eternal keys," she means the Christian Heaven reached after death that ends just one embodied existence. Speaking in this vein, Paderewski's music is said to bring to his listeners "a brief glimpse of Heaven" (Lines to an Artist... by A.B.), or "the melodies of Heavens" (When 'Padi' Comes to Town by George W. Hootman), since "his heart is Heaven half" (Paderewski by Kate Slaughter McKinney). After all, as the Australian Josephine observed in 1904, citing another poet, Paderewski was among God's minstrels sent to this earth "That they might woo the hearts of men / And lure them back to heaven again."

---

62 The "I AM" teaching and activities are associated with the writings of the St. Germain Foundation, a post-Theosophic spiritual movement that swept through America since 1930, reaching a million followers worldwide. See Godfre Ray King (pseudonym of Ray Ballard, the founder of the St. Germain Foundation), Unveiled Mysteries (Chicago: St. Germain Press, 1935), and The Magic Presence (reprint, 1989).

As Dorothy Hull Beatty wrote, *Genius* (1938) was one who acted "With measured tread, and dauntless heart / Unconquerable…" The Polish virtuoso pianist was a living embodiment of such a Genius, "to the throb of the universe attuned / Interpreter of every living thing /Way-shower, prophet, wingèd king."[63]

During more than 50 years, dozens of poems about Ignacy Jan Paderewski were written in English by amateur and professional poets. Their language is often archaic and typically rather too florid for modern tastes, though their classical, musical and religious erudition coupled with the skill of sonnet-writers deserve our admiration. These unusual verses evoke a range of fascinating relationships between dominant tropes in the poetic images of the Polish pianist-statesman: from the musician, virtuoso, through the seraph, divine messenger and Polish patriot, to the immortal Master invoking the spiritual and revelatory worlds of the sublime.

Figure 6: Paderewski on the cover of The Etude, *May 1931.*

---

[63] Dorothy Hull Beatty, *Genius,* signed typescript, Los Angeles, April 1938, AAN Paderewski Poems, p. 2.

PART III

ABOUT PADEREWSKI

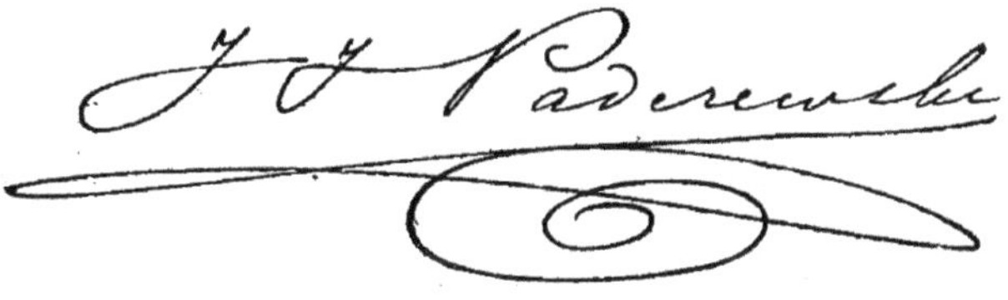

Edited by Maja Trochimczyk

Paderewski: A Calendar of Life

Maja Trochimczyk

1860	Ignacy Jan Paderewski was born on 6 November [O.S. 25 October] 1860, on the estate of Kuryłówka, in the Podolia district of former Polish lands, occupied by the Russian Empire since 1795 (returned to Poland in 1918, incorporated into Soviet Union in 1945, and a part of the Ukraine since 1990). His father, Jan Paderewski, was an estate administrator, and his mother, Poliksena, née Nowicka, was a daughter of a patriotic friend of famous Polish poet Adam Mickiewicz (1798-1855). She died soon after Ignacy Jan's birth. He had an older sister, Antonina.
1863	Jan Paderewski is arrested and imprisoned for one year in Kiev for assisting participants in the January Uprising against the Russian Empire, seeking to liberate Poland. During their father's incarceration, Ignacy Jan and Antonina are cared for by their aunt.
1865	After the father's release from prison, the family moves to Sudyłków in the Zasław County in the district of Volhynia, where Jan becomes administrator of the Szaszkiewicz estate. He continues in this role and periodically moves to other gentry estates in the same general area.
1867	Jan Paderewski marries his second wife, Anna née Tańkowska. They have three children: Józef (1871-1958), Stanisław (1873-1914), and Maria (1876-1952). Ignacy studies piano with home teachers: Filip Runowski, Piotr Sowiński, and Michał Babiański
1871	Birth of Ignacy's half- brother, Józef Paderewski (1871-1958) who later becomes a schoolteacher in the Bydgoszcz area and a writer; Józef publishes studies about the Grunwald Monument (1910), the city of Kraków, and various agricultural topics.
1872	At the age of 12, Ignacy is admitted to the Warsaw Institute of Music while residing with the Kerntopf family.
1873	January – Ignacy enrolls in the piano class of Jan Śliwiński, followed by Juliusz Janotha. He studies music theory with Karol Studziński. June 27 – Paderewski plays the trombone in the Institute's orchestra. July 2 – his debut as a pianist, he plays a duet with Antoni Rutkowski at the second students' concert (Friedrich Kalkbrenner's Duet for Two Pianos).
1874	February – Ignacy moves to the piano class of Henryk Koman, while Klemens Podwysocki (1832–1903) teaches literature,

	Polish, and French. The pianist starts studying German. In June-July, he plays the trombone in four benefit concerts of the school orchestra. October 25 – Paderewski and two other students (Antoni Sygietyński and Henryk Pachulski) are removed from the list of Institute's students.
1875	October 29 – after his father's letter to the Board of the Institute, Ignacy is reinstated for a trial period, as an unenrolled student.
1876	February – first composition, *Valse mignonne*, dedicated to his harmony and counterpoint teacher, Gustaw Roguski. October – with violinist Ignacy Cielewicz and cellist Michał Biernacki, Ignacy goes on a concert tour of cities in Russia and Northern Poland.
1877	Ignacy discontinues the tour, visits St. Petersburg; with his father's help, he returns to Warsaw.
1878	January, Warsaw – with the consent of Principal Apolinary Kątski and after passing exams, Ignacy returns to school. February-June – he performs several times during school concerts (as a soloist, accompanist, or in the orchestra). June – Ignacy passes final exams and graduates (certificate No. 186). June 29 – he performs with Antoni Rutkowski while his future wife, Antonina Korsak, recites a poem. June 30 – the second students' concert features his song "Życzenie" to poem by Władysław Syrokomla. Ignacy is a soloist in the first movement of Edward Grieg's Concerto in A minor. October – Ignacy becomes a piano teacher at his alma mater. December – he stays with the Adamowskis in Warsaw, at 12 Włodzimierska Street.
1879	January – Paderewski composes *Romance* from the Suite in E-flat major for piano. June-August – he accompanies violinist Władysław Górski in concerts in Warsaw and in summer resorts. His Impromptu in F major for piano is published in *Echo Muzyczne*.
1880	Paderewski marries a fellow student Antonina Korsakówna on 7 January, in her family's estate, Rudnia in Volhynia. March – a concert in Warsaw. April – a concert in Piotrków. July – concerts in resorts Druskienniki and Libawa (2), with Stanisław Barcewicz, violinist. Birth of disabled son Alfred on 9 October is followed by the death of wife of injuries during childbirth, on 18 October.
1881	January-June, Warsaw – Ignacy continues his work at the Warsaw Institute of Music and composes: Three Pieces, Op. 2, Elegy in B-flat minor, Op. 4 (dedicated to the memory of Antonina), and *Old Suite* (for three voices), Op. 3.

	July/August, Zakopane resort in Tatra Mountains – Vacation with friends, Helena, née Rosen Górska (who later becomes Paderewski's second wife) and her then husband, violinist Władysław Górski.
1882	Ignacy leaves his son with his grandmother, Julia Korsak, and travels to Berlin. January-June, Berlin – composition studies with Friedrich Kiel; collaboration with the Bote und Bock publishing house. 2 July – Concerts in Nałęczów and Busko (solo, duet with violinist W. Górski). September – he returns to work at the Warsaw Institute of Music. He completes composing *Chants du voyageur*, Op. 8 (dedicated to Helena Górska), 1881-82, in five movements, published in 1883. 30 October – Institute of Music's concert with his Piano Sonata.
1883	January 12, Berlin (Roma Hotel Concert Hall) – the first concert as a composer. January – April. Concerts with W. Górski in Berlin, Kraków, Lublin, Warsaw, and Kutno. 24 July – he performs in Szczawnica, and Zakopane. August – visit to Zakopane; starts composing the Tatra Album, Op. 12. The pianist befriends Dr Tytus Chałubiński who encourages him to collect folk melodies for use in his music. They travel together into the Tatras with Bartek Obrochta's ensemble and others. Summer – Jan Kleczyński and Paderewski travel through the Tatras and their foothills (Podhale), notating about 70 melodies of górale. He later uses "the most characteristic" in the cycle *Album tatrzanskie* op. 12. First published in October 1883 in *Echo muzyczne i teatralne*. 16 November – a concert in Kiev.
1884	January-July, Berlin – composition studies with Heinrich Urban; friendship with the family of composer Richard Strauss. Paderewski composes the first orchestral works: Overture, Suite, and miniatures for wind instruments. On 18 August, Paderewski, Chałubiński, and Kleczyński collect new tunes in the Tatras, with folk musicians, Bartek Obrochta, fiddler, and Kuba Gut, bassist. His transcriptions of górale melodies are used by Kleczyński (who lost his own) in the first publication of Tatra music. Paderewski completes *Album tatrzańskie* [Tatra Album], Op. 12 (4 mvts.) in 1883 (No. 1-3) and 1884 (No. 4). Arrangement for four hands, *Tatra Album*, dedicated to Tytus Chałubiński in 6 movements is published in Berlin: Ries und Erler, 1884. He composes Piano Concerto in Zakopane and meets actress Helena Modjeska (Modrzejewska, 1840-1909) through Chałubiński. Modjeska becomes his life-long supporter, she arranges a joint appearance as a fundraiser for the pianist's further studies,

	held in Kraków's Hotel Saski on 3 October. November – departure for Vienna to study with Theodore Leschetitzky.
1885	February-March – Concerts in Lwów and Kraków. April, Warsaw – Concert of Paderewski's compositions with Helena Weychert, Władysław Górski, and Antoni Rutkowski: Song, Op. 7, to words by Adam Asnyk, Variations and Fugue in A minor for piano, Op. 11, and Sonata in A minor for violin and piano, Op. 13. August – Paderewski visits Paris with Górski, meets Pablo de Sarasate and Edward Lalo, among other musicians. January to April – he composes Sonata in A Minor, Op. 13, for violin and piano, dedicated to Pablo de Sarasate, published by B&B, in 1886.
1886	Autumn 1885 to July 1886 – he teaches piano, harmony, and counterpoint at the Strasbourg Conservatory, recommended by his piano teacher, Theodore Leschetitzky.
1887	January – Paderewski travels to Vienna for further studies with Leschetitzky; Anetta Yesipova (aka Essipov), an outstanding pianist, Leschetitzky's wife, plays his Minuet in G major, Op. 14, No. 1, *Album Majowe*, Op. 10, Variations in A minor, Op. 11. October 22, Strasbourg – Paderewski gives a concert with violinist Florián Zajíc. December 9, Vienna (Musik-Verein) – a concert with singer Marie van Zandt. He composes six pieces in two sets of *Humoresques de concert*, Op. 14 (dedicated to A. Essipov/Yesipova), published by B&B, including the famous Minuet in G Major (written before 8 Nov. 1886) and *Cracovienne fantastique* in B Major.
1888	January–February – two group concerts in Vienna. 3 March, Paris (Salle Erard) – a successful debut (after several private recitals in aristocratic salons) starts his international piano career. March-April – Concerts in Paris, Brussels, and Prague. November-December – Concerts in Brussels, Ischl, and Liège. Hailed as "The Lion of Paris" by music critics. He completes Concerto in A Minor Op. 17 for piano and orchestra (dedicated to Theodore Leschetitzky), started in 1882.
1889	January 20, Vienna (Musik-Verein) – premiere of Piano Concerto in A minor by Anetta Yesipova, cond. Hans Richter. February-April – Recitals in France and Belgium – Lyons, Bordeaux, Liege, Paris (8. Including some chamber with W. Górski), Nantes. October – concerts in Kraków (2), Lwów (2), Tarnów, and Przemyśl; then in Germany – Hamburg, Schwerin, Frankfurt; in Romania – Bucharest, and in December, in Switzerland – Neuchatel, Lausanne (2), Basel, Geneva, and Vevey. In Vienna Paderewski meets Jewish writer Alfred Nossig (1864-1943) who sends him ideas for

	an opera, the plans culminate with *Manru* in 1901, based on a story about Gypsies and Górale by Jozef Ignacy Kraszewski (1812-1887), *Chata za wsią*. Paderwski receives Order of the Crown from the King of Romania.
1890	January – concerts in Toruń, and Poznań, Poland. 27 February to 14 May – a series of 15 concerts in Paris at Salle Erard, Concert Lamoreux, and other venues, some with W. Górski, violinist. 29 April – Fundraiser for charities in Montmartre. 30 April – Fundraiser for St. Casimir Society. 3 May – Concert Lamoreux, fundraiser for victims of hunger in Galicia. Other concerts in Nantes, France, and the Netherlands: Utrecht, Arnhem, The Hague, Rotterdam; later in Berlin. On 9 May, London (St. James's Hall) – debut in England, first of planned four London concerts. July-August, vacations in Vienna, he composes, learns English, and rests. October-November – Concert tour of Great Britain. 20 October – Edinburgh, then London (3 concerts, at St. James's Hall and the Crystal Palace), Liverpool, Edinburgh, Glasgow, Newcastle. Modjeska's friend, British painter Edward Burne-Jones (1833-1898) makes a drawing of the pianist as "an archangel" with a halo of hair. The pianist is also portrayed in pre-Raphaelite style by another Modjeska associate, Dutch painter living in England, Lawrence Alma-Tadema (1836-1912). The "archangel" becomes his preferred stage image, while Alma-Tadema joins the ranks of his friends, Laurence, the painter's younger daughter becomes one of the pianist's translators and promoters. December – concerts in Germany: Frankfurt am Mein, Berlin (with the Philharmonic, conducted by Hans von Bülow, 1830-1894), plus 2 solo recitals; a concert in Dresden.
1891	January-February – concerts in Germany: Dresden (2), Brunswick, Hamburg, Breslau (now: Wrocław, Poland), Berlin (2 concerts), and Nuremberg. March-April – concerts in Brussels, Paris (9 concerts), and Amsterdam. June-July – concerts in London (6 concerts) and Clifton. October – a tour of the UK: Hastings, Liverpool (2 concerts), Manchester (2), Clifton, Wolverhampton, Edinburgh, Glasgow, Bradford, Birmingham, London. Most of these are solo recitals, some are with violinist W. Gorski and some with orchestras. First American Concert Tour organized by Steinway piano makers. 11 November – arrives in New York. 17 November, New York (Music Hall, now Carnegie Hall) – Paderewski's first concert in the U. S., followed by 7 concerts in New York, 4 in Boston, 3 in Brooklyn, 2 in New York, and 3 in Boston.

	The tour lasts to March 1892 – he gives 109 concerts during 130 days of touring the U.S. and Canada. Through Modjeska's recommendation, in New York, he befriends the family of Richard Watson Gider, editor of *The Century Magazine* and poet. Music critic Henry Krehbiel becomes a supporter.
1892	The first American Tour continues. January – Chicago (2), Cincinnati, St. Louis (2), Buffalo, Detroit, New York (4), Brooklyn, Philadelphia (3), Orange N.J. February – Washington DC (4), Baltimore, New York, Montreal, Toronto, Chicago (2), Milwaukee (2), Boston (4), Portland. 2 March – benefit concert for Boston Symphony Orchestra, with Arthur Nikisch conducting. March – Chicago (4), Cincinnati (2), New York, Boston. 11 June – concert in London, July – concert and exhibition in Vienna, October – London. December – 6 concerts in London, followed by Liverpool, Wolverhampton, & Brighton, the last concert before his departure for the U.S. Second American Tour begins. 28 December – Binghampton NY. Paderewski is among sponsors of the construction of the Washington Arch in New York. The first Paderewski biography is published by Henry T. Finck in New York. He is named an honorary member of the Royal Academy of Music, London.
1893	The Second American Tour continues. January – New York (3), Boston (5), New Haven (2), Rochester, Albany, Hartford, Buffalo, Philadelphia, Brooklyn, Portland (2). February – Philadelphia (2), New York (2), Buffalo, Geneva NY, Providence, Boston, Brooklyn, Detroit, Ithaca. March – Chicago (3), Cleveland, New York (4), Baltimore, Boston (2), Philadelphia, Morrison NY, Providence, Springfield, Washington DC, Orange NY. April – Boston, Baltimore, Brooklyn, Poughkeepsie, New York, Chicago, St. Louis (2), Kansas City (2), Denver, Omaha, Pittsburgh, Philadelphia, New York (2), Northampton. 2-3 May – Chicago (2 concerts before returning to Europe). 20 June, London – first concert in Europe. August – Paderewski visits Switzerland and Normandy, devotes himself to creative work (including 6 Songs to lyrics by Adam Mickiewicz and Polish Fantasy, performed on October 4, 1893, at the Norwich Festival). He completes composing *Fantaisie polonaise sur des thèmes originaux* (Polish Fantasy on Original Themes) for piano and orchestra, started in 1891. Completes composing Six Songs Op. 18 to texts by Adam Mickiewicz, started in 1887, dedicated to Władysław. Mickiewicz, and published by B&B, 1893.

	October – tour of the UK: Norwich, Brighton, Glasgow, Edinburgh, Dunder, Aberdeen, London (2), Cheltenham, Liverpool (2), Manchester (2), Chester, Dublin (2), Huddersfield, Middleborough, Hull, Bradford, Portsmouth, Bournemouth, Birmingham. December – continued UK tour: Clifton, Edinburgh, Glasgow, Sydenham, London, Leeds, Brighton, Leighton, Sheffield, Manchester, Hampstead.
1894	13-15 May – Festival in Aachen, with Paderewski's participation. 5 July – concert in London. November – death of Jan Paderewski, the pianist's father. December – 2 concerts in Amsterdam, then Arnhem and The Hague.
1895	January – UK concert tour: Cardiff, Plymouth, Edinburgh, Glasgow, Preston, Manchester, Birmingham, Leeds, Oxford, Nottingham, Hanley, and Norwich. February – concerts in Cambridge, Bournemouth, Dublin (2), Manchester, Bradford, Leamington, Dresden (2), Leipzig. March-April – 3 concerts in Paris, followed by a return to the UK: Reading, Bedford, Sheffield, Chester. April – Bristol, Cheltenham, Turnbridge Wells, York, Sunderland. 24 June – London, then Maidstone, Brighton, Ipswich. The Third American Tour starts with two concerts on 4 & 9 November in New York, at Carnegie Hall, with the orchestra conducted by Walter Damrosch. November – concerts in Philadelphia (2), New York, Poughkeepsie, Brooklyn, Albany, Boston (3), Portland (2), Worcester, Springfield, Troy. December – Hartford, New Haven, Providence, New York, Richmond, Philadelphia, Washington DC, Baltimore, Pittsburgh (2), Cleveland, Buffalo, Brooklyn. Bote and Bock publishes *Polish Fantasy* for piano and orchestra (1891-1893). Paderewski receives Order of Albert from the Kingdom of Saxony.
1896	The Third American Tour continues. January – New York (2), Boston, Syracuse, Cincinnati, Louisville, Indianapolis, Chicago (2), St. Louis (2), Nashville, Atlanta, Memphis, New Orleans (3), Houston.February – San Antonio TX, San Diego. 6 February – two concerts in Los Angeles. 10 February – first of seven concerts in San Francisco. Then – Oakland, San Jose. March – Sacramento, Salt Lake City, Denver, Kansas City, Des Moines, Chicago (2), Duluth, Minneapolis, St. Paul (2), Milwaukee, Toledo, Columbus, Boston. April – Boston, Montreal (2), Toronto, Detroit, New York, Brooklyn, Northampton, Philadelphia, New York. Summer – before his departure for Europe, Paderewski donates US $10,000 to establish The Paderewski Foundation for Young American

	Composers that supports a triennial Paderewski Prize competition held since 1901 at Stanford University.
1897	In January, Jan Styka's Golgotha panorama, created at Paderewski's initiative and with his financial support, is unveiled in Warsaw. It is now located in Glendale, California. January – Italian concert tour: Monte Carlo, Nice, Milan, Rome (2 concerts). February – Concerts in Germany: Leipzig and Dresden. March – UK concerts: London (2), Bath, Brighton, Cambridge, Ryde, Southampton, Salisbury, Reading, Dover, Canterbury, Derby, and Warrington. April – 2 concerts in Paris, 2 concerts at Queen's Hall, London. Summer-Autumn – first family vacation at the Riond-Bosson villa near Morges. Paderewski bought the manor house of the former Duchess of Otrante. 18 October – starts a UK tour. November – Purchase of the Kąśna Dolna estate near Ciężkowice in the area of Tarnów; this estate becomes his summer residence from 1897 to 1902 (currently the manor houses the Paderewski Center in Kąśna Dolna in Poland).
1898	3, 5 February – two concerts at the Gewandhaus in Leipzig. Paderewski launches a composition contest for young composers in Leipzig and funds its prizes. End of March – concerts in Bristol, Cardiff, and Cologne. Summer – A competition is announced for the construction of a hotel (later Hotel Bristol), in which Paderewski holds significant stakes. 1 July – deadline for submissions to Polish Young Composers' Competition, funded by the pianist, with the conductor Arthur Nikisch, as the jury president. The competition has three categories – symphony, concerto with orchestra, and chamber music. The 1st prize goes to Zygmunt Stojowski (Symphony in D Minor, Op. 21), two 2nd prizes – to Henryk Melcer (Piano Concerto in E Minor) and Emil Młynarski (Violin Concerto in D minor, Op. 11). Two 3rd prizes to – Wojciech Gawroński (String Quartet), and Grzegorz Fitelberg (Violin Sonata). 5-12 December – concerts in the UK: Brighton, Huddersfield, Middlesbrough, Manchester, and two concerts in London.
1899	12 January – Paderewski arrives in Warsaw for three benefit concerts for: scholarships for poor students, a children's hospital, and shelters and support for the poor. Then, he gives two concerts in Łódź, followed by Białystok, Wilno, St. Petersburg (2). February-March – more concerts in St. Petersburg (4), then in Riga (2), Wilno, Mińsk (2), Moscow (5), Kiev (4), and Odessa. 13 March – the start of a British tour with a concert in Portsmouth, followed by Bourne-

	mouth, Eastbourne, Norwich, Folkestone, Bath, Torquay, Exeter, Sheffield, Handley, Chester, Preston, Manchester, Glasgow, and Edinburgh. 9 April – the first of four concerts in Paris is held at the Concert Colonne, the rest at Salle Erard. Spring – Paderewski funds a second composition competition, won by Lucjan Rydel and Józefat Nowiński. He creates scholarship funds for students at the Moscow Conservatory and the Saint Petersburg Conservatory. 31 May 1899 – The pianist marries his second wife, Helena Paderewska (née von Rosen, 1856–1934), after the annulment of her prior marriage to violinist Wacław Górski. She earlier cared for the pianist's son Alfred (1880–1901). The couple spends the summer in Kąśna Dolna; Paderewski prepares for the Fourth American Tour, attends the harvest festival, and makes numerous trips around the area. 27 November – a concert in Liverpool, 28 Nov. – in London. 6 December – arrival in New York for the Fourth American Tour. Concerts in New York (3), Boston (4), Philadelphia, Richmond, and Washington DC.
1900	December 1899 to mid-May 1900 – continued Fourth American Tour; the artist traveled with his wife for the first time. January – Portland, Providence, New York, Brooklyn, Hartford, New Haven, Philadelphia, Baltimore, Pittsburg, Troy NY, New York (3), Syracuse Buffalo, Cleveland, Toledo, Columbus, Chicago. February – Milwaukee, Chicago (2), Louisville, Cincinnati, Kansas City, Lincoln, Des Moines, St. Louis (2), Memphis, Nashville, Chattanooga, Atlanta, Birmingham, Mobile, Nowy Orleans (2). March – Houston, Galveston, Austin, Dallas, Forth Worth, SanAntonio, Mexico City (2). Los Angeles (2), San Diego, San Francisco (4), Oakland. April – Fresno, San Francisco (3), San Jose, Portland, Tacoma, Seattle, Vancouver, Spokane, Helena MT, Butte, Salt Lake City UT, Denver, Sioux City, Minneapolis, St. Paul, Chiago, Detroit. May – Toronto, Buffalo, Brooklyn, Washington DC, Philadelphia, Northampton, New Haven, New York, Newark NJ. 8 June – first of two concerts in Paris, then in London.
1901	January-April – concerts on the Riviera, in Rome and other Italian cities, as well as in Great Britain and Spain. February – concerts in Monte Carlo (2), Nice, Cannes, Rome. 4-16 March – UK concert tour: Birmingham, Sheffield, Manchester, Liverpool, Glasgow, Edinburg, Aberdeen, Newcastle, Bradford, Leeds, Colchester, Bournemouth. March 20 – Alfred, Paderewski's only son, dies during a medical treatment in Göggingen, Bavaria, while he gives a concert in Bilbao, Spain.

	20 April – performances resume in Copenhagen (Grieg attends one of 3 concerts), Stockholm. 5 May – a recital in Dresden, followed by Bonn. May 29, Dresden (Opernhaus) – world premiere of the opera *Manru*, conducted by Ernst von Schuch. In the audience: violinist Josef Joachim, composer and Paderewski's teacher, Theodore Leschetizky, composer Hugo Wolff, and other music celebrities. The opera, the first Polish "music drama" (with Wagnerian-inspired leitmotifs and continuous musical structure without set arias and recitatives) is then staged in Nice, Monte Carlo, Cologne, Prague, Zürich, and Bonn. Positive reviews of *Manru* by Ludwig Hartmann, A. H. Geiser, Henryk Opieński, Stanisław Niewiadomski, Frederic Hegar, Charles Phillips, and others. 8 June, Lwów (Municipal Theatre) – the Polish premiere of *Manru*, conducted by Francesco Spetrino. After 11 performances the troupe moves to Kraków. 12 June – concert in London. 29 June – Buxton. October – concerts in Wrocław, Katowice, Poznań, Hamburg. 5 November, Warsaw – the inaugural concert of the new Warsaw Philharmonic site, with the participation of Paderewski who is also a shareholder in the building. November-December – concerts in Germany: Leipzig, Magdeburg, Nuremberg, Munich, Mannheim, Frankfurt am Mein, Karlsruhe, Wiesbaden, Düsseldorf, Cologne, Hanover. Concerts in Austria (Vienna, Stuttgart), Hungary (Budapest), and the Czech Republic (Brno, Prague). The year ends with concerts in Dresden and a benefit in Morges.
1902	1 January – performance of *Manru* in Cologne, then in Zurich and Geneva. The Fifth American Tour starts on 5 February in New Haven CT, followed by concerts in Poughkeepsie NY, New York (3), Boston, Hartford, Northampton, Scranton PA, Washington DC, Richmond, and Baltimore. 11 February – the American premiere of *Manru* at the Metropolitan Opera House in New York, followed by performances in Philadelphia, Boston, Chicago, Pittsburgh, and Baltimore. March – concerts in Philadelphia, Boston, Rochester, Toronto (Canada), Syracuse, New York, Pittsburg, Columbus, Cleveland, Cincinnati, St. Louis, Kansas City, Chicago, Davenport, Milwaukee, Detroit, Troy NY, New York, Brooklyn. April – Providence, Philadelphia, Utica NY, Ottawa (Canada), Louisville KY, Indianapolis, Rockford IL, Wichita, Lincoln NE, Cedar Rapids IA, Peoria IL and Grand Rapids. May-June – concerts in London (8 May), Warsaw, Madrid (4), Lwów (3). 27 June – a benefit for the Society of Polish Journalists. 24 May – Warsaw premiere of *Manru*, later

	shown in Moscow, and Kiev. Paderewski receives the Order of Charles II from the King of Spain. 8-11 October – the Tenth Bristol Music Festival with Paderewski' participation. 10 October – another UK tour starts in Bristol, followed by Southport, Glasgow, and Leeds. November – Bath, London, Preston, Bournley, Warrington, Bradford, Cardiff, and Bristol. December – Ipswich, Middlesbrough, London (Crystal Palace), Llandudno, Dublin, Belfast, Inverness, Aberdeen, Dundee, Ryde, Eastbourne, Tunbridge, Wells, Blackpool, Harrogate, Huddersfield, Kendal, Derby, and Birmingham. 29 December, Zakopane – opening of a sanatorium for tuberculosis, built at the initiative of Kazimierz Dłuski and with significant financial participation from Paderewski.
1903	In March, Paderewski sells the estate in Kąśna Dolna, ruined by its administrator. He spends almost the entire year in Riond-Bosson; during this time he writes: the Piano Sonata in E-flat minor, Op. 21, *Douze Mélodies sur des Poésies de Catulle Mendès*, Op. 22 (cycle of 12 songs, dedicated to M. Trélat). The songs appear in Paris (Heugel et Cie, 1904), then in German in 1911. He composes the Variations and Fugue in E-flat Minor and starts sketches of the Symphony in B Minor, completed in 1909. The composer spends his free time playing bridge and solitaire, taking trips (a cruise on the Leman River), and going to the cinema. December – concerts in Lausanne (benefit for the construction of Lausanne concert hall), Morges (a charitable benefit), and Kraków.
1904	2, 4 January – two concerts in Kraków. 8 January – concert of his music at the Warsaw Philharmonic, 9 January – renewed performances of the opera *Manru* in Warsaw. After another concert in Łódź, he tours Russia. January – Moscow, Vilnius, Minsk, Smolensk, Riga, St. Petersburg, Kiev, February – Ekaterinoslav, Odessa (2), Kiev. April – he performs at Concerts Colonne in Paris, then in Zurich, and in Paris again, where 8 of 12 Mendes songs are presented. More concerts in Geneva and Cologne. 7 July to 25 October – Paderewski, accompanied by his second wife and a whole entourage, including secretaries and three Erard pianos, gives concerts in Australia and New Zealand, in collaboration with a Polish-French composer-pianist Henri Kowalski. July – 5 concerts in Melbourne. August – 4 concerts in Sydney, followed by 2 concerts in Brisbane, 2 more in Sydney and 2 in Auckland. September – two concerts in Wellington, then Napier, Christchurch (2),

	Dunedin (2), Invercargill. October – Hobart, Launceston, Melbourne (2), and Adelaide (2). He returns to the U.S. in December (with a new parrot!) and soon starts the Sixth American Concert Tour with concerts in San Francisco at the Alhambra Theatre (3), Oakland, Fresno, Santa Clara, and Los Angeles. Paderewski then visits Arden – Helena Modjeska ranch in Orange County, California.
1905	The Sixth American Tour continues. January – concerts in Fresno, Seattle, El Paso TX, New Orleans (2), Mobile and Birmingham AL, Savannah GA, Columbia SC, Charleston, Charotte NC, Norfolk VA, Washington DC. February – Baltimore, Harrisburg and Reading PA, Trenton NY, Troy, Worcester, Hartwell, Springfield MA, Rochester and Buffalo NY, Pittsburg PA, Cincinnati, St. Louis MO, Springfield IL, Plymouth IN, Fort Wayne, and South Bend IN. March – Detroit, Toledo OH, Danville, Indianapolis, Terre Haute IN, Bloomington, Milwaukee, Chicago, Philadelphia, New Haven, Poughkeepsie, New York, Brooklyn Newark NJ, Providence RI, April – Boston, Cleveland, Columbus, Dayton, Chicago (2), Ds Moines, Topeka KS, St. Joseph MO, Omaha, Richmond, Youngstown OH, Boston (2), followed by a tour of Canada – Montreal, Ottawa, Toronto, and London, Ontario. 2 May – a benefit concert for Helena Modjeska organized by Paderewski (he is sick and does not appear). Later, in May, he records music for Welte-Mignon piano rolls. In July, Paderewski is again sick, but travels to Paris and Austria.
1906	27 February – Paderewski continues recordings on Welte-Mignon piano rolls (two movements of Beethoven's Moonlight Sonata). 21 March – he gives a benefit concert for the Lausanne Orchestra. He also plays in Bern, Strasburg, Nancy, and Bordeaux. April – concerts in Marseille, Lyon, Lisbon, Porto. May – concerts in Madrid (2) and Barcelona.
1907	January – concerts in Switzerland: Lausanne and Montreux. February and March – a tour of Great Britain: Bristol, Brighton, Hanley, Oxford, Reading, Newcastle, Aberdeen, Dundee, Glasgow, Edinburgh, and Liverpool. June – 3 concerts in Paris, followed by more concerts in the UK London (2), and in Switzerland (Geneva). 28 October – start of the Seventh American Tour in Bridgeport CT, then in Baltimore. November – New York, Hartford, Boston, Pittsburgh (2), Philadelphia, Springfield MA, Boston (2), Washington DC, Wilmington, New York (2), Montreal and Toronto (Canada), and Buffalo. December – Philadelphia, Washington DC, Baltimore, New York (3),

	Brooklyn (2), Troy NY, Newark NJ, Philadelphia, Boston (2), and Portland ME.
1908	The Seventh American Concert Tour continues. January – Akron OH, Cincinnati, Evansville IN, St. Louis, Chicago, Winnipeg, St. Paul, Minneapolis, Cleveland, Milwaukee, Kansas City. February – Salina KS, Denver, Colorado Springs, Salt Lake City, Boise City ID, Spokane WA, Victoria and Vancouver (Canada), Seattle, Tacoma WA, Portland OR, Oakland. March – San Francisco, Los Angeles, Santa Barbara, San Diego, Albuquerque NM, Fort Worth, Waco, and Dallas TX, Little Rock AR, Memphis, St. Louis, Atlanta, Nashville, Indianapolis, Louisville KY, April – Richmond, Pittsburgh, Chicago, Detroit, Schenectady NY, Brooklyn, New York. 2 May – concert at Carnegie Hall, New York, with Marcelina Sembrich-Kochańska & the Adamowski brothers, a benefit for the Legal Aid Society. The end of the tour and return to Europe. 23 June – recital at Queen's Hall, London.
1909	January – concerts with orchestra, cond. Emil Młynarski, in Edinburgh and Glasgow. 30 January – the first concert of the Eighth American Tour in Newark NJ, followed by concerts in New York, Boston, and Worcester. February – and Philadel-phia, Washington DC, Baltimore, Brooklyn, New York, Mont-real, Toronto, and Hamilton (Canada). 12 February – Boston, the world premiere of the Symphony in B minor, Op. 24, conducted by Max Fiedler. March – Brooklyn, Richmond, Norfolk, Lynchburg, Washington DC, St. Louis, Chicago, St. Paul, Minneapolis, Milwaukee. He returns to Europe in May. 23 May – Concert for the benefit of Conservatoire National de Musique in Paris, with revenue of 12,000 francs; Paderewski plays two piano concerti, Beethoven's No. 5, and Saint-Saens' No. 4, with the Symphony in B Minor "Polonia" (composed in 1903-1909) also on the mammoth program. The funds are for scholarships at the Conservatory. August – Paderewski receives the Legion of Honor from the French government. 31 October – a concert in Edinburgh. November – Glasgow, Newcastle, Sheffield, London, Dublin, Belfast, Bristol, Man-chester, Liverpool, Cardiff, and Exeter. December – concerts in Mühlhouse, and London.
1910	January-March – European concert tour: Vienna, Budapest, Lausanne, Paris (benefit for flood victims), and concerts on the Riviera. 15-17 July, Kraków – the ceremony of unveiling of King Władysław Jagiełło monument (known as the Grunwald Monument), sculpted by Antoni Wiwulski (1877-1919) and funded by the Paderewski Foundation. He delivers

	a patriotic speech at the unveiling. October 23, Lwów – the celebration of the 100th anniversary of Fryderyk Chopin's birth and the 1st Congress of Polish Musicians; Paderewski lectures about Chopin. November – he receives an honorary membership from the Warsaw Music Society.
1911	January - Symphony in B minor, Op. 24, *Polonia* is performed in Warsaw, with Henryk Opieński conducting. March – the Symphony is played in Berlin. 26 May – Paderewski gives a concert in Freiburg for the benefit of Polish students there. After several European concerts, a major tour of South America (The Ninth American Tour) begins on 1 August: 5 concerts in Rio de Janeiro, 3 concerts in Sao Paulo, and 7 in Buenos Aires, the last concert is on 6 October. Paderewski returns to Europe, on 18 October in Paris – he has the first recording session for Gramophone Company Ltd., "His Master's Voice."
1912	February 13 and 14 – further recordings for the Gramophone Company Ltd. March – a tour of South Africa, with planned 20 concerts: two in Cape Town, three in Johannesburg (more than three thousand people waited for him at the train station), more concerts in Kimberley, Pretoria, Bloemfontein, Maritzburg, and Durban. June – Jan Kazimierz University in Lwów awards Paderewski an honorary doctorate. He also becomes an Honorary Citizen of the City. June – concerts in London, Harrogate, & Brighton. October-November – concerts in Bristol, London, Sheffield, and Torquay. December – a concert in Lausanne.
1913	February – a concert in Monte Carlo. 6 March – a symphony concert in Leipzig (Gewandhaus orchestra conducted by Arthur Nikisch, the Symphony in B Minor on the program). Then concerts in Kraków (2), Lwów, Łódź, and Warsaw (2). 18-21 May, Vevey – Celebrations of Saint-Saens, whose Polonaise and Scherzo for two pianos is presented by the composer & Paderewski; Symphony in B Minor also played. His sister Antonina Wilkonska moves to Riond-Bosson and remains the manager of the estate to her death in 1941.Heena Paderewska continues her agricultural project, breeding thousands of poultry, some of which become food for refugees after the outbreak of WWI. Paderewski also owns a nearby ranch, with apple, peach, cherry orchards, and farm animals – sheep and pigs among them. 9 October – the pianist arrives in New York for his Ninth American Concert Tour that continues through December. 13 October – the first concert in Trenton NY, then in Jersey City

	NJ. November – New York (3), Buffalo, Worcester, Boston (2), Baltimore, Washington DC, Scranton, Philadelphia, Brooklyn, Springfield MA. December – Columbus, St. Louis, Milwaukee, Boston, Minneapolis, Fargo, St. Paul, Madison, Cleveland, Pittsburgh.
1914	The Ninth American Tour continues. January – Colorado Springs, Salt Lake City, Boise City, and Vancouver (Canada). 14 January – the pianist cancels his concert in Seattle due to neuritis, nerve inflammation in the right hand. 17 January – he travels to hot springs in Paso Robles CA for a cure of neuritis, and to rest during the tour. February-April – further concerts in the United States and Canada start on 9 February in Fort Worth TX, then Wichita KS, St. Joseph and Springfield MO, Cedar Rapids IA, Lincoln NE, Birmingham AL, Louisville KY, Cincinnati OK, Chicago. March – Ann Arbor MI, Detroit, New York, Toronto (Canada), Boston, Philadelphia, Washington DC, Baltimore, Brooklyn, Newark, Providence RI, Troy NY, Harrisburg PA. April - Philadelphia, Hartford CT, Boston, Rochester, Erie PA, Chicago, Kansas City. 4 February – the pianist purchases 1520 acres of land in Paso Robles, in San Luis Obispo County, in California's Central Coast region. Additional successive purchases of 900, 80, 44, and 320 acres together form Rancho San Ignatio where he grows almond trees and adds vineyards later. Paderewski returns to Europe in May, on 15 June to perform at Queen's Hall in London and on 20 June – to give a symphonic concert in Harrogate, UK. 28 July – start of the Great War, Austria-Hungary attacks Serbia, then Germany declares war against Russia and France, invades Belgium. Great Britain declares war. The Paderewskis host about 60 guests in Riond-Bosson who came to celebrate his name day on 31 July (St. Ignatius Day); the guests are stranded due to the outbreak of the war and closures of banks and railways.
1915	Paderewski, along with patriotic writer and Nobel Prize winner Henryk Sienkiewicz (1846 – 15 November 1916), leads the General Committee for Aid to War Victims in Poland (Comité Général des Secours aux Victimes de la Guerre en Pologne), in Vevey, Switzerland. Branches of the Committee are established in Paris, London (March), and New York, under the name Polish Victims' Relief Fund. May 22, New York – Paderewski appeals to Poles living in America, requesting assistance for Poles affected by the war.

	The Tenth American Concert Tour. May 30, Chicago – Poles rally at the Tadeusz Kościuszko Monument; the artist delivers the first of over 300 patriotic speeches in the U.S., calling for the establishment of "Labor Day for Poland" to fundraise for war victims, on 15 July 1915, the anniversary of the Battle of Grunwald against the Teutonic Knights. 6 July – world premiere of symphonic prelude *Polonia* Op. 76 by Edward Elgar (1857-1934), dedicated to Paderewski, with quotations from the Polish National Anthem *Mazurek Dąbrowskiego*, the *Warszawianka*, other Polish patriotic songs, and themes by Chopin and Paderewski's *Polish Fantasy*. The concert was a benefit for the Polish Victims' Relief Fund and was conducted by the composers at Queen's Hall, London. Denoting "Poland" in Latin, the title may have been a tribute to Paderewski's Symphony in B Minor, *Polonia*. From May 1915 to May 1917, the pianist's concerts become patriotic appeals for assistance for Poland ravaged by the war. He plays Chopin's music and gives rousing speeches. The proceeds are donated to Polish Victims' Relief Fund. 27 August – benefit concert for the Relief Fund at the San Francisco World Exhibition. 1 October – speech at the General Meeting of the Polish National Alliance in Schenectady NY, followed by concerts in New York, Boston, Wilkes-Barre PA, Schenectady & Binghamton NY, Newark, Pittsfield MA, Philadelphia. December - Hartford, New York, Milwaukee, and Boston (2).
1916	The Tenth American Tour continues with patriotic lecture-recitals. January – Chicago, Milwaukee, Minneapolis, Des Moines IA, Columbia MI, Moline IL, Omaha NE, Chicago, Detroit, Toledo OH, St. Louis, Kansas City and Joplin MO. February – Oklahoma City, Tulsa OK, Chicago, Pittsburgh, Wheeling WV, New York, Washington DC, March – New York, Albany NY, Boston, Chicago, Springfield MA, Brooklyn, New Haven, Providence RI, Reading, Waterbury CT. April – Youngstown OH, Washington DC, Bridgeport CT, Wilmington NC, Syracuse NY, New York. 7 May, New York – benefit concert for children of composer Enrique Granados (1867 to 24 March 1916), with violinist Fritz Kreisler (1875-1962) and cellist Pablo Casals (1876-1973). Paderewski becomes acquainted with "Colonel" Edward M. House (1858-1938), the closest aide of Democratic President Thomas Woodrow Wilson (1856-1924, serving in 1913-1921). The pianist seeks to interest the U.S. government in the restoration of Polish independence. 22 February,

	Washington DC – concert at the White House in the presence of President Wilson, one of the most important of the year. 6 November, New Jersey – meeting with President Wilson, discussions about the joint manifesto of the German and Austrian emperors, announced the day before, to create "the Kingdom of Poland" only on the partitions they occupied (excluding the part taken over by Russia). Paderewski sends protests to state leaders against this act. September-October – the pianist continues to give patriotic lecture-recitals in San Francisco, Los Angeles, San Diego, Salt Lake City, Denver, Buffalo, and Philadelphia. November – New York, Cleveland, Boston, Elmira NY, Rochester NY, Chicago, Indianapolis, Dayton OH, Cincinnati, Charleston WV. December – Washington DC, New York, Brooklyn, Boston, and Providence RI. 27 November, Chicago – the pianist speaks at a memorial service of writer Henryk Sienkiewicz who died on the 15th.
1917	January 11, New York – Paderewski as the leader of the Polish diaspora delivers a memorandum to the US President about Poland and the need to restore its independence. 22 January – President Wilson presents his Peace Plan to the Senate, with 13th Point of Poland's Independence. Since April 1916, Paderewski has been speaking publicly to Poles in the U.S. with increasing frequency, appealing for financial support for his compatriots, political pressure to create a Polish army to be sent to Europe, and efforts to achieve recognition of Poland's independence. January – concerts in New York, Boston, Spartanburg SC, Baltimore, Washington DC, Raleigh NC, Columbia, Jacksonville FL, Miami. 7,9 February – two concerts in Havana (Cuba). March – Boston and New York. April – concerts in Pittsburgh, Boston, Canton OH, Detroit, Chicago, St. Louis. 4 April – Speech for the Polish Hawks (Sokolstwo Polskie) a paramilitary youth organization to appeal for recruits to join the Polish Army and to assist the U.S. in the war. 10 May – concert in New York, June – in Chicago. 23 May, New York – Paderewski sends a memorandum to the American authorities advocating for the creation of a Polish Army fighting on the side of the Allies. In New York, he composes his last work, the battle anthem *Hej, Orle Biały. Hymn bojowy poświęcony Armii Polskiej w Ameryce* [Hey, White Eagle. Military Anthem dedicated to the Polish Army in America], to his own words for male voices and piano.

	20 June, New Haven CT – Paderewski receives an Honorary Doctorate from Yale University. September – he expands his California holdings and purchases 2,626 acres of land near Santa Maria, CA, owned jointly with wife Helena. After September 20, the pianist sends a letter to President Wilson asking for the recognition of the Polish National Committee (established on August 15 in Lausanne with Chairman Roman Dmowski and Paderewski) as Poland's official representative in the U.S. He also discusses the need to form a Polish Army in France, supporting the Polish-French military mission visiting the U.S. with this request. 6 December – Paderewski sends a cable to Roman Dmowski requesting 600 Polish officers from Russia to be sent to the newly established Polish Army in America.
1918	8 January – President Wilson, in his Peace Address, recognizes Poland's independence as one of the conditions for future peace in Europe, point 13 of the Peace Plan: "An independent Polish state should be erected, which should include the territories inhabited by indisputably Polish populations which should be assured a free and secure access to the sea, and whose political and economic independence and territorial integrity should be guaranteed by international covenant." 3 March – Paderewski gives a speech about Poland to the National Security League. June-July, Washington – Paderewski begins establishing the Polish White Cross (Helena Paderewska becomes its leader). 9 June – he gives a speech to the soldiers of new Polish Army being trained in Niagara-on-the -Lake. He funds purchases of equipment, and his name is included in the soldiers' rolls called out daily. 26 August, Detroit – the pianist speaks at the First Polish Exile Parliament in America. Recognized as the spiritual leader of the Polish diaspora, he addresses their aspirations to regain an independent, united Poland, including Gdańsk and access to the Batic Sea. He raises funds for the Polish War Victims' Relief Fund. 13 September – Meeting with President Wilson; Paderewski, along with Roman Dmowski, argues for Poland's rights to the Eastern Borderlands (now in Lithuania, Belarus and Ukraine), as well as Silesia, Wielkopolska, and Pomerania, including Gdańsk. British politicians (lord Balfour) also support plans for Polish independence and secure military transport, a cruiser with minesweepers, to take the pianist to Poland. 25 December – Paderewski arrives in Gdańsk on a

	British cruiser *Concord,* on 26 December he goes to Poznań, this visit gives impetus to the outbreak of the Greater Poland Uprising, that helps restore the province's independence..
1919	1 January – Paderewski arrives in Warsaw. January 16 – After lengthy negotiations, he assumes the positions of President of the Council of Ministers and Minister of Foreign Affairs; three days later, he presents the composition of his cabinet to Chief of State Józef Piłsudski. 9 January – he becomes an Honorary Citizen of Warsaw. Paderewski receives Honorary Doctorate from Jagiellonian University in Krakow. 10 January – Inaugural concert of the Warsaw Philharmonic, conducted by Henryk Melcer, with fragments of *Manru* and Tatra dances by Paderewski. 16 January – Paderewski officially becomes Prime Minister and Foreign Minister. 25 January – First meeting of Paderewski's cabinet. 28 June, Paris – Peace Conference – Paderewski, along with Roman Dmowski and the Polish delegation, defends Poland's interests (including the rights to Gdańsk, Pomerania, Greater Poland, Upper Silesia, Cieszyn Silesia, Eastern Galicia, and the Vilnius region); he signs the Treaty of Versailles. Controversies surround new country's borders with Germany, Lithuania, Ukraine, and Czechoslovakia: last minute changes, detrimental to Poland, are made, ceding portions of Silesia and other areas to the neighboring countries (some are restored after the Silesian Uprisings). Paderewski is attacked by his political opponents in the country, led by socialists but he also loses the support of peasant party's leader, Wincenty Witos. 4 December – The cabinet resigns, and due to a lack of support, attempts to form a new government are abandoned (10 December). This is the end of Paderewski's service in a political office in Poland. 17 December – the Symphony *Polonia* is played at the 60th Anniversary of the Warsaw Conservatory.
1920	3 January – Paderewski resigns from his role as representative of Poland to the Peace Conference in Paris. He receives the title of the Honorary Citizen of Poznań, Poland. February – The Paderewskis depart for Riond-Bosson, Switzerland. 18 July – he is nominated to represent Poland at international organizations and meetings. July – following reports of Piłsudski's Kiev campaign, attacking the Soviet Union and seeking to expand Polish borders eastward (which Paderewski did not approve of), and in the face of the Red Army counter-offensive that eventually reached Warsaw, Paderewski informs Prime Minister Grabski of his readiness

	to place himself at the government's disposal to defend Poland's interests; he becomes the Polish government's delegate to the Conference of Ambassadors and the London Conference, as well as to the League of Nations. December – he is granted an Honorary Doctorate by Oxford University in England.
1921	January – Paderewski resigns as the Polish delegate to the Council of Ambassadors due to his critical attitude towards Piłsudski's foreign policy relating to Lithuania and Soviet Russia. May – Paderewski resigns as Poland's delegate to the League of Nations. Resignation accepted on 23 June. He is awarded Polish highest distinction, Order of the White Eagle. Mansion Riond-Bosson in Switzerland becomes his primary residence, continuing the various poultry breeding projects of his wife, Helena, managed by his sister when they travel abroad. He continues to visit Paso Robles, California, annually for winter rest and hot springs cures, staying two to four weeks at a time, in 1921-24. July – he attempts to sell his Paso Robles ranch at auction to raise funds, but the price requirements are not met and the auction is canceled. Paderewski continues to grow almonds and later plants a vineyard of 35,000 vines on his ranch, bringing Petit Syrah and Zinfandel grapes to California. 16 December – gives 25 acres in Paso Robles to stepson Wacław Górski.
1922	Difficult financial circumstances prompt the artist to resume concertizing; Paderewski resides in Paso Robles, where he works on a new repertoire in January and February. November 9 – The Eleventh American Tour commences with its first concert in Worcester, MA, The pianist returns to concert stages worldwide with concerts in the United States and Canada. November – New Haven, Ithaca NY, Rochester, Toronto (Canada), Baltimore, New York (he receives Honorary Doctorate from Columbia University in New York), Syracuse, and Boston. December – Springfield MA, Philadelphia, New York, Providence RI, Lowell MA, Brooklyn Portland ME, and Boston.
1923	Eleventh American Concert Tour continues. January – Buffalo, Cleveland, Ann Arbor MI, Detroit, Pittsburgh, Erie PA, Milwaukee, Minneapolis, St. Paul, Chicago, Dayton OH, Cincinnati, Lexington KY, Montgomery, New Orleans, February – Houston, Dallas, Fort Worth TX, Oklahoma City, Austin, El Paso, Phoenix AZ, San Diego, Los Angeles (3), 28 February – he receives Honorary Doctorate from the University of Southern California In Los Angeles. March –

	concerts in Santa Barbara, Fresno, San Francisco, Denver, Wichita KS, Kansas City, Omaha NE, Des Moines IA, Chicago, Indianapolis. April – Columbus, Springfield OH, Grand Rapids MI, Toledo OH, Akron OH, Troy NY, Philadelphia, Scranton PA, Poughkeepsie NY, Hartford MA, New York, Newark NJ, Boston and, in May, Brooklyn. 3 May – Paderewski receives Polonia Restituta Order from Polish government. 9 June – he gives a benefit concert to sponsor Edouard Colonne Monument in Paris. 14 June – a benefit concert to sponsor scholarships from Paris's Ecole Normale. He continues giving concerts in Paris, London, and Eastbourne. 3 November – he leaves for New York for the Twelfth American Concert Tour. 16 November – Schenectady. January – Baltimore, Richmond, Raleigh and Charlotte NC, Atlanta GA, Asheville NC, December – Lynchburg VA, Philadelphia. Paterson NJ, Providence RI, Montreal (Quebec, Canada) New York (4), Brooklyn, and Boston (2),
1924	January – The 12th American Tour continues with concerts in Philadelphia, Wilkes Barre PA, Toronto (Canada), Buffalo, Canton OH, Cleveland, Detroit, Columbus OH, Pittsburg PA, Youngstown OH, Akron OH, Louisville KY, Chicago, Milwaukee, Springfield IL, February – St. Louis MO, Chicago, Evansville IN, Nashville TN, Birmingham AL, Memphis TN, Pine Bluff AR, Shreveport LA, Fort Worth TX, Tulsa OK, Dallas, Abilene TX, Tucson AZ, Los Angeles,, San Francisco. March – Santa Barbara, Medford OR, Portland OR, Tacoma WA, Vancouver, (Canada), Seattle, Spokane WA. April – Great Falls MT, Duluth MT, Winnipeg (Canada), Grant Forks ND, St. Paul MA, Eau Claire WI, Sioux Falls SD, Rockford IL, Galesburg IL, Terre Haute IN, Cincinnati OH, Jamestown NY. May – Bethlehem PA, Brooklyn, Utica NY, New York. 26 May – Arrives in Brussels to give benefit concert for the victims of war (27 May), and another one in June in Paris. He is awarded Order of Saints Maurice and Lazarus in Italy and Order of Leopold in Belgium. 20 October, Vevey – The pianist chairs the committee for the transfer of Henryk Sienkiewicz's remains to Poland; he speaks at the ceremony. 21-29 October, Poznań – he receives an Honorary Doctorate from the University of Adam Mickiewicz in Poznań, during his last visit to Poland.
1925	January – concerts in Vevey, Geneva (8 Jan. benefit for the Red Cross), and Rome (2). February – recital in London. March – Bournemouth. April – Venice. May – Florence, Rome, Napoli, Vevey, London. 26 May, London –he receives Order of the

	Knight of the Grand Cross of the British Empire and a noble title. The pianist is granted an Honorary Doctorate from the University of Glasgow in Scotland. The 13th American Concert Tour commences. 4 November – arrives in New York. November –Princeton, New Haven, Philadelphia, Hagerstown, Roanoke, Baltimore, New York, Boston. December – Worcester MA, Waterbury CT, Springfield MA, Providence RI, Lowell MA, New York (3), Philadelphia, Washington DC, Boston, Trenton NY.
1926	The 13th American Tour continues. January – Brooklyn, Toronto (Canada), Buffalo, Chicago, Detroit, Fort Wayne IN, Pittsburg, Cleveland, Dayton OH, St. Louis MO, Urbana IL, Indianapolis, Cincinnati, Lexington KY, Atlanta GA. February – Chattanooga and Nashville TN, Daytona Beach FL, Palm Beach, Miami (2), St. Petersburg FL, Havana (Cuba, 2 concerts), Jacksonville FL, Jackson MI, New Orleans. March – Houston, San Antonio, El Paso, Phoenix, Pasadena, Los Angeles (2), San Diego, Santa Barbara, San Francisco. April – Sacramento, Salt Lake City, Denver, Pueblo CO, Kansas City, Davenport IA, Milwaukee, Chicago, Saginaw MI, Toledo OH, Scranton PA, and in May – Hartford CT followed by a return to Europe. November – Paderewski receives an Honorary Doctorate from Cambridge University in England.
1927	The 14th American Concert Tour. January – after concerts in Long Beach and Oakland, he travels to Hawaii, for a concert in Honolulu in February. March – Concert Tour of Australia and New Zealand starts with 3 concerts in Sydney, 2 in Brisbane. April – 2 concerts in Sydney, 2 in Adelaide. May – 8 concerts in Melbourne, one in Bendigo, June – after one concert in Syndey, a series of performances in New Zealand – 3 in Wellington, 2 in Christchurch, two in Dunedin, and one in Auckland. July – Auckland (2), and one in Honolulu. Paderewski returns to Europe and, on 29 October, gives a concert in Zurich.
1928	January – he becomes a honorary president of Association of Young Polish Musicians in Paris, supports the Association with a donation of 10,000 francs. The 16th American Concert Tour starts in January – New Rochelle and Orange NY, Philadelphia, Brooklyn, Troy NY, Springfield MA, Boston, Lancaster PA, Baltimore, Washington DC, Charlottesville VA, Richmond VA, Norfolk, Greensboro NC. February – Atlanta, Knoxville and Nashville TN, Louisville KY, Columbus and Cleveland OH, Pittsburg, Cincinnati, St. Louis MO, Kansas City MO, Wichita KS, Pittsburgh, Omaha NE, Des Moines IA,

	Minneapolis. March – Mankato MA, Milwaukee, Green Bay WI, Madison, Chicago, Detroit, Lansing MI, Buffalo, Toronto (Canada), Syracuse, New York, New Haven CT, Philadelphia, Rochester NY, Chicago. April - Indianapolis, MemphisTN, New Orleans LA, Beamont TX San Antonio, Austin, Dallas, Los Angeles, (2), San Diego, San Francisco, followed by a concert in New York in May. 16 May – a Tribute Dinner in New York for the 10th Anniversary of Poland's independence honoring Paderewski, documented in a book published by The Kościuszko Foundation. Return to Europe. 23 June – a benefit concert in Paris for sanatoria in mountains.
1929	January – a concert tour in Switzerland and France starts in Freiburg, followed by concerts in Bordeaux, Nantes, Lille, Strasburg, Toulouse, Marseilles, Monte Carlo, Cannes, Nice, Brussels, Zurich, and Paris; 300,000 francs in revenue dedicated to assistance of widows and children of war victims through the Marshall Foch Fund. May – Paderewski receives Grand Croix of the Legion of Honor from other French Government. Autumn – Paderewski cancels his American tour due to an appendicitis surgery; he prepares his will before a notary in Morges, with a bequest to the Jagiellonian University, after the expiration of his life, and annuity for his wife and sister (in 1930, Paderewski deposited his will in a Morgan Bank vault in Paris, paid for from his account; it was not discovered until 1949).
1930	January – Paderewski's 70th birthday concert in Vilnius. Paderewski leaves Lausanne sanatorium after three months of recovery. The 70th birthday of Paderewski – gala concerts in Poznań, and Warsaw. The opera *Manru* is performed in Poznań and Warsaw. 20 October – the 17th American Concert Tour commences in Syracuse NY. October – Schenectady and Binghamton NY, Providence RI, Portland ME. November – New York, Harrisburg PA, Toronto (Canada), Fort Wayne IN, Kalamazoo and Grand Rapids MI, Chicago, Detroit MI, Boston, Springfield MA, Philadelphia MA, Baltimore MD, Washington DC, and New York. December – Pittsburgh PA, Columbus and Toledo OH, Milwaukee and Appleton WI, Minneapolis MA, Chicago, Dayton OH, Wheeling WV, Philadelphia, Boston, and New York.
1931	January – The 17th American Concert Tour continues – Brooklyn, Hartford CT, Richmond VA, Raleigh and Charllotte NC, Lynchburg VA, Charleston WV, Indianapolis, Cincinnati, Louisville and Lexington KY, Evansville IN, Nashville TN, Chattanooga TN, Spartanburg SC. February – Atlanta GA,

	Birmingham and Montgomery AL, Shreveport LA, Houston and Fort Worth TX, Abilene and Wichita Falls TX, Amarillo and El Paso TX, Phoenix AZ, San Diego. March – Riverside, Fresno, and San Francisco. After vacations in Paso Robles Paderewski continues the tour in April – Los Angeles, Pasadena, Salt Lake City, Denver CO, Lincoln NE, Minneapolis, Lawrence KS, Warrenburg and St. Louis MO, Bloomington IL, Toronto (Canada). May – Lancaster PA, New Haven CT, New York, Ann Arbor MI, Evanston IL, White Plains NY. Paderewski returns to Europe in June and gives the first concert on 6 June in Paris, with revenue dedicated to the Claude Debussy Monument in Paris. Paderewski is awarded Honorary Doctorate by the University of Warsaw, Poland. June, Riond Bosson – master classes for Polish pianists: Henryk Sztompka, Stanisław Szpinalski (winner of the 2nd Prize at the 1st Chopin Competition), Aleksander Brachocki, Zygmunt Dygat, Albert Tadlewski, and others. Their concert is on 26 June. Autumn – Paderewski on a concert tour of England and Scotland, gives a series of concerts, ending on 15 November – London, at the Royal Albert Hall. December – the pianist becomes a corresponding member of the American Academy of Literature.
1932	18th American Concert Tour continues. January – Ithaca and Montclair NY, Englewood NY, Philadelphia PA, Northampton MA, Boston, New York, Washington DC, Hartford CT, Worcester MA, Boston. February – Troy NY, Toronto (Canada), Rochester NY, Brooklyn, New York, Reading PA, Baltimore MD, Columbia SC, Daytona Beach FL, Orlando, St. Petersburg FL, Miami, West Palm Beach, Macon GA, Memphis TN, Little Rock AR. February 8, New York (Madison Square Garden) – Paderewski's exceptional concert, attended by a record audience of 16,000; Proceeds from the concert are donated to unemployed American musicians. March – Dallas, Tulsa and Oklahoma City OK, Wichita KS, Des Moines IA, Cedar Falls IA, Chicago IL, Madison WI, Bloomington IN, Detroit MI, Cleveland OH, Buffalo, Brooklyn, and Chicago. Paderewski becomes Honorary Citizen of Chicago, with a memorial plaque erected in a park. April – Chicago, Kansas City MO, Los Angeles, Oakland, Vancouver and Victoria (Canada), Portland OR, Seattle and Tacoma WA, Spokane WA, Ogden UT, Cheyenne WY. May – Colorado Springs CO, Manhattan KS, Muncie IN, Greenwich CT, Orange NY, New York. 9 November – concert in Vevey, then Florence, Rome,

	Napoli, Venice. 25 June - another benefit concert in Paris for the victims of war. December – Triest, Milan.
1933	5 January – U.K. Concert Tour starts in Birmingham. 12 January, London – a benefit concert for insurance fund for unemployed musicians. Paderewski also offers support to Jewish intellectuals in Paris (benefit concert on 28 June) . 19th American Concert Tour commences. He arrives on 26 January. February – New Haven CT, Boston, New York, Providence RI. March – Chicago, Pittsburgh PA, Washington DC, White Plains NY. April – New York, Symphony in B Minor conducted by F. Schelling. May-June – concerts in Paris start on the 15th then on the 28th at the Théâtre des Champs-Elysées, he gives a benefit concert for Jewish intellectuals. May – Ignacy and Helena Paderewski become Honorary Citizen of the city of Lausanne, he is awarded Honorary Doctorate by the University of Lausanne in Switzerland and a second Honorary Doctorate by the New York University.
1934	January 16 – Helena Paderewska dies; the artist withdraws from concert life for a year, his life is also marred by bad health. Paderewski biography by Rom Landau is published in London.
1935	Concerts and academies are organized to mark the 75th anniversary of Paderewski's birth in Poland. A compete issue of *Życie Muzyczne i Teatralne* is dedicated to his music.
1936	February, Morges – At the initiative of Władysław Sikorski, Józef Haller and Wincenty Witos arrive in Riond-Bosson to rebuild national unity and form the so-called Front Morges – opposing the government of Marshall Piłsudski. Summer, Denham near London – Paderewski begins work on the film *Moonlight Sonata*, directed by Lothar Mendes, produced by Pall Mall Production Limited. The film features a 20-min. recital – Chopin's Polonaise in A-flat Major, Liszt's *Hungarian Rhapsody*, Beethoven's *Moonlight Sonata*, and his Minuet. Autumn, Riond-Bosson & Paris – Paderewski, with American journalist Mary Lawton, works on *Memoirs*.
1937	18 February – Lausanne benefit concert for those unemployed in the Vaud canton of Switzerland. 28 February – concert in Solothurn for the benefit of Kosciuszko Museum in Switzerland. The pianist's health deteriorated significantly (hypertension, smoking habit, and advanced age). April – a tour of the UK, concerts in Brighton, Leeds, Bristol, Leicester, Newcastle, Manchester. Summer, Morges – collaboration with delegates of the Fryderyk Chopin Society in Warsaw on the *Complete Works* of Fryderyk Chopin (published after the

	war). Editors: Jan Turczynski, Ludwik Bronarski, Bronislawa Wójcik Keuprulian.
1938	Autumn – concerts in Great Britain starting on 8 October in Eastbourne, then in Leeds, Birmingham, Newcastle on Thyne, Manchester, Cheltenham, and Brighton. December – concerts in Lausanne and Vevey, Switzerland.
1939	February 26 – Paderewski's first radio recital in America, broadcast by Radio City New York. March – 20th American Concert Tour commences with recitals in Newark, Cleveland, Cincinnati, Columbus, Detroit, Chicago, Milwaukee, Minneapolis, Omaha. April – Los Angeles, San Francisco, Denver, San Antonio, Dallas, Houston, Atlanta, Raleigh. May – Newark, Philadelphia, Pittsburgh, Boston, Providence, New Haven. 21 May – Rochester, the last public concert. 5 May, New York – Paderewski's statement broadcast by NBC regarding Józef Beck's rejection of the German ultimatum (with the support of Polish diplomacy). 31 May – Appeal to the Polish American community, printed in almost all Polish diaspora newspapers. 1 July – Paderewski returns to Switzerland aboard the *Normandy*. 1 September – From the outbreak of war, Paderewski engages in political and patriotic activities, organizing aid for war victims in Poland, sending memorials and letters to politicians, and speaking via radio to the American, British, and French communities, as well as to his compatriots in the US and Poland. *The Paderewski Memoirs* published by Collins in London.
1940	23 January, Paris – Paderewski speaks during the inaugural meeting of the National Council of the Republic of Poland in exile. He was elected Chairman of the National Council. May – Paderewski appeals on the radio to the Americans, British, and French for help for the victims of invaded Poland. 23 September – Paderewski travels via Spain and Portugal to the United States. Before leaving, he records a farewell radio address to the Swiss, explaining his reasons. 6 November – Paderewski arrives in New York on his 80th birthday; he resides at the Buckingham Hotel; delivers speeches on the airwaves in French, English, and Polish; speaks at rallies and political meetings, and publishes articles in the press.
1941	January – The artist records further speeches, encouraging Poles to fight; appealing to the world for help for Poland, insisting on the use of the Polish language by Polonia (speeches to the Polish Diaspora Council, etc.). 3 February – Paderewski leaves for Florida and stays in Palm Beach to the end of April; he hosts journalists, artists, and politicians

	(including Władysław Sikorski and Stanisław Mikołajczyk). He returns to New York in May. Paderewski's American activities are supported by his secretary, Sylwin Strakacz, representing the pianist on numerous occasions. 15-22 February – concerts are scheduled across the U.S. celebrating 50th anniversary of Paderewski's first American concerts – these Paderewski-themed events collect funds for Polish victims of war. The Paderewski Week features over 6,000 concerts in his honor. The 80-year-old artist restarts his Polish Relief Fund; his speeches are recorded and broadcast. The last of the speeches on 22 June is recorded and filmed in Oak Ridge, NJ, at the Polish Army Veterans' Convention; this is his final public speech. 27 June – Paderewski falls ill. 29 June, New York (Buckingham Hotel) – Paderewski dies of pneumonia. 3 July – the funeral Mass at the St. Patrick Cathedral, in New York is followed by burial at the Arlington Cemetery on 5 July. At the Cathedral, Paderewski's coffin is draped in the Polish banner; crowds of residents bid farewell on the city streets and at the Buckingham Hotel. The funeral procession, carrying the coffin on an eight-horse carriage, travels to Pennsylvania Station and then to the Polish Embassy in Washington, D.C. 5 July – Funeral ceremonies, with the highest military honors, at Arlington National Cemetery, in the rotunda of the heroes of the battleship USS Maine, thanks to a special act by President Franklin Delano Roosevelt, approved by the Senate and Congress. After his 1941 death, Paderewski receives Order of Virtuti Militari, Silver Cross (posthumous) from the Polish Government in Exile in London. The music publisher Boosey & Hawkes commissions 17 prominent composers to contribute a solo piano piece each for an album to commemorate the 50th anniversary of Paderewski's American debut in 1891. This becomes a posthumous tribute to Paderewski's life and work, Homage to Paderewski (1942). The Polish Museum of America in Chicago receives a donation of his personal possessions after his death in June 1941, as a bequest from Paderewski and his sister, Antonina Paderewska Wilkonska. The Paderewski Room is officially opened on 3 November 1941.
1948	The Ignacy Paderewski Foundation is established in New York City by Edward and Jeannette Witkowski to provide scholarships to gifted musicians. Today, the Paderewski Foundation of Cleveland, Ohio, FEIN 13-1673648, is listed as

	still active, with a purpose of granting scholarships, albeit with no assets, activities, nor 990 Tax Returns on record.
1960	Installation of a Paderewski star, honoring him as a musician, on the Hollywood Walk of Fame in California.
1961	The Music Society in Bydgoszcz, Poland, organizes an International Paderewski Piano Competition, held every three years, in 2025 – the 13th Competition takes place.
1963	9 May – Arlington Cemetery: the President John F. Kennedy funds and unveils a plaque announcing that the remains of the Polish statesman are temporarily buried there.
1964	Polonia Paderewski Chorus of New Britain Inc. is incorporated in Connecticut; it continues to be active as a community music organization until this day.
1986	Antonina Wilkońska, Paderewski's sister, entrusted the artist's heart to the care of the Polish community. First kept in hospital vaults, in 1986 it is placed in the National Shrine of Our Lady of Częstochowa in Doylestown, Pennsylvania. In Bydgoszcz, Poland, the Music Society (Towarzystwo Muzyczne), in operation since 1922, changes its name to Towarzystwo Muzyczne im. I. J. Paderewskiego and adds to its mission the promotion of Paderewski's music.
1992	29 June – The coffin containing Paderewski's ashes is brought back to Poland, to the vault of St. John's Cathedral in Warsaw; with the participation of President Bush and Lech Wałęsa. In accordance with Paderewski's will, his ashes are buried in finally independent Poland.
1993	The first of two music festivals honoring Paderewski is initiated in the United States, both in November. Organized annually since 1993 in Paso Robles, California, after a hiatus, it is reorganized and expanded in 2007. with support of the Polish government, in collaboration with Polish Music Center at the University of Southern California, Los Angeles (an initiative of Director Marek Żebrowski).
2002	To recognize the most eminent Polish composers, promote their achievements in America, and commemorate Paderewski's 1923 Honorary Doctorate from the University of Southern California, the Polish Music Center at USC initiates Annual Paderewski Lecture Recitals in Los Angeles, established by Dr. Maja Trochimczyk.
2006	The Paderewski Association in Chicago is formed in 2006, by Stefan and Diana Bernacki, to "secure the legacy of Ignacy Jan Paderewski in America by restoring the prominence of his timeless virtues" – in practice, by providing support the

	Polish Museum of America and various Paderewski-themed projects in Chicago.
2008	The Paderewski Music Society in Los Angeles is created in 2008, upon the initiative of Boenig engineer, Christopher Onzol, to promote Paderewski's music. The Society organizes international piano competitions every three years; it is managed by professional pianists and community volunteers, with the artistic director Dr. Wojciech Kocyan.
2012	The Paderewski Foundation is established in Warsaw, Poland, with a "mission is to stimulate social and economic development through the implementation of tasks related to the development of science, culture and economy." Another new Polish-Ukrainian Foundation of Ignacy Jan Paderewski of Warsaw has a purpose of furthering Polish Ukrainian collaborations.
2014	The second Paderewski Festival is held since 2014 in Raleigh, North Carolina (The Ignacy Jan Paderewski Festival Of Raleigh Inc.) organized by Honorary Consul of Poland, Dr. Mark A. Fountain III and his wife, pianist Brenda Bruce.

Ignacy Jan Paderewski with his crew on his personal railroad carriage that he lived on instead of lodging in hotels while touring the U.S. and Canada. About 1894-1900, Los Angeles. Wikimedia Commons.

Paderewski Writings

By Maja Trochimczyk

Books and Editions

- *The Paderewski Memoirs*, by Ignacy Jan Paderewski and Mary Lawton. New York: Charles Scribner's Sons, 1938.
- *Pamiętniki,* ed. Mary Lawton. Polish trans. Wanda Lisowska and Teresa Mogilnicka. Krakow: PWM, 1986, 6th ed.
- *Pamiętniki: 1912-1932* [Memoirs: 1912-1932]. Edited by Mary Lawton. Translated, edited and introduced by Andrzej Piber. Krakow: Polskie Wydawnictwo Muzyczne, 1992.
- *The Paderewski memoirs, Part II, 1914-1932* by Ignace Jan Paderewski, eds. Mary Lawton and Christopher Onzol. Los Angeles: Paderewski Music Society, 2011.
- Ignacy Jan Paderewski, Halina Janowska (ed.), *Archiwum polityczne Ignacego Paderewskiego*. Polska Akademia Nauk and Archiwum Akt Nowych. Wrocław: Zakład Narodowy im. Ossolinskich, 1973-2007.
- *F. Chopin, Dzieła wszystkie*, [Complete Works]. Ignacy Jan Paderewski, Editor-in-Chief. Krakow: PWM, 1949-61.
- *The Century Library of Music* vol. 1-20. New York: The Century Co., 1900-1902. Editor-in-Chief of the series. Co-edited by Fanny Morris Smith and Barnard Boekelman.

Articles

- "Korespondencje muzyczne z Berlina," [Musical correspondence from Berlin]. *Echo Muzyczne i Teatralne* 18 and 26 (1884).
- "*Konrad Wallenrod* Władysława Zelenskiego" [review]. *Tygodnik Ilustrowany* 115 (1885): 175-6.
- "Antoni Rutkowski (Wspomnienie posmiertne)." *Echo Muzyczne Teatralne i Artystyczne* (EMTA) 168 (18 December 1886): 543.
- "Impressions and Opinions." *The Independent* 52 (24 May 1900): 1234-1235.
- "What Good Piano Playing Calls For." *Ladies Home Journal* 24 (February 1907): 8.

- "Tempo rubato" in Henry Finck, *Success in Music and How It Is Won*. New York: Macmillan, 1909, 454-61. I Polish in *Słowo Polskie* 49 (1910). Reprint "Poetic Piano Playing" in *Ladies' Home Journal* 27 (March 1910): 17, 84. Reprint "Tempo rubato: The Best Way to Study the Piano," in *The Paderewski Paradox/Le paradoxe Paderewski*. Lincoln: Klavar Music Foundation, 1992. Reprint online in *Polish Music Journal* 4: (summer 2001).
- "Helpless Poland." *The Independent* 83 (9 Aug. 1915): 192.
- "Paderewski Pleads for Food for Poland's Starving Millions." *Musical America* (16 October 1915).
- "W gorę serca i oczy w gorę! Apel Mistrza Paderewskiego," [Raise up your hearts and your eyes. An appeal by Paderewski], article in *Jednodniówka of the Polish Roman-Catholic Union in Chicago*, May 1915; reprinted in Jozef Orłowski, ed. *Paderewski i Odbudowa Polski*, vol. 2. Chicago: The Stanek Press, 1940, 49-50.
- "Paderewski's Letter to Polish Organizations of 22 May 1915," in Jozef Orłowski, ed. *Paderewski i Odbudowa Polski*, vol. 2. Chicago: The Stanek Press, 1940, 66-67.
- "Independent Poland: Why the Ancient Democratic Nation Should be Resurrected." *World's Work* 37 (December 1918): 173-179.
- "Future of Poland." *Living Age* 301 (28 June 1919): 779-782.
- "Paderewski on Rhythm." *Etude* 42 (December 1924): 882.
- "Chopin." *Etude* 44 (February 1926): 95-96.
- Introduction to Charles Kellog, *Jadwiga, Poland's Great Queen,* New York, 1931.
- "O stylu narodowym w muzyce," reprint of one of music reports from Berlin of 1884, *Muzyka* 3-4, (1932): 79.
- *Poland and Peace*. London: Wishart & Co., 1933.
- "Musical Opinion," *Musical Digest* (October 1933), 9. Reprinted as "The Arts in the Wilderness," in *Polish Music Newsletter* 7: 11 (November 2001).
- "Z mych wspomnien" *Muzyka* 4-6 (1933): 117-19 (trans. of an interview in *The Daily Mail* "My Sixty Years of Music").
- Introduction to Henryk Opienski, ed. *Lettre de Chopin*, Paris, 1933.
- "Muzyka jedna jest istotnie zywą sztuką (wypowiedz)" [Music is really a live art. A statement] in "Trzy głosy o muzyce," [Three voices about music]. *Muzyka* 2 (1933): 3.
- "Poland's So-Called Corridor." *Foreign Affairs* 11 (April 1933): 420-433.

- "Wizje przyszłosci" [Visions of the future] *Muzyka* 1-2 (1936): 887.
- "Mysli uwagi, refleksje." [Thoughts, remarks, reflections]. *Muzyka* 2 (1934): 49-51.

Selected Speeches and Lectures

- "Chopin, mowa" in *Obchód setnej rocznicy urodzin Chopina i Pierwszy Zjazd Muzyków Polskich we Lwowie,* Lwow 1912, 195-202, reprinted in *Kompozytorzy polscy o Fryderyku Chopinie* (ed. M. Tomaszewski), Krakow: PWM, 1959, 69-107. Reprinted as *Chopin: A Discourse,* trans. Laurence Alma-Tadema, London: Addlington, 1911. French trans. Laurence Alma-Tadema. New York, 1911. Reprint in *Polish Music Journal* 4: 2 (winter 2001).
- "Paderewski's Speech." in "Paderewski as Orator and Pianist in San Francisco." *Musical Courier* (9 February 1915). Reprint in *Polish Music Journal* 4: 1 (winter 2001).
- "Paderewski Pleads for Food for Poland's Starving Millions. *Musical America* (16 October 1915). Reprinted in *Polish Music Journal* 4: 1 (winter 2001).
- "Polska straznikiem całej Europy! Polska Obroncą Chrzescijanstwa!" (Poland as the guardian of Europe! Poland as the Defender of Christianity). Paderewski's speech at the Kosciuszko Monument on 15 May 1915, in Jozef Orłowski, ed. *Paderewski i Odbudowa Polski*, vol. 2. Chicago: The Stanek Press, 1940, 54-55.
- *Poland Past and Present.* Address by Ignacy Jan Paderewski. New York, 1916.
- "Mowa Mistrza I. J. Paderewskiego wygłoszona na wieczornicy załobnej [...] z powodu smierci Henryka Sienkiewicza" [Speech of Master Paderewski given on the memorial evening on the occasion of the death of Henryk Sienkiewicz], Chicago 1917; reprinted in Jozef Orłowski, ed. *Paderewski i Odbudowa Polski*, vol. 2. Chicago: The Stanek Press, 1940, 173-175. Reprinted in English transl. by Maria Piłatowicz in *Polish Music Journal* 4: 2 (winter 2001).
- "Paderewski w sprawie utworzenia Armii Kosciuszkowskiej," [Paderewski about the creation of a Kosciuszko Army], speech at the Extraordinary Seym of the Sokolstwo, Pittsburgh, 8 April 1917,

in Jozef Orłowski, ed. *Paderewski i Odbudowa Polski*, vol. 2. Chicago: The Stanek Press, 1940, 199-200.

- "W Stuletnią Rocznicę Zgonu Kosciuszki," [On the hundredth anniversary of Kosciuszko's death], speech of 17 October 1917, Chicago, Dexter Pavilion; in Jozef Orłowski, ed. *Paderewski i Odbudowa Polski*, vol. 2. Chicago: The Stanek Press, 1940, 213-216. English trans. by Maria Piłatowicz in *Polish Music Journal* 4: 2 (winter 2001).

- "W rocznicę zgonu T. Kosciuszki w Jersey City, 25 Listopada 1917. Porywająca Mowa Paderewskiego." [On the anniversary of the death of Kosciuszko, in Jersey City, 25 November 1917. Sublime Speech by Paderewski], in Jozef Orłowski, ed. *Paderewski i Odbudowa Polski,* vol. 2. Chicago: The Stanek Press, 1940, 232-234.

- "Speech to the National Security League, 3 March 1918," in Jozef Orłowski, ed. *Paderewski i Odbudowa Polski*, vol. 2. Chicago: The Stanek Press, 1940, English version 242-244; reprint *Polish Music Journal* 4: 2 (winter 2001). Polish trans. J. Orłowski, 239-241.

- "Paderewski w odpowiedzi na mowę mayora Detroit," [Paderewski in response to the speech of the Mayor of Detroit], at the Wielki Seym Wychodzstwa Polskiego w Ameryce, [Great Seym of the Polish Emigration in America], Detroit, 26-30 August 1918, in Jozef Orłowski, ed. *Paderewski i Odbudowa Polski,* vol. 2. Chicago: The Stanek Press, 1940, 279-281.

- "Przemowienie sejmowe z 20 II 1919 (na I posiedzeniu Sejmu Ustawodawczego)," [A Seym Speech of 20 February 1919, at the First Session of Seym], *Kurier Warszawski* no. 52 (21 II 1919).

- „O chwili bieżącej w Rzeczpospolitej" (Przemowienie sejmowe 12 XI 1919) [About the present moment of the Republic. A Speech at the Seym, 12 November 1919]. Krakow, 1919.

- *Discours prononcé à Vevey, le 20 octobre 1924 a l'occasion de la translation des cendres de Henryk Sienkiewicz en Pologne.* Lausanne 1925, see also "Mowa Mistrza..."

- "Remarks in Self-Defense," speech at a testimonial dinner of 1928, New York (originally untitled); reprinted in Part III of "Paderewski and the Tenth Anniversary of Poland's Independence (1928)" ed. Maja Trochimczyk, *Polish Music Journal* 4: 1 (Summer 2001).

- *Poland and Peace.* Garden City, 1932.

- "La Pomeranie Polonaise," *La Pologne et la Paix*, Warszawa 1933.

- *L'Allemagne et le Corridor polonais*, H. Strasburger. Paris: le Comite Polonais. n.d.

- "Buy a Share in America" [flyer, printout of a radio appeal], Washington D.C.: U.S. Treasury and U.S. Government Printing Office, 1941.

≡ ∭ ≡

Paderewski's Compositions

by Maja Trochimczyk

Notes

Paderewski's compositions have been published by
- Bote und G. Bock in Berlin, abbreviated to "B&B"
- 19th-century Polish periodical *Echo Muzyczne Teatralne and Artystyczne,* abbreviated to „EMTA" and its predecessors, EM and EMT.
- *Utwory fortepianowe Ignacego Jana Paderewskiego* [Paderewski's Piano Works]. Ed. R. Smendzianka. vol. 1-8. Published as facsimile of early prints, Warsaw: Akademia Muzyczna im. F. Chopina, 1996.
- Series *Dzieła Wszystkie* [Complete Works] vol. 1-12 (ed. M. Perkowska-Waszek). Krakow: Musica Iagellonica, 1998 -2007. Abbreviated to "CWP" below. Eight volumes published so far. Vol. I, II, III i IV - *Utwory fortepianowe* (Piano Works); Vol. V - *Utwory Kameralne* (Chamber Music], Vol. VI – *Pieśni* (Songs); Vol. VIII - *Fantazja polska gis-moll, Op. 17* (Polish Fantasy in G-sharp minor); Vol. X *Uwertura Es- dur i Suita G-dur* (Overture in E-flat major and Suite in G major). Volumes in preparation: Vol. VII - *Koncert fortepianowy a-moll* (Piano Concerto in A minor); Vol. IX - *Symfonia h-moll* (Symphony in B minor); Vol. XI - Opera *Manru*; and Vol. XII - *Varia.*

Music for and with Orchestra

Overture in E-flat major, 1884. CWP, Vol. 10, 1997.

Suite in G major for string orchestra, 1884. CWP, Vol. 10, 1997.

Symphony in B minor, "Polonia," 1903-1909, Paris: Heugel et Cie, 1911.

Concerto in A minor, Op. 17 for piano and orchestra (dedicated to Theodor Leschetitzky), 1882-89. B&B, 1890.

Fantaisie polonaise sur des themes originaux (Polish Fantasy or Fantasia) in G-sharp minor, Op. 19 (dedicated to R. de Brancovan), 1891-93. B&B, 1895.

Manru. Lyric Drama in 3 acts to a libretto by Alfred Nossig, based on Jozef Ignacy Kraszewski's novel, *Chata za wsią* [A hut beyond the village] 1893-1901, Published: Berlin Bote and Bock, 1901. Piano Reduction in English translation by Henry Krehbiel, New York: G. Schirmer, 1901. Premiered: Dresden, 29 May 1901.

Music for Piano Solo

Waltz in F major, ca. 1876, CWP, Vol. 4, 1997.

Impromptu in F major, 1878/79 (dedicated to R. Stroblow), Wwa 1879 EM No. 11, CWP, Vol. 4, 1997.

Suite in E-flat major, Op. 1 (dedicated to "F.L.?]"), 1879, 4 mvts.:
> 1. Preludium a Cappriccio in E-flat major, Op. 1 ,No. 1;
> 2. Menuetto in G minor (published with changes as Minuetto in *Zwei Klavierstücke,* Op. 1, No. 2, B&B 1886),
> 3. Romans in A-flat major
> 4. *Burleska* in E-flat major

Trois morceaux, Op. 2 (dedicated to Wlasoff) 1880, Warszawa: Kruzinski and Levi, 1881:
> 1. *Gavotte* in E minor
> 2. *Mélodie* in C major
> 3. *Valse mélancolique* in A major

Stara Suita, na trzy głosy [Old suite for 3 voices] Op. 3 (dedicated to A. Zarzycki), 1880/81, 4 mvts.; (dedication on manuscript: "for my wife" "for you"] 1880, published B&B, 1882:
1. Preludium in D minor   2. Intermezzo in B-flat major
3. Aria in F major   4. Fugue in D minor

Danses polonaises, Op. 5 (dedicated to Nathalie Janotha) 1881, Publ.: B&B, 1882:
> 1. Krakowiak in E major

2. Mazurek in E minor

3. Krakowiak in B-flat major

Introduction et toccata, Op. 6 (dedicated to P. Schlozer), 1881-1882, Publ.: B&B, 1884.

Chants du voyageur, Op. 8 (dedicated to Helena Gorska),1881-82, five movements. Publ.: B&B, 1882:

  1. *Allegro agitato*   2. *Andantino*

  3. *Andantino grazioso* 4. *Andantino mistico*

  5. *Allegro giocoso*

Danses polonaises, Op. 9 (dedicated to H. Toeplitz), 1882 (No. 2-4) and 1884 (No. 1, 6), Publ.: B&B, 1884:

  1. Krakowiak in F major 2. Mazurek in A minor

  3. Mazurek in A major 4. Mazurek in B major

  5. Krakowiak in A major 6. Polonez in B major

Album de Mai. Scenes romantiques, Op. 10 (dedicated to A. Essipov, i.e., Anna Yesipova, pianist) before January 1884, 5 movements; B&B, 1884.

  1. *Au soir*   2. *Chant d'amour* 3. *Scherzino*

  4. *Barcarola*   5. *Caprice-valse*

Powódź [Flood] in A minor, 1884, publ. in *Na pomoc* [Help!], an occasional brochure, Warsaw, 1884. CWP, Vol. 4, 1997.

Intermezzo in C minor, 1882 (part of an unfinished piano sonata), EMTA No. 77, 89, 1885; CWP Vol. 4, 1997.

Variations et fugue sur un theme original in A minor Op. 11 (dedicated to E. d'Albert), 1882/3 and 1884, B&B 1885.

Album tatrzańskie [The Tatra Album], Op. 12, in four movements, 1883 (No. 1-3), 1884 (No. 4).

  1. *Allegro cómodo,* Publ.: Warsaw, 1883 EMTA No. 1

  2. *Andantino grazioso*

  3. *Maestoso, vivace*

  4. *Allegro poco moderato,* Publ.:1884 EMTA No. 314, 41, 51

Tatra Album. Tänze und Lieder des polnischen Volkes aus Zakopane [Polish folk dances and songs from Zakopane, arranged by the composer for 4 hands], (dedicated to Tytus Chałubinski) 1884, in six movements; published Berlin: Ries und Erler, 1884.

  Part I:

1. *Allegro con brio.* 2. *Andantino,* 3. *Allegro con moto;*
Part 2:
4. *Allegro maestoso,* 5. *Allegretto* 6. *Allegro ma non troppo,*

Suite in E-flat major (unfinished; individual movements published separately):
    1. Toccata, 1886-87 (published as Op. 16)
    2. Preludium. 1885 (published as Op. 1, No. 1)
    3. Scherzo [missing]
    4. Romans, 1885/86 (publ. *Melodia* or *Legenda* Op. 16)
    5. Intermezzo, 1886 (published as Op. 14, Part 2, No. 2)
    6. Variations and Finale, 1885-87 (publ. Op. 16, No. 3 & Op. 23)

Zwei Klavierstücke Op. 1 (dedicated to A. Rutkowski):
    1. *Praeludium et capriccio* in E-flat major, 1885,
    2. *Minuetto* in G minor 1879, B&B 1886;

Humoresques de concert, Op. 14 (dedicated to A. Essipov), 6 works:
Cahier 1, à l'antique, B&B, June 1887:
    1. Minuet in G major (before 8 Nov. 1886)
    2. Sarabande in B minor (Jan. 1887)
    3. *Caprice* (genre Scarlatti) in G major (Jan. 1887)
Cahier 2, moderne. B&B, Oct. 1887:
    4. *Burlesque* in F major (ca. 1887)
    5. *Intermezzo polacco* in C minor (1885/86)
    6. *Cracovienne fantastique* in B major (Nov. 1886, Publ.: Warsaw. 1887. EMTA No. 171, without opus, dedicated to A. Michałowski).

Dans le désert. l. *Tableau musical en forme d'une toccata* in E-flat major Op. 15 (dedicated to A. Essipov, prob. Anna Yesipova, Russian pianist) 1886-87, published B&B, 1887.

Miscellanea. Série de morceaux Op. 16, 7 works, editions: No. 1-3, B&B ca. 1888, No. 1-4, ca. 1892, No. 5, ca. 1895, Op. 16, ca. 1895-96:
    1. *Légende* No. 1 in A-flat major, written in 1886 or 1888 (dedicated to C. Scheurer-Kastner),
    2. *Mélodie* in G-flat major, 1885 (dedicated to M. Trelat),
    3. *Thème varié* in A major, 1885-87 (dedicated to A. Weber-Schlumberger),
    4. Nocturne in B major, ca. 1890-92 (dedicated to R. de Brancovan),

5. *Légende* No. 2 in A major, ca. 1894 (dedicated to H. Bibesco), Publ.: New York, Nov. 2, 1894 in *The Strand Magazine*.
6. *Un moment musical*, 1891, Published: New York, 2 Oct. 1891 *The New York Herald*.
7. Minuet in A major, 1890-1896. Publ.: London, Wilcocks, ca. 1896;
8. *Canzone. Chant sans paroles*, ca. 1890-1903, Publ.: B&B, ca. 1907, CWP vol. 4 1997.

Mazurka in G major, 1896, facsimile, Publ.: Philadelphia, 1896 in *Ladies' Home Journal*. CWP, Vol. 4, 1997.

Miniatura in E-flat major, no date. Publ.: CWP, Vol. 4, 1997.

Sonate pour piano in E-flat minor Op. 21, 1887 and 1903 (dedicated to Austrian Prince Karol Stefan), Publ.: B&B, ca. 1906, CWP, Vol. 3, 2000.

Variations et fugue sur un theme original in E-flat minor, Op. 23, 1885 and 1903 (dedicated to W. Adlington), Publ.: B&B, no date. ca. 1906, CWP, Vol. 3, 2000.

Music for Chamber Ensembles

Piece in F major for violin and piano (dedicated to Jozef Ignacy Kraszewski), 1878.

Romance in A major for violin and piano, Op. 7, ca. 1881-82 (dedicated to Władysław Gorski).

Sonata in A minor, Op. 13, for violin and piano, composed in January to April, 1885 (dedicated to Pablo de Sarasate), pub. B&B, 1886.

Variations and Fugue for String Quartet, 1882; 3 sketches, 1882, 1884, 1887 (incomplete).

Ćwiczenia [Excercises] for wind ensemble, 1884 (unpublished).

Songs and Choral Music

Vier Lieder, Op. 7, to texts by Adam Asnyk 1882-85 (dedicated to Adam Asnyk), Publ.: B&B, ca. 1888:
    1.   *Gdy ostatnia róża zwiędła* [when the last rose withers]

2. *Siwy koniu* [Grey horse]
3. *Szumi w gaju brzezina* [The birch rustles in the grove]
4. *Chłopca mego mi zabrali* [They took my boy away from me]

Konwalijka [Lily of the valley], (incipit, "Nie będę ci rwała"...) to words of A. Asnyk, Op. 7, No. 5, 1882, not in the edition by B&B.

Six Songs, Op. 18 to texts by Adam Mickiewicz 1887-93 (dedicated to Władysław. Mickiewicz), Publ.: B&B 1893:
1. *Polały się łzy* [The tears flowed]
2. *Idę ja Niemnem* [and go along Niemen] (Dudziarz)
3. *Moja pieszczotka* [My darling]
4. *Nad wodą wielką* [Upon the great water]
5. *Tylem wytrwał* [I have endured so much]
6. *Gdybym się zmienił* [If and should change]

Dans la forêt to text by Theodore Gautier, ca. 1896 (dedicated to Maurel), New York, G. Schirmer, 1896.

Douze Mélodies sur des Poésies de Catulle Mendès, Op. 22, to poetry of C. Mendes, 1903 (dedicated to M. Trelat), Paris, Heugel et Cie, ca. 1904, later published in German in 1911:

1. *Dans la forêt*	2. *Ton coeur est d'or pur*
3. *Le ciel est très bas*	4. *Naguère*
5. *Un jeune pâtre*	6. *Elle marche d'un pas distrait*
7. *La nonne*	8. *Viduité*
9. *Lune froide*	10. *Querelleuse*
11. *L'Amour fatal*	12. *L'Ennemie;*

Hej, Orle Biały! Hymn bojowy poświęcony Armii Polskiej w Ameryce. [Hey, White Eagle. Military Anthem dedicated to the Polish Army in America], to a text by the composer; song for male chorus and piano or wind ensemble. Composed in 1917 in New York, published in 1918. Reprinted in *Songs* CWP vol. VI, 2001. Text reprinted and translated into English by Maja Trochimczyk in her paper, "Master of Harmonies or Poland's Savior? Paderewski in Poetry," *Polish Music Journal* 4: 1 (summer 2001).

Paderewski Archives and Musea

Maja Trochimczyk

- *Archiwum Ignacego Jana Paderewskiego* (Paderewski Archive) in Archiwum Akt Nowych (Archives of New Records), Warsaw. Archival collections from 1880 to 1941.
- *Ignacy Jan Paderewski's Personal Library* at the Osrodek Dokumentacji Muzyki Polskiej XIX I XX wieku im. I. J. Paderewskiego. Jagiellonian University, Institute of Musicology, Krakow, Poland.
- *The Paderewski Room.* Polish Museum of America, Chicago.
- *Paderewski Archive – The Paso Robles Collection.* Polish Music Center, University of Southern California, Los Angeles. Donated by Henry Blythe III.
- *Musée Paderewski*, Le Chateau, Rue du Chateau, 1110 Morges, paderewski-morges.ch (near his former estate in Riond Bosson).
- *Muzeum Wychodźstwa Polskiego im. Ignacego Jana Paderewskiego* w Warszawie. Oddział Muzeum Łazienki Krolewskie w Warszawie, ul. Agrykola 1, 00-460 Warszawa, Poland, www.lazienki.ueu.pl.
- *Paderewski Centre/Centrum Paderewskiego* w Kąsnej Dolnej. Kąsna Dolna 17 | 33-190 Ciężkowice, Poland. centrumpaderewskiego,pl.

≡ ∫∫∫ ≡

Selected Bibliography

by Maja Trochimczyk

Andress, Bart. *Ignace Jan Paderewski: Artist, Humanitarian, Statesman: A Digest of Material for Speakers, Writers and Campaign Workers.* New York: Paderewski Fund for Polish Relief, 1940 or 1941.

Baughan, Edward Algernon. *Ignaz Jan Paderewski.* London, New York: J. Lane Co., 1940, 3nd ed.

Biskupski, Mieczysław B. 'Paderewski as Leader of American Polonia, 1914-1918,' Polish American Studies 43:1 (1986), 37-56.

Biskupski, M. B. "Paderewski, Polish Politics, and the Battle of Warsaw, 1920." *Slavic Review*, 46 (1987), 503.

Biskupski, M. B. "The Origins of The Paderewski Government In 1919: A Reconsideration in Light of New Evidence." *The Polish Review*, 33 (1988), 157.

Biskupski, M. B. „Wilson, Paderewski, and the Polish Question, 1914-1921: Eugene Kusielewicz's Historical Works." *Polish American Studies*, 56 (1999), 89.

Borland, Andrew. *Paderewski, Polish Pianist and President.* Kilmarnock: John Ritchie, 19—n.d.

Braun, Kazimierz. *Dzieci Paderewskiego. Paderewski's children. Paderewski wraca. Paderewski returns. Dwa dramaty. Two dramas.* Warsaw: Instytut Dziedzictwa Mysli Narodowej im. Romana Dmowskiego i Ignacego J. Paderewskiego, 2021.

Braun Kazimierz. *Dramaty Zebrane. Collected Plays. Tom 1. Volume 1. Teatr Jednego Aktora. Plays for One Actor (Maestro Paderewski in Polish and English).* Los Angeles: Moonrise Press, 2025.

Braun Kazimierz. *Dramaty Zebrane. Collected Plays. Tom 4. Volume 4. Teatr Pamięci. Theater of Memory* (two plays about Paderewski in Polish and English). Los Angeles: Moonrise Press, 2025.

Cartwright, Jim. *Immortal Performances Discographic Data: No. 6, Ignace Jan Paderewski Recordings.* Austin: J. Cartwright, 1978.

Cieplinski, Jan. *Ignacy Jan Paderewski (w setną rocznicę urodzin).* Wykonano w drukarni Społki Wydawn. Czas, New York, 1960.

Dobrzanski, Slawomir. "From Paderewski to Penderecki: The Polish Musician in Pennsylvania." *The Polish Review*, 63: 1, (January 2018), 99.

Dodson, Alan. "Metrical Dissonance and Directed Motion in Paderewski's Recordings of Chopin's Mazurkas." *Journal of Music Theory*, 53 (2009), 57.

Drozdowski, Marian Marek. *Ignacy Jan Paderewski: pianista, kompozytor, mąż stanu.* Warsaw: Wydawnictwo DiG, 2001.

Drozdowski, Marian Marek. *Tradycja Kościuszkowska w życiu i twórczości Ignacego Jana Paderewskiego.* Polska Fundacja Kosciuszkowska, 1991.

Dulęba, Władysław, Zofia Sokołowska, and Wiktor Litwinski. *Paderewski.* New York: Kosciuszko Foundation, 1979.

Dziadek, Magdalena, Michał Jaczynski, Justyna Kica. "The Grand Piano of Ignacy Jan Paderewski in Cartoons." *Fontes Artis Musicae* 70 (2023), 34.

Finck, Henry T. *Paderewski and His Art.* New York: Wittingham and Atterton, 1892.

Giron, Simone. *Tajemnica testamentu Paderewskiego* [Mystery of Paderewski's Last Will]. Krakow: PWM, 1996.

Hoskins, Janina W. *Ignacy Jan Paderewski, 1860-1941: A Biographical Sketch and a Selective List of Reading Materials.* MLibrary, Prepared for Publishing by HP, Ann Arbor, 2011.

House, Edward Mandell. "Paderewski, the Paradox of Europe." *The Harper's Magazine*, December 1925.

Howard, Lord of Penrith. "Paderewski: Musician, Patriot, Statesman." *Foreign Affairs* 14: 1 (1936), 309.

Jenner, Aleksander. "The 'Paderewski Edition' of Chopin's Works." *Musicus* 32: 1 (January 2004), 128.

Jezierski, Bronislas A. "Paderewski and the Treaty of Versailles." *Polish American Studies* 11 (1954), 42.

Kellog, Charlotte. *Paderewski.* New York: Viking Press, 1956.

Kędra, Władysław. *Ignacy Paderewski.* Warsaw: Czytelnik, 1948.

Kozubek, Lidia. *Manru Ignacego Jana Paderewskiego.* Katowice: Wydawnictwo Unia, 2001.

Krehbiel, Henry Edward. *Analytical Notes on M. Paderewski's Programmes.* New York: [No publisher], 1899.

The Kosciuszko Foundation. *To Ignace Jan Paderewski, Artist, Patriot, Humanitarian.* New York: The Kosciuszko Foundation, 1928.

Krzyzanowski, Jerzy R. *Henryk Sienkiewicz and Ignacy Paderewski.* New York: The Polish Institute of Arts and Sciences in America, 1970.

Kulisiewicz, Eugene. "Paderewski and Wilson's Speech to the Senate, January 22, 1917." *Polish American Studies*, 13 (1956), 65.

Landau, Rom. *Paderewski.* London: Ivor Nicholson and Watson, 1934.

Lisandrelli, Elaine. *Ignacy Jan Paderewski: Polish Pianist and Patriot.* Morgan Reynolds Publishing, January 1999, for youth.

Lorkowska Halina. *Ignace Jan Paderewski: The Man and His Work.* Beata Brodniewicz, Transl., Poznan: I.J. Paderewski Academy of Music, 2015.

Majewska, Magdalena. *Paderewski.* Brief biography in English transl. by Magdalena Majewska. Krakow: PWM, 2025.

Majewska, Magdalena. *Paderewski.* In Polish. Krakow: PWM, 2025.

Marcus, Kenneth, H. "Modjeska, Paderewski, and the California Landscape." *Southern California Quarterly*, 100 (April 2018), 69.

Marczewska-Zagdanska, Hanna and Janina Dorosz, 'Wilson – Paderewski – Masaryk: Their Visions of Independence and Conceptions of how to Organize Europe.' *Acta Poloniae Historica* 73 (1996), 55–69.

McGinty, Brian. *Paderewski at Paso Robles.* Scottsdale, AZ: Overland Books, 2004.

Michell (n.n). *The Brighton Album.* Untitled album of press clippings, photos, ephemeral documents, and writings, 1890-1914. Unpublished.

Modelski, I. *Ignacy Paderewski w walce o wielką Polskę.* Drukiem Przewodnika Katolickiego, New Britain, Conn., 1933.

Modjeska, Helena (Helena Modrzejewska). *Memories and Impressions of Helena Modjeska: An Autobiography.* New York: McMillan, 1910.

Moran, Michael. *The Pocket Paderewski: The Beguiling Life Of The Australian Concert Pianist Edward Cahill.* Melbourne: Australian Scholarly, 2016.

Orłowski, Jozef, ed. *Ignacy Jan Paderewski i odbudowa Polski.* Chicago: The Stanek Press, Vol. 1, 1939, Vol. 2, 1940.

Paderewska, Helena. *Paderewski: The Struggle for Polish Independence (1910–1920),* Ilias Chrissochoidis, ed. Stanford: Stanford University Press, 2015.

Paderewski: Twentieth American Tour Souvenir Program. Los Angeles: J. Paul Huston for Peter D. Conley, 1939.

The Paderewski Foundation. *Ignacy Jan Paderewski, 1860-1941; memorial album.* New York: The Paderewski Foundation, 1953.

The Paderewski Foundation. *Paderewski Notes.* A magazine of The Paderewski Foundation in New York, no. 1, 1976.

Paderewski, Jozef. *Wieniec grunwaldzki z 1910-go roku : wydawnictwo historyczne, pamiątkowe ilustrowane: zbiór aktów i dokumentów historycznych z 1910 r. ku uczczeniu 500 letniej rocznicy wiekopmnego zwycięztwa Polaków nad Krzyżakami.* Krakow: Skład Głowny w Księgarni Gebethnera i Społki, 1910.

Paja-Stach, Jadwiga. *Polish music from Paderewski to Penderecki.* English transl. Cara Emily Thornton. Krakow: Musica Iagellonica, 2010.

Perkowska, Małgorzata and Włodzimerz Pigła, "Katalog rękopisow I.J. Paderewskiego" [Catalogue of manuscripts by Paderewski], *Muzyka* 33 No. 3 (1988): 53-70.

Perkowska, Małgorzata. *Diariusz koncertowy Ignacego Jana Paderewskiego.* Krakow Polskie Wydawnictwo Muzyczne, 1990.

Perkowska-Waszek, Małgorzata. *Ignacy Jan Paderewski (1860-1941) : portrait of man, artist, and statesman : an exhibition on the 50th anniversary of the artist's death : Museum of Jagiellonian University-- Collegium Maius, 31 May-23 June 1991.* Krakow: The Museum, 1991.

Perkowska-Waszek, Małgorzata. *Paderewski i jego twórczość : dzieje utworów i rys osobowości kompozytora.* Krakow: Musica Iagellonica, 2010.

Phillips, Charles. *Paderewski: The Story of a Modern Immortal.* New York: McMillan, 1933.

Piber, Andrzej. *Droga do sławy: Ignacy Jan Paderewski w latach 1860- 1902* [Way to fame: Ignacy Jan Paderewski in the years 1860-1902] Warsaw: PIW, 1982.

Poniatowska, Irena. *Chopin w poezji.* Warsaw: NIFC, 2020.

Prazmowska, Anita. *Ignacy Paderewski. Poland.* Series Makers of the Modern World. London: Haus Publishing, 2010.

Prazmowska, Anita and Françoise Stonborough. *Ignace Paderewski et la renaissance de la Pologne en 1919.* Lausanne: Les Editions Noir sur Blanc, 2014.

Pylee, M.V. *Annual Symposium 1962: Paderewski Scholars in India.* New Delhi: Paderewski Foundation, 1963.

Rich, Ruth Anne. "Paderewski: America's Million-Dollar Pianist." *American Music Teacher,* 30 (1981), 44.

Richards, Mrs. George S. *Ignace Jan Paderewski, world's greatest pianist.* Duluth, Minn., n.p., 1924.

Roman, Kazimierz and Haag Czekaj. *Ignacy Jan Paderewski: album Międzynarodowego Towarzystwa Muzyki Polskiej im. Ingacego Jana Paderewskiego w Warszawie.* Warsaw and Basel: Die Internationale Vereinigung-Paderewski zur Forderung der Polnichen Musik, Warszawa, Basel, Switzerland, 2010.

Sieradz, Małgorzata. „Riond-Bosson i Ignacy Jan Paderewski w relacji Ludwika Bronarskiego." *Muzyka,* 69 (2024).

Sitarz, Andrzej and Wojciech Marchwica. *Warsztat kompozytorski, wykonawstwo i koncepcje polityczne Ignacego Jana Paderewskiego* [Composers workshop: Performance and political conceptions of I. J. Paderewski]. Conference proceedings from Jagiellonian, U., 1991. Krakow: Musica Iagellonica, 1991.

Steinway & Sons. *Paderewski.* Booklet published ca. 1895 by piano-maker Steinway & Sons.

Stevenson, Ronald and Harriette Brower. *The Paderewski paradox = Le paradoxe Paderewski.* Lincoln [England]: Klavar Music Foundation 1992.

Strakacz, Aniela. *Paderewski as I Knew Him.* Trans. Halina Chylewska. New Brunswick: Rutgers University Press, 1949.

Szombara, Justyna. "The Collection of Musical Manuscripts in I. J. Paderewski's Personal Library" (at the Jagiellonian University, Institute of Musicology). *Fontes Artis Musicae,* 61 (2014).

Towarzystwo Muzyczne im I. J. Paderewskiego w Bydgoszczy. *Rok Ignacego Jana Paderewskiego.* Bydgoszcz: Towarzystwo Muzyczne im. Ignacego Jana Paderewskiego w Bydgoszczy, 2001.

Trochimczyk, Maja. "Paderewski in Poetry: Master of Harmonies or Poland's Savior?" in "Paderewski and Polish Emigres in America;" special issue of the *Polish Music Journal* 4:1 (Summer 2001).

Trochimczyk, Maja, ed. 'Paderewski and the Tenth Anniversary of Poland's Independence (1928),' in "Paderewski – Lectures and Documents," *Polish Music Journal* 4: 1 (2001), online.

Trochimczyk, Maja. "Searching for Poland's Soul: Paderewski and Szymanowski in the Tatras," in *A Romantic Century in Polish Music,* Maja Trochimczyk, ed., Moonrise Press, 2009, 179-219.

Trochimczyk, Maja. "An Archangel at the Piano: Paderewski's Image and his Female Audience." *Polish American Studies* 67: 1 (Spring 2010): 5-44.

Trochimczyk, Maja. "Romantic, Sublime, Heroic, Immortal – Paderewski in American and English Poetry" a chapter forthcoming in Stephen Downes, ed. *Modern Constructions of "Polish" Music outside of Poland,* 2025.

Trochimczyk, Maja, ed. *Polish Music Journal.* Online, peer-reviewed journal for research in Polish music (1998-2003). Founder and Editor. Two issues dedicated to Paderewski. 4:1 (2001, "Paderewski and Polish Emigres in America"), and 4:2 (2001, "The Unknown Paderewski").

Wapinski, Roman. *Ignacy Paderewski.* Wrocław, 1999.

Windakiewicz, Helena. "Stosunek dzieł Paderewskiego do muzyki ludowej. Studium analityczne." [Relation between Paderewski`s works and folk music.] *Echo Muzyczne, Teatralne i Artystyczne,* nos. 956, 958, 959, 961 (1902).

Zamoyski, Adam. *Paderewski.* New York: Atheneum, 1982.

Zebrowski, Marek. *Celebrating Chopin and Paderewski.* Warsaw: Ministry of Foreign Affairs, Department of Public and Cultural Diplomacy, 2010.

Zebrowski, Marek. *Paderewski in California.* Torun: Tumult Foundation, 2009.

www.ingramcontent.com/pod-product-compliance
Lightning Source LLC
Chambersburg PA
CBHW060330100426
42812CB00003B/946